I0799916

IMAGES
of America

KILLINGLY

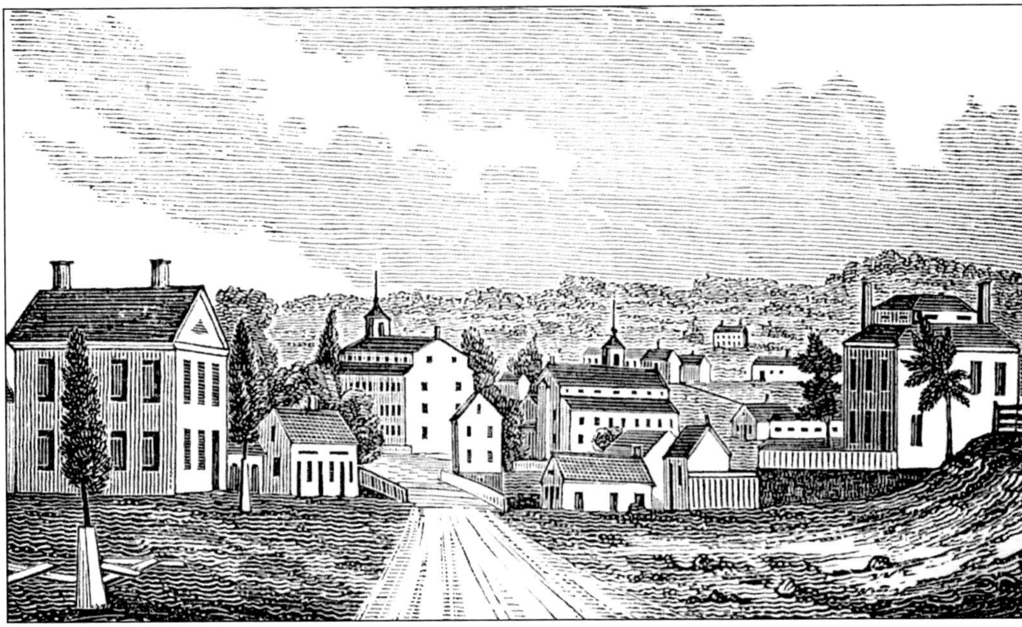

A View of Danielsonville from South Main Street in Brooklyn. This early woodcut, by John Warner Barber, is the earliest available image of Danielsonville. It shows the wooden Danielson mill and, to the right of it, the Cundall woolen mill, which in later years made satinette.

IMAGES
of America

KILLINGLY

Natalie L. Coolidge
and Robert A. Spencer

ARCADIA
PUBLISHING

ISBN 978-0-7385-1920-3

Published by Arcadia Publishing
Charleston, South Carolina

Printed in the United States of America

Library of Congress Catalog Card Number: Applied For

For all general information contact Arcadia Publishing at:
Telephone 843-853-2070
Fax 843-853-0044
E-mail sales@arcadiapubishing.com
For customer service and orders:
Toll-Free 1-888-313-2665

Visit us on the Internet at www.arcadiapublishing.com

Contents

Acknowledgments

The majority of photographs in this book are from the Killingly Historical Society's collections. In addition, members and friends have kindly donated or loaned some of their personal photographs. We are especially grateful to Wayne Magao, who generously allowed us to go through his entire collection to find items of interest.

Thanks also go to Maureen (Lyon) Girard for use of her daguerreotype, and to Grace Wilson, Avery Tillinghast, Anthony Barber, the South Killingly Congregational Church, and Logee's Greenhouses for sharing photographs and information. Members of the Historical Society were most helpful in the research. We all increased our knowledge of the town and its surrounding villages.

Our families have been most patient with the clutter, telephone calls, and endless hours spent on research. They deserve the most thanks.

INTRODUCTION

Killingly was established as a town in 1708. Most of the land was dispensed to a few individuals in large land grants by the General Court of Connecticut. Some 1,500 acres of the best land went to Maj. James Fitch. John Chandler received 2,400 acres in the Chestnut Hill area, now known as East Killingly. James Danielson purchased about 2,000 acres between the Assawaga and Quinebaug Rivers. Until it was settled by Jacob Spaulding in 1721, South Killingly was controlled by residents of Plainfield. By 1708, some 30 families resided east of the Quinebaug River, north of Plainfield. The farmland was not of the highest quality but was suitable for smaller family farms.

Throughout the town there were many watercourses that had falls. Sawmills and gristmills were developed at these falls. The mill sites made nearby properties better adapted to manufacturing than to agricultural uses. The Danielson family, along with other local residents and entrepreneurs from Rhode Island, started industrial development in 1809 when they built the first textile mill in town at the confluence of the Five Mile (Assawaga) and Quinebaug Rivers. Power looms came into use in Danielson by 1819, just a few years after they appeared in America. By the early 1850s, Irish families (and later, French-Canadian families) lived in lower Danielson in tenement houses built by the mill companies. The state legislature granted a charter in 1854 to the Borough of Danielsonville, primarily for the purpose of providing better fire protection.

Killingly was the first town in Connecticut to benefit from the Industrial Revolution, triggered by the mechanization of the textile industry. As a result, the community abounds with small mill villages. Many, like Ballouville and East Killingly, survive in a remarkably complete state of preservation. These mill villages contain not only the mill itself but also many of the peripheral buildings, such as the churches, schools, stores, and tenements, that were so important to these nuclear communities. South Killingly is the only village that was not settled around a mill. In its day, this village was an important center along a stage route to Providence, Rhode Island. With the coming of the railroad in 1839–40, the depot village of Danielsonville blossomed into a flourishing commercial center.

This photographic history presents Killingly from its earliest days. Through vintage photographs, c. 1840 to the mid-1900s, it shows how residents lived, what they wore, and where they worked and played in each of the villages that comprise the town.

One

Danielson:

Danielsonville

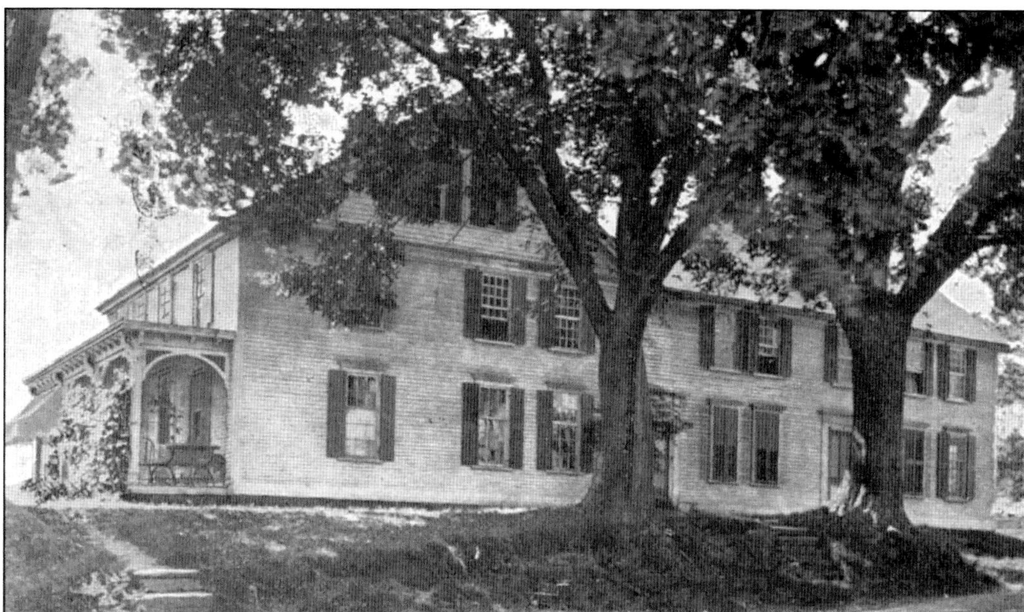

The Danielson Homestead, 1786. This was the home of Col. William Danielson, a Revolutionary War officer. It was erected on a portion of the original 1707 purchase of James Danielson, for whom the borough is named. The house remained in the Danielson family throughout the 19th century. Several successive supervisors of the Danielson Manufacturing Company textile mill occupied the ell.

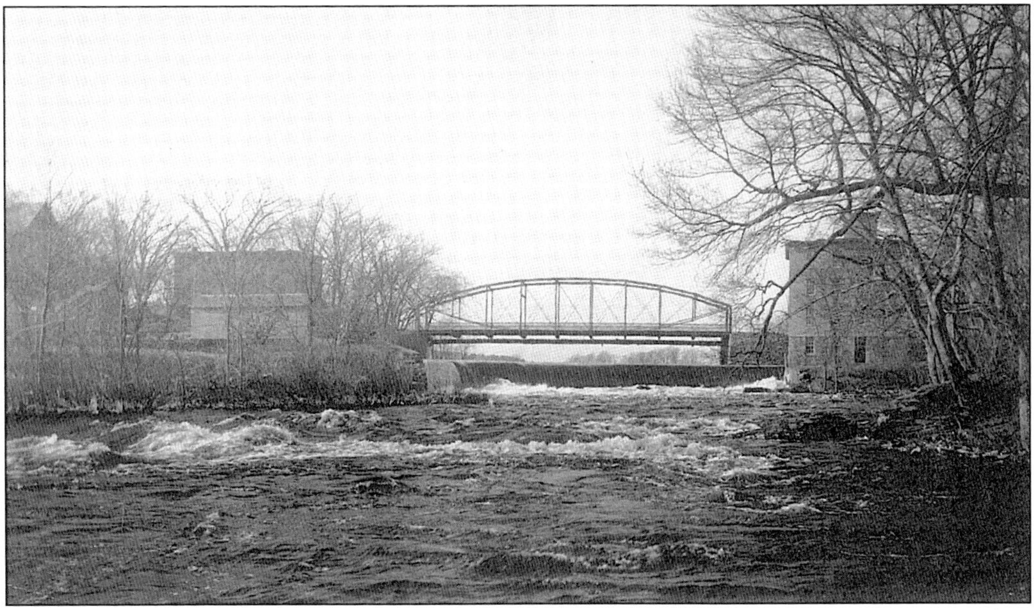

BROOKLYN BRIDGE. In 1722, John Sabin built the first bridge across the Quinebaug River, below the High Falls. A new bridge was built over the Quinebaug at Capt. Samuel Danielson's place in 1750. In 1770, this bridge was rebuilt. The iron bridge, *c.* 1885, survived the Freshet of 1886, the Hurricane of 1938, and was the only local bridge across the Quinebaug River to remain after the Flood of 1955.

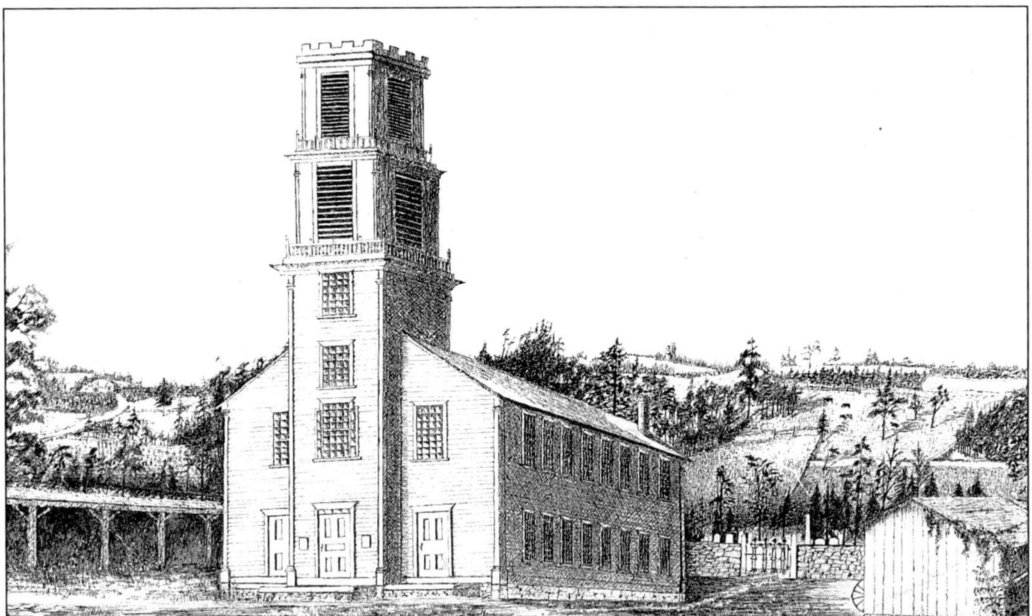

THE CHURCH OF WESTFIELD, 1796. A meetinghouse was built in West Killingly on a lot donated by Dr. Penuel Hutchins and Robert Howe. It was on the east side of Main Street, near the junction of North Street. Organized in 1801, the church was named the New Church of Christ in the West Society in the Town of Killingly. The Rev. Gordon Johnson was ordained as the first pastor in 1804.

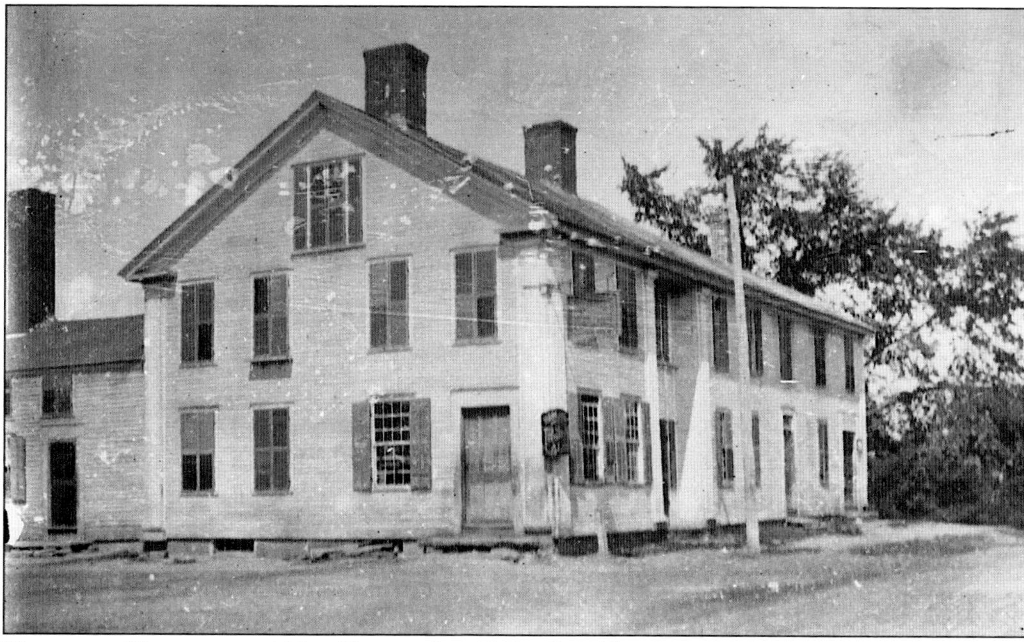

HUTCHINS TAVERN, C. 1831. During the 1800s, Franklin Street was a main stagecoach road between Providence and Hartford. Randall and Joseph Davis erected the tavern west of the Dyer Street intersection to serve as a stage stop and boardinghouse for factory workers and railroad laborers. The tavern was sold to Silas Hutchins in 1837. At various times, it was called the old Hutchins Stand and the Railroad House.

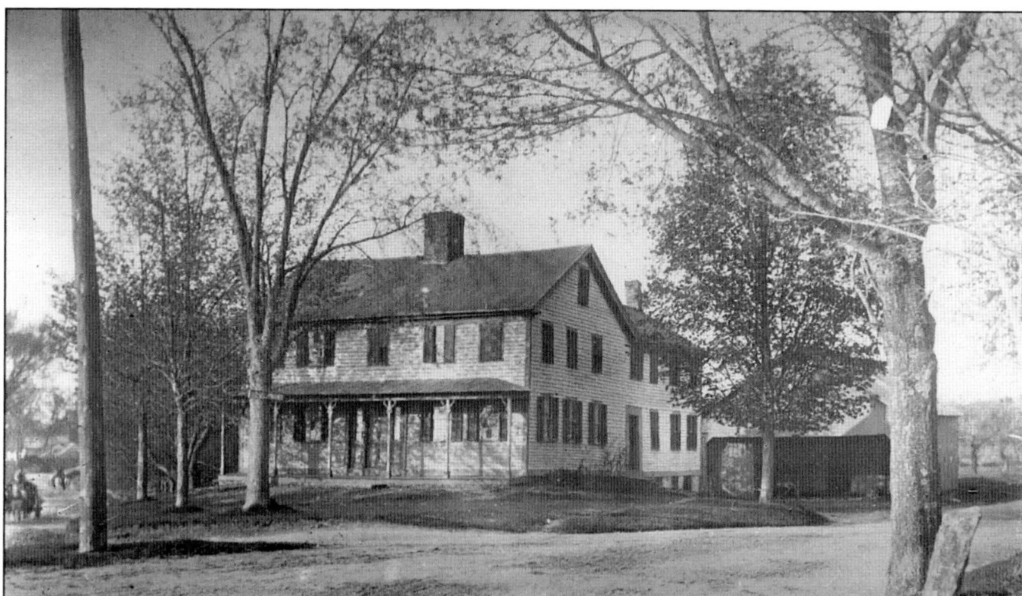

THE BENJAMIN FRANKLIN HOUSE, C. 1835. The second tavern on Franklin Street was erected at its intersection with Broad Street and Green Hollow Road, the junction of two stagecoach roads from Norwich to Worcester and Providence to Hartford. It was soon called Kies Tavern after the new owner, Harris Kies. The arrival and departure of the different stages were events not to be missed.

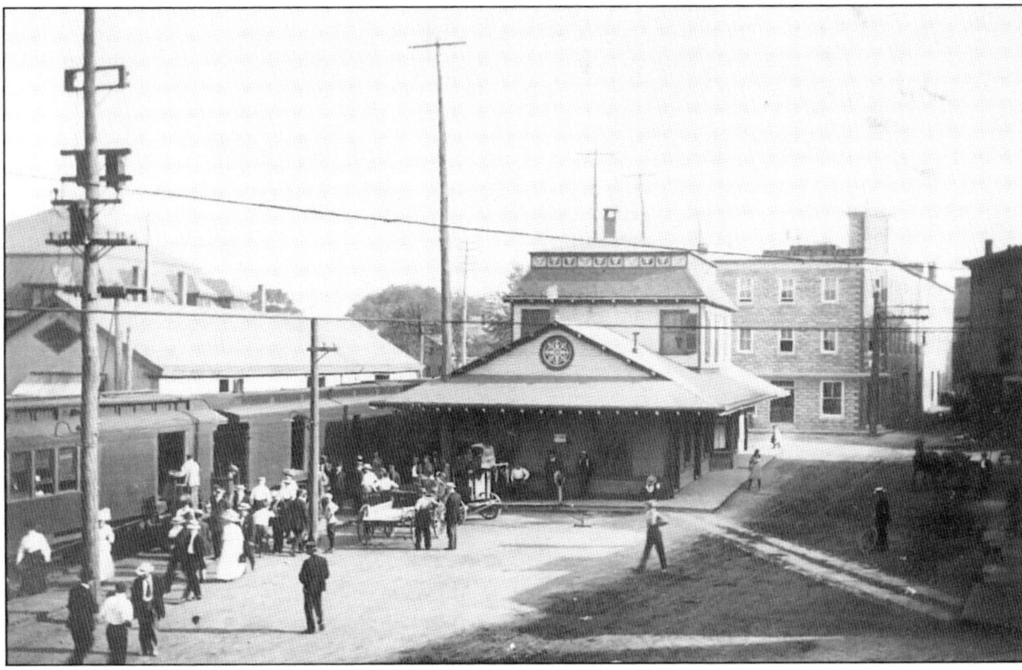

RAILROAD DEPOT, 1839. The first depot and freight house of the Norwich & Worcester Railroad were built or begun in 1839. The first depot was on the west side of the track. Capt. Samuel Reynolds was the first station agent. In 1860, the depot was moved to the east side of the track. During the early 1900s, 14 passenger trains a day stopped at Danielson, in addition to a great many freight trains.

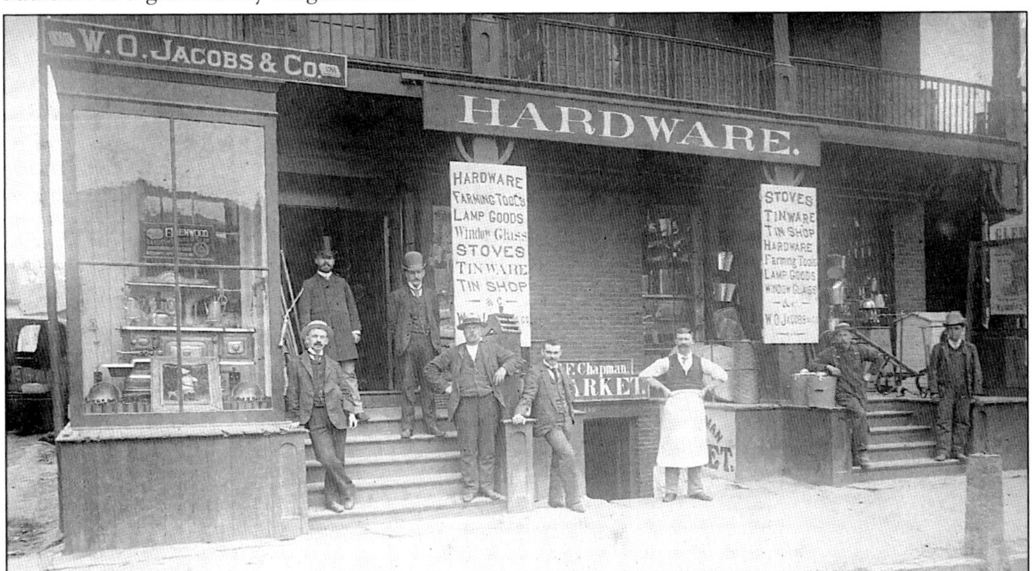

THE W.O. JACOBS & CO. AND B.F. CHAPMAN, C. 1844. The hardware portion of the business of E.H. & O.P. Jacobs was sold to William O. and Oliver P. Jacobs. Benjamin F. Chapman started a meat business in the basement in 1840, supplying the depot and other villages with fresh meat. These stores were in the building that later housed Woodward's Drug Store, *c.* 1844, located on the southeast corner of Main and Center Streets.

THE EARLY METHODIST CHURCH, 1842. The first Methodist church stood on the northwest corner of Main and Central Streets. Lloyd Baldwin of Willimantic built it in 1842. Later a brick-walled basement called Washington Hall was built beneath the church. A steeple replaced the belfry in 1867. Because of noise at the site's busy street corner location, a new church was built on Spring Street in 1902.

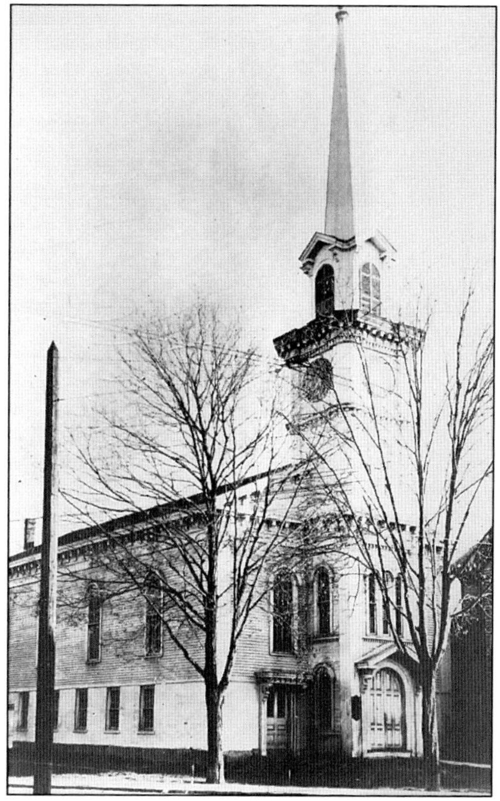

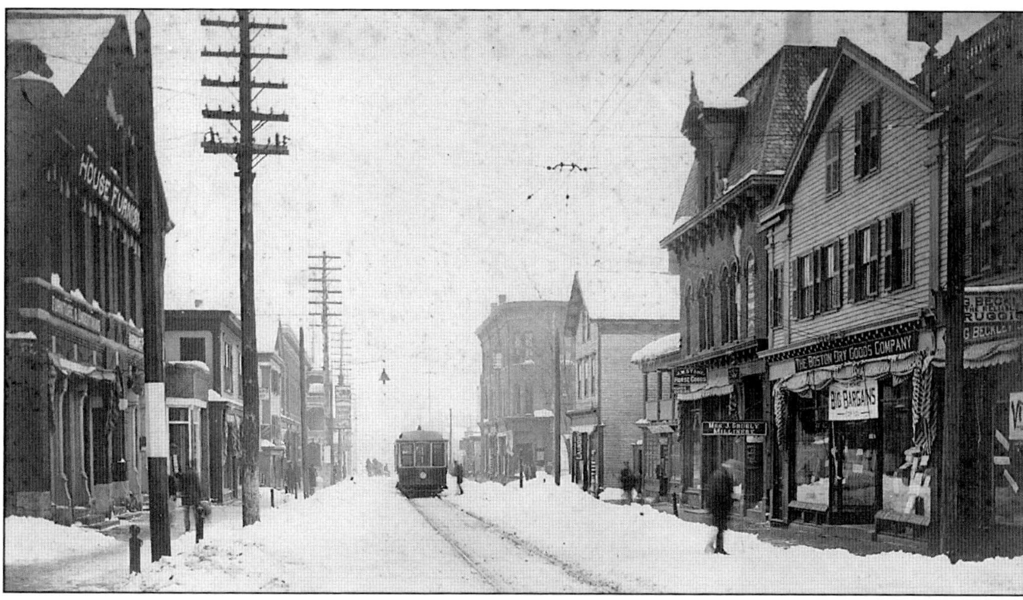

THE EARLY METHODIST PARSONAGE, 1873. An extensive revival stirred the Methodist church and gave it new life, which led to the construction of a new parsonage. The building was erected next to the church on Main Street. Its first floor was used as a store. In thisphotograph, the parsonage is the second building to the right of the trolley, with the barber pole in front of it.

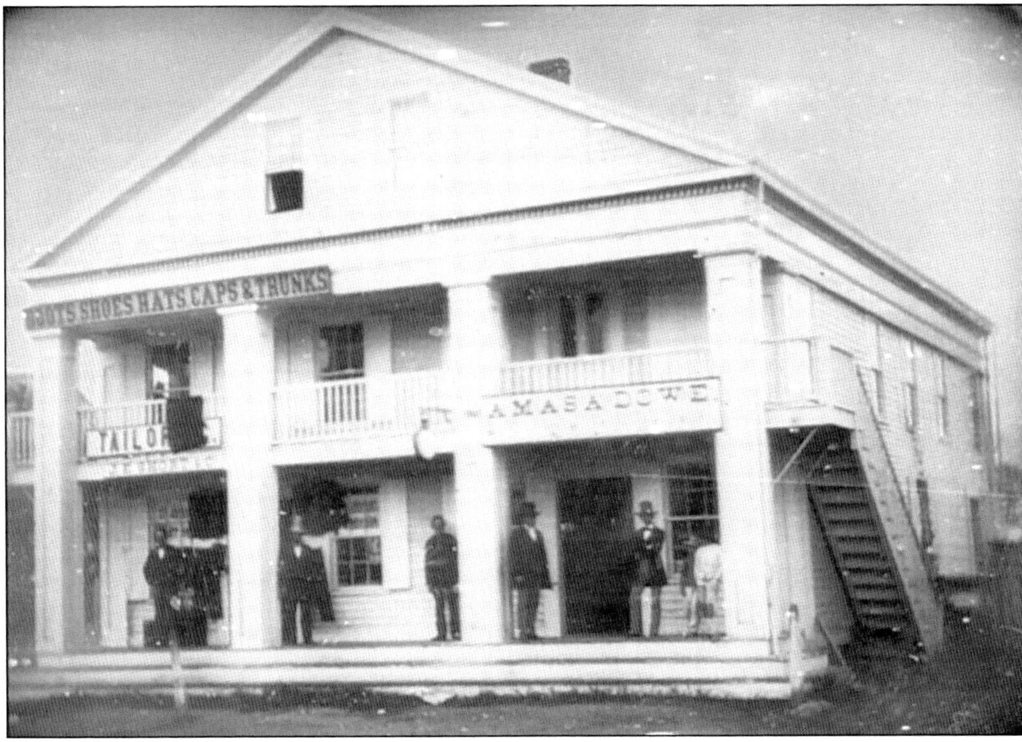

THE DAY BUILDING, 1846. Constructed in 1846 by Luther Day, this building is perhaps the oldest one in continuous commercial use in Danielson. It is located on the corner of Main and Union Streets, where they join Commerce Avenue, and is now known as the Jodoin block. This daguerreotype was likely taken by the first daguerrian, a Mr. Langley, who came to the village in 1847. Langley charged $1 per picture.

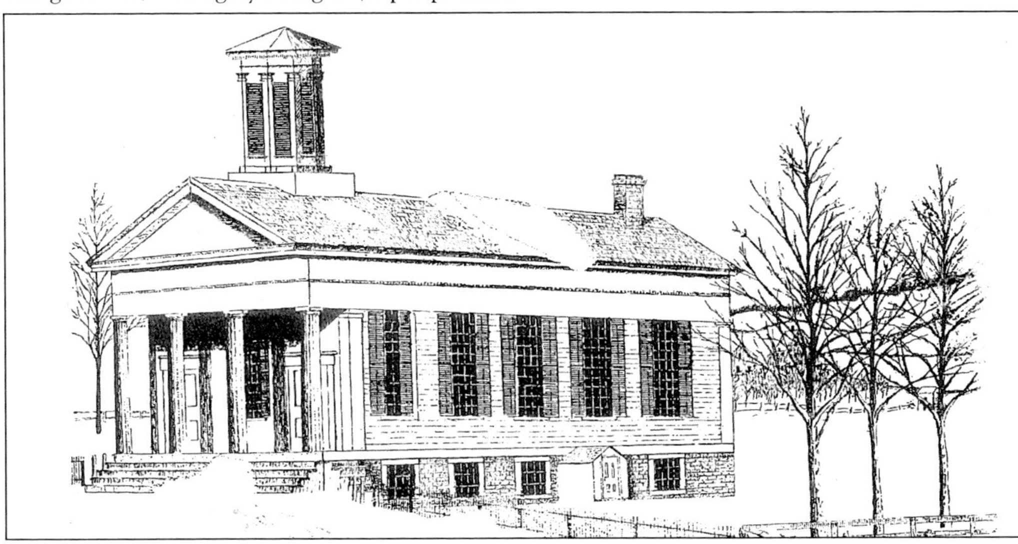

WEST KILLINGLY ACADEMY. A private school was built on Broad Street in 1847 in order to fill Killingly's need for its own secondary school. Previously, students had to travel to Plainfield or Woodstock to complete high school. The school was closed in 1862. It was purchased by St. Alban's Episcopal Church and was renovated in 1865.

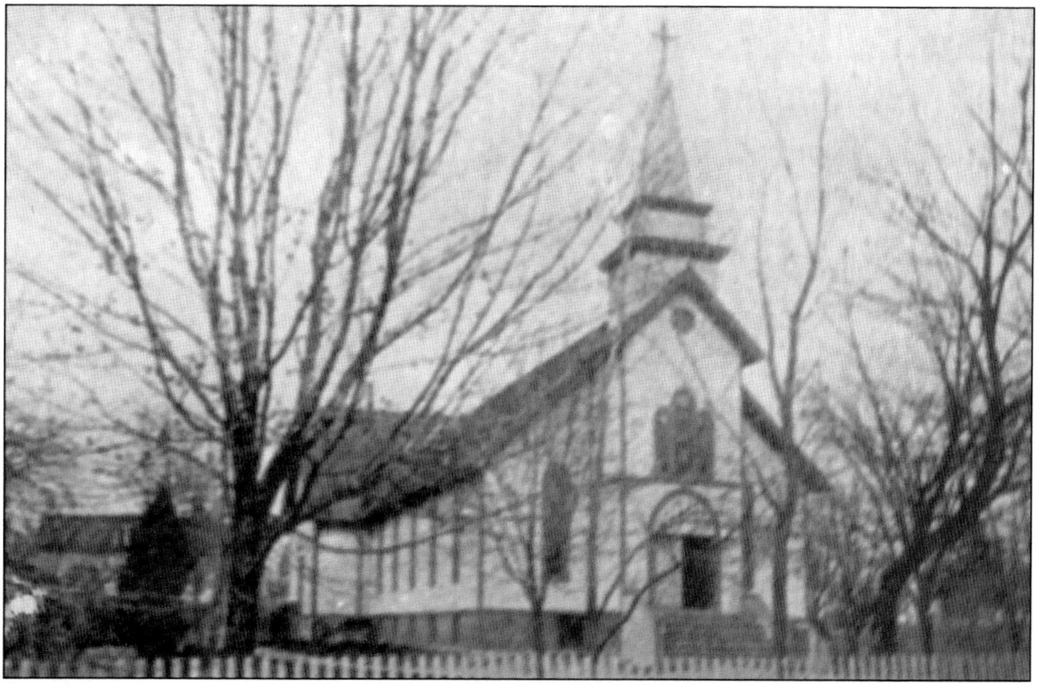

St. James Church and School, Winter Street. Killingly's first Catholic Mass was held in a house on Franklin Street in 1848. In 1864, the church purchased an old Second Adventist chapel on Winter Street. The first parochial school was opened in the basement of that church but was discontinued four years later because of its distance from Quebec Village, where most of the pupils lived. The building burned in April 1903.

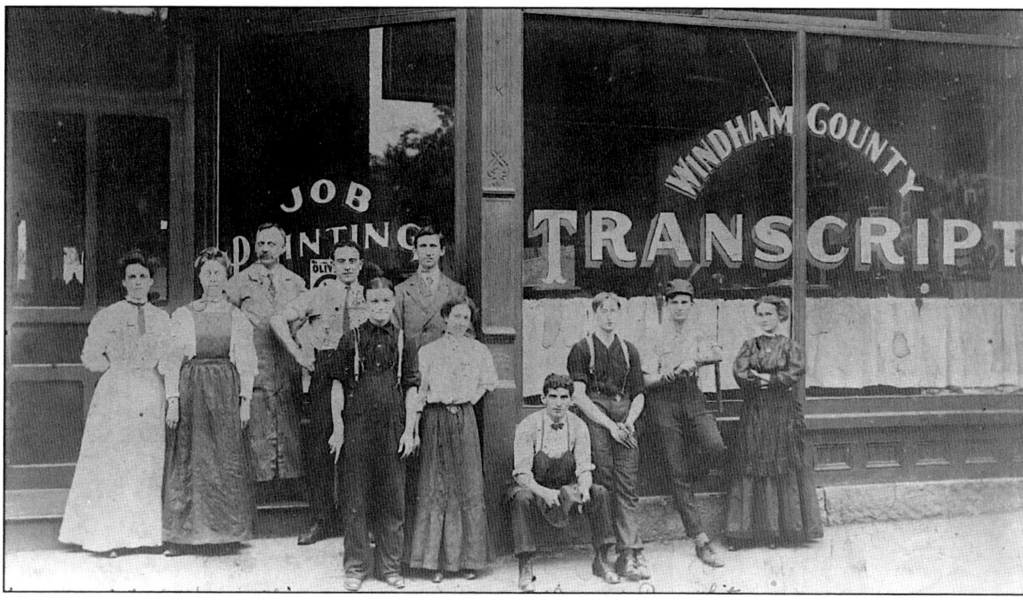

The Transcript Office. The *Windham County Transcript* was founded in 1848. During its lifetime, the local newspaper has occupied many different locations. This photograph shows staff members standing in front of the Burroughs and Hopkins premises on Center Street in the Phoenix Hall block. The newspaper was printed at that location during the early 1900s.

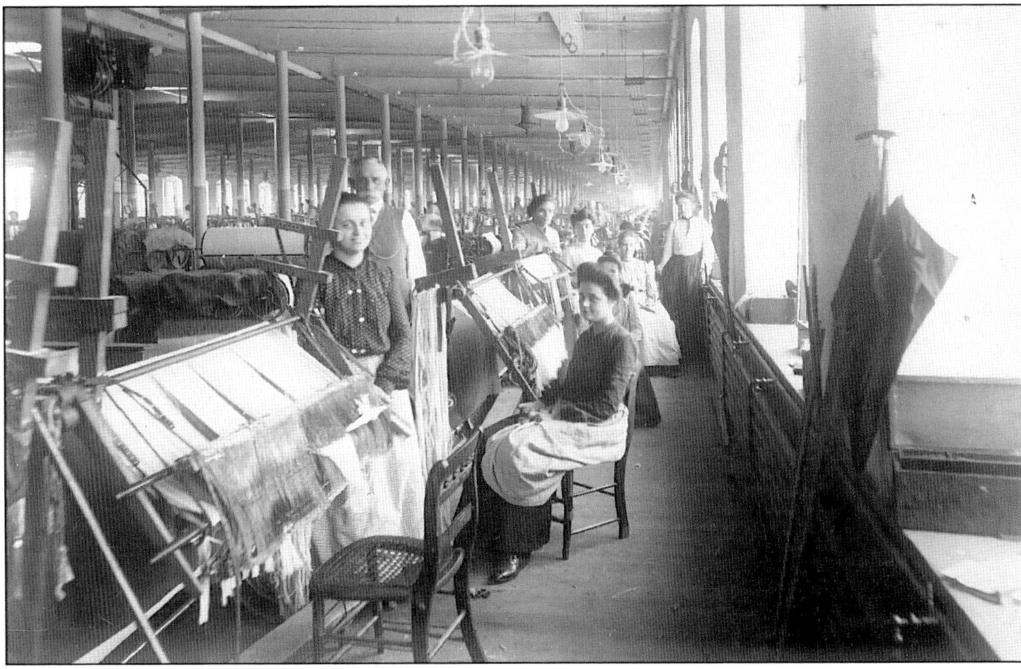

Women at Work. In the 1850s, employees worked 69 hours a week. The factories operated by lamplight, fueled by fish oil, during the fall and winter months. On Saturdays, the workday ended at 3:30 p.m. During the summer months, employees spent the rest of their Saturdays tending garden plots assigned to each family by the mill. Only four workdays during the year were recognized as holidays: Fast Day in April, the Fourth of July, Thanksgiving, and Christmas.

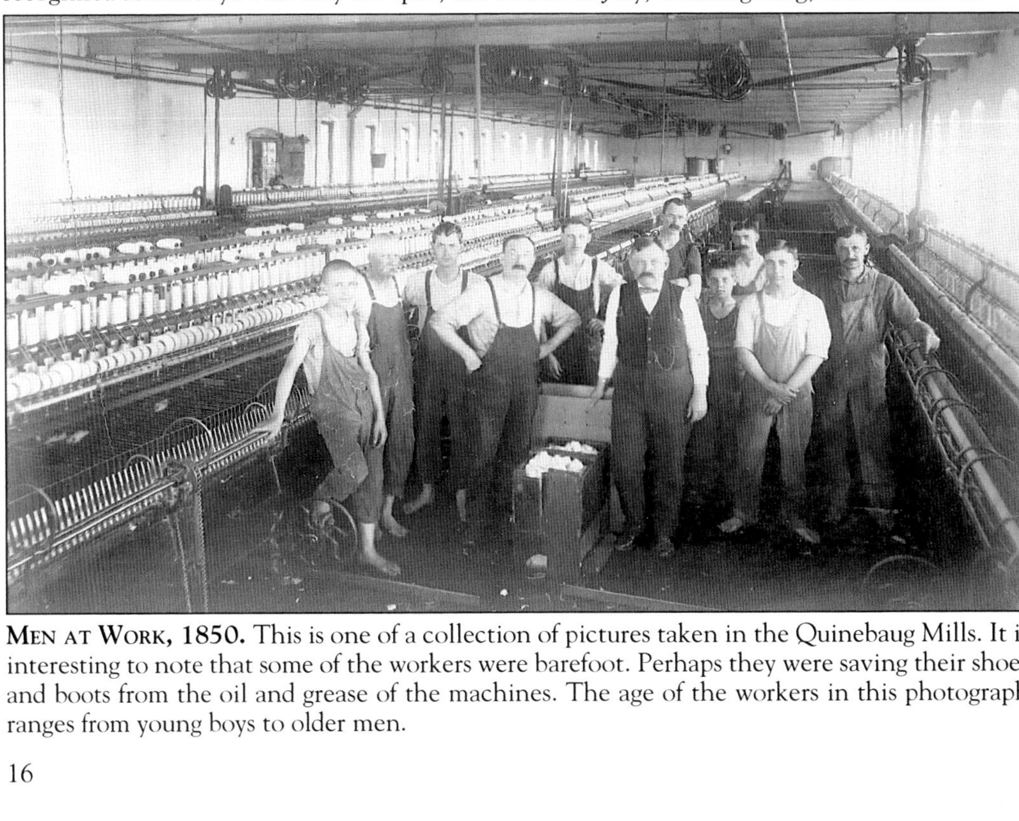

Men at Work, 1850. This is one of a collection of pictures taken in the Quinebaug Mills. It is interesting to note that some of the workers were barefoot. Perhaps they were saving their shoes and boots from the oil and grease of the machines. The age of the workers in this photograph ranges from young boys to older men.

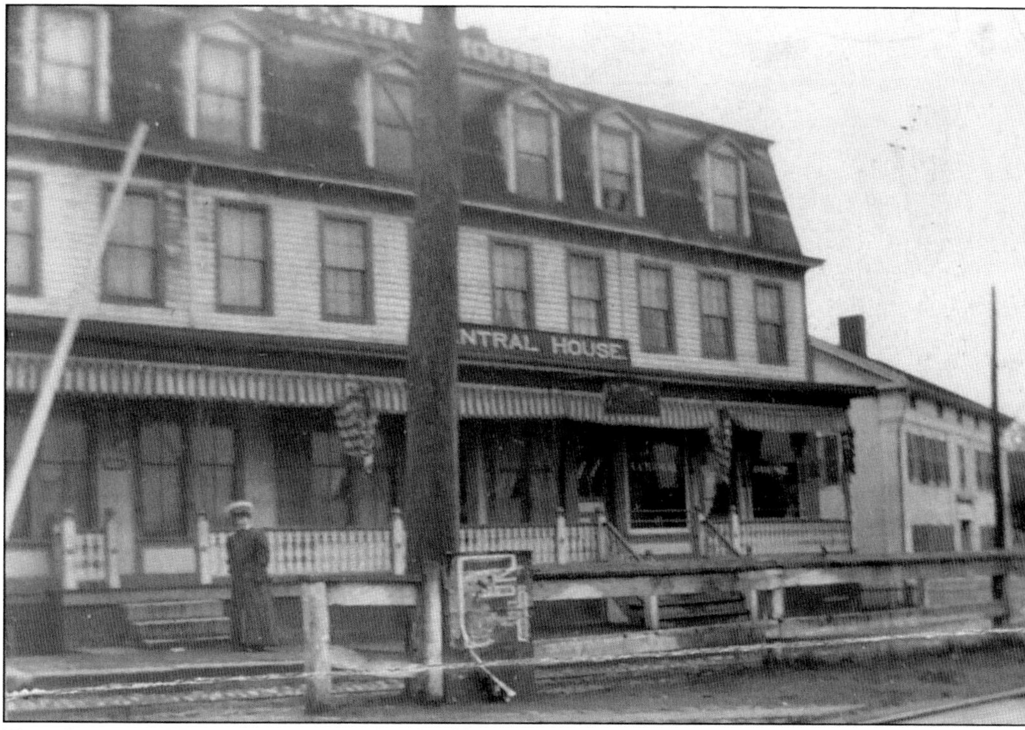

The Central House, c. 1854. This building was originally known as the Currier, or Courier, Building. For a time it was a clothing store. Tenants occupied the rooms on the second floor. At a later date, the building was remodeled and became the Central House, with S.P. Humphrey as proprietor. Since the early 1900s, it has been called the Danielson Inn.

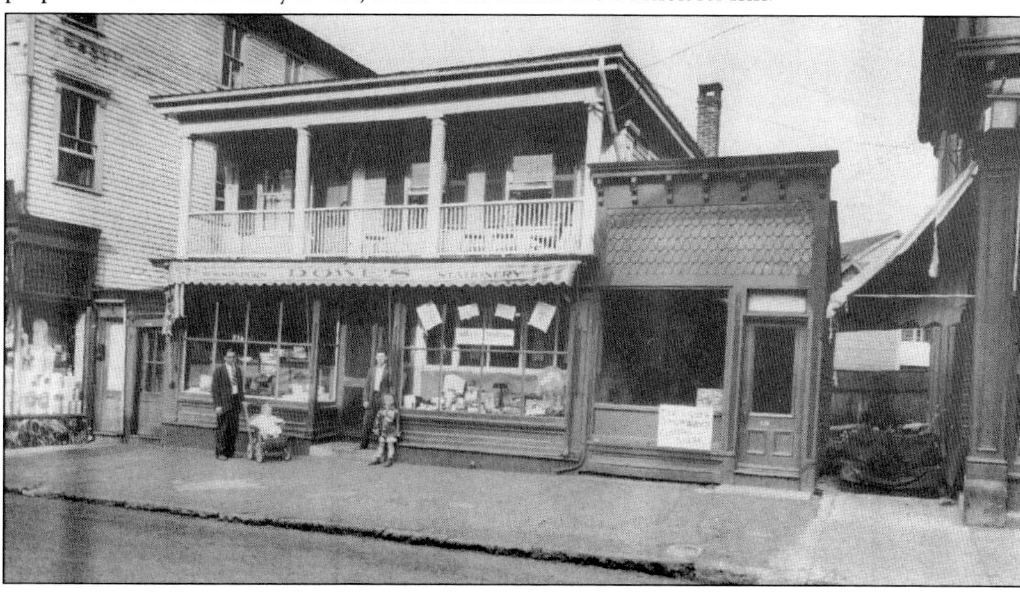

Dowe's, 1854. Dowe's stationery store was started in 1854 when Amasa Dowe, proprietor of a jewelry store, gave his son, Marshall P. Dowe, room for the sale of stationery. In 1860, Marshall P. Dowe started his own stationery and bookstore. In 1927, Dowe's Card and Gift Shop was constructed on the west side of Main Street.

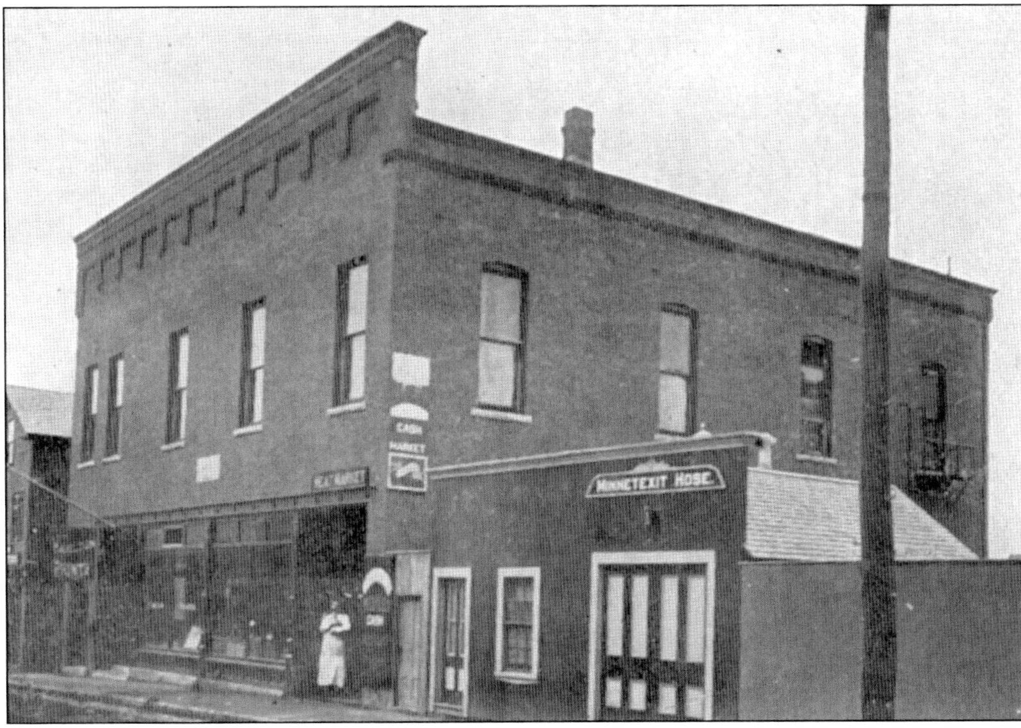

THE MINNETEXIT HOSE COMPANY. In 1854, a fire department was organized. An engine was purchased and named the Quinebaug. Twelve fire cisterns were built. In 1855, the borough purchased the brick building on Cottage Street near the railroad tracks for a firehouse. That same year the Minnetexit Fire Company was formed and was moved into a building next to the Phoenix Hall block on Center Street. The engine was renamed the Minnetexit.

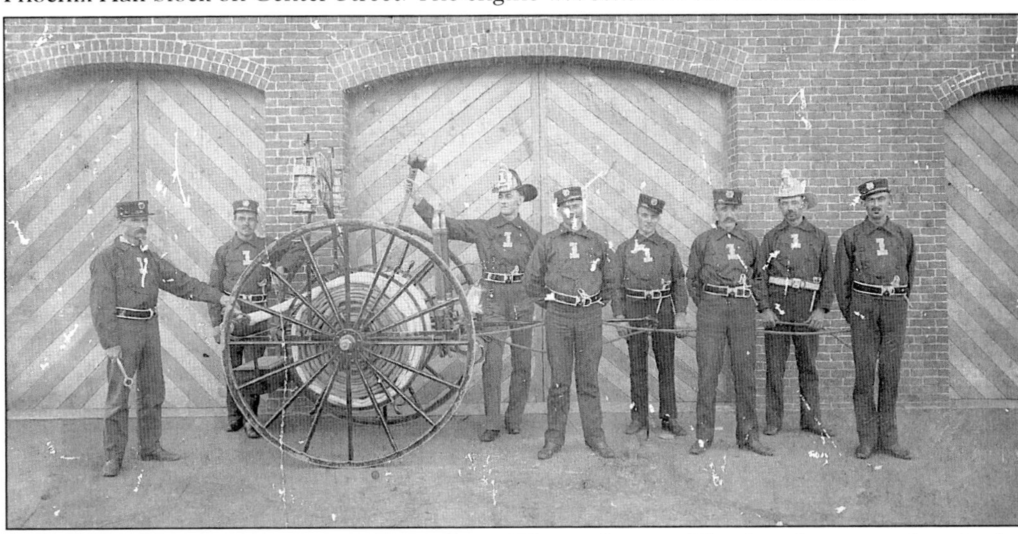

THE VILLAGE FIRE DEPARTMENT, BORO HALL, WATER STREET. The first floor served as the fire station. The lockup was in the basement. Boro Hall was on the second floor. The fire alarm system progressed from "a promiscuous ringing" of the Methodist church bell to an efficient alarm system. The Quinebaug Brass Band, with Albert Burrows as bandleader, also held its meetings in Boro Hall.

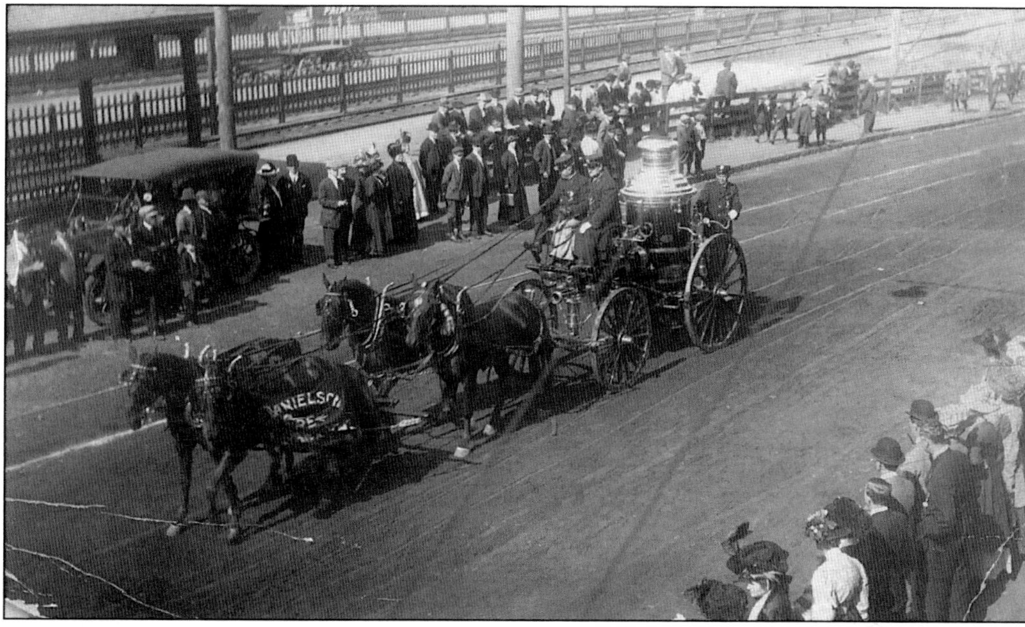

THE GENERAL PUTNAM. THE Danielson Fire Department grew from the Minnetexit, a hand engine, to the General Putnam, a horse-drawn, steam fire engine. The department used the General Putnam from the 1870s to the early 1950s. In 1936, the department demonstrated the engine at a convention of firemen held in Plainfield. In this photograph, the department proudly paraded the new steam engine in the town of Putnam.

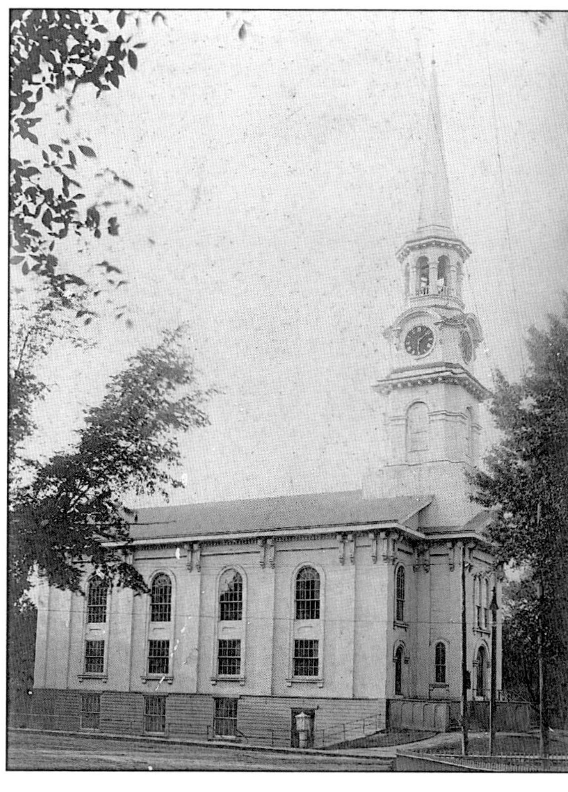

THE WESTFIELD CONGREGATIONAL CHURCH, 1855. The new Congregational church was built on Main Street at the corner of and parallel to Reynolds Street, as stipulated by Capt. Samuel Reynolds, who donated the land. The church was built by George Truesdell, a carpenter from Dayville. It replaced the old meetinghouse on North Main Street, and was dedicated in June 1855. The Rev. Thomas O. Rice served as minister.

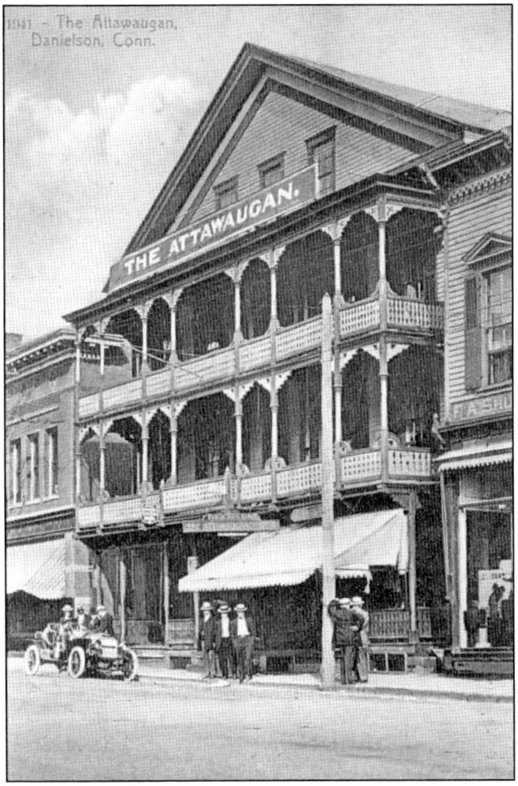

The Attawaugan Hotel, 1856. The Attawaugan Hotel, on the east side of Main Street near the railroad station, was the principal hotel in Danielsonville. The first manager was Henry Peckham, who was soon followed by Lewis Worden. There were 41 guest rooms, which lodged visitors from all areas of the country. Often the names and hometowns of these visitors were published in the newspaper.

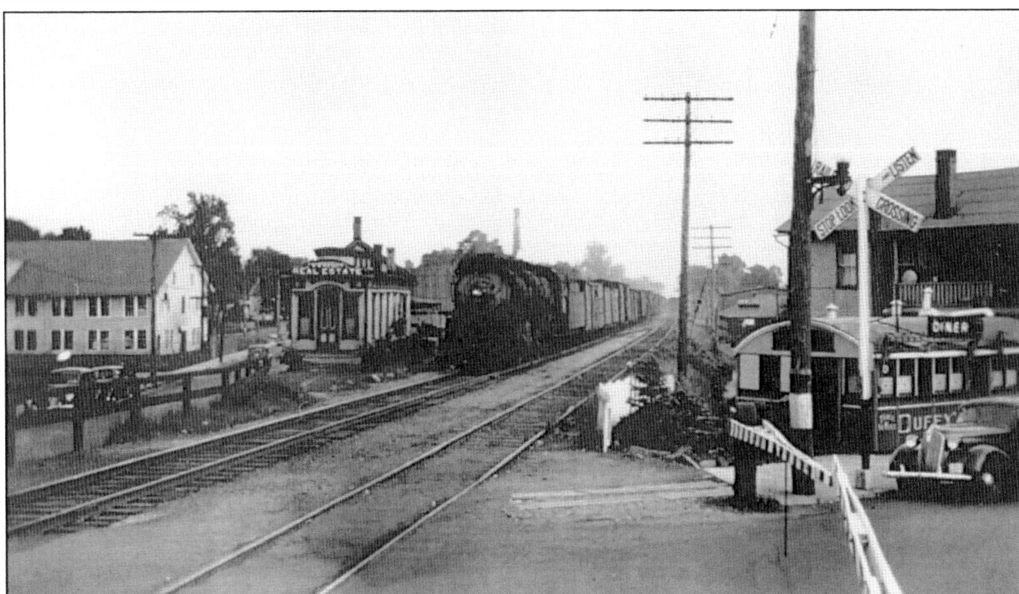

Keystone-Shaped Building, c. 1860. In 1859, photographer Samuel P. Davis established a studio between Furnace Street and the railroad tracks, in a shape that conformed to the property. On the left is Plant #1, purchased in 1919 by J.W. Powdrell and J.S. Alexander for their first curtain-making operation in Danielson. On the right side of the tracks is Duffy's Diner and the People's Clothing Store.

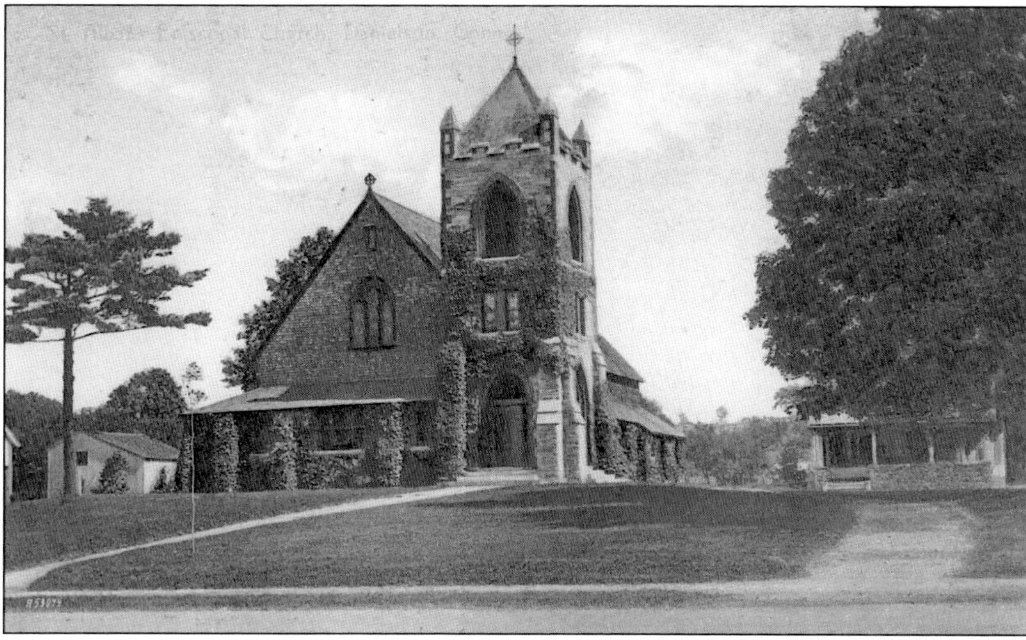

St. Alban's Episcopal Church. Through the efforts of six individuals, an Episcopal church was established in Danielsonville in 1865. The six men purchased the West Killingly Academy on Broad Street and refurbished it. The parish house was erected in the mid-1920s. For 24 years, from 1928 until his death in 1952, Rev. John Rees Jones served as rector and was held in high esteem by the whole community.

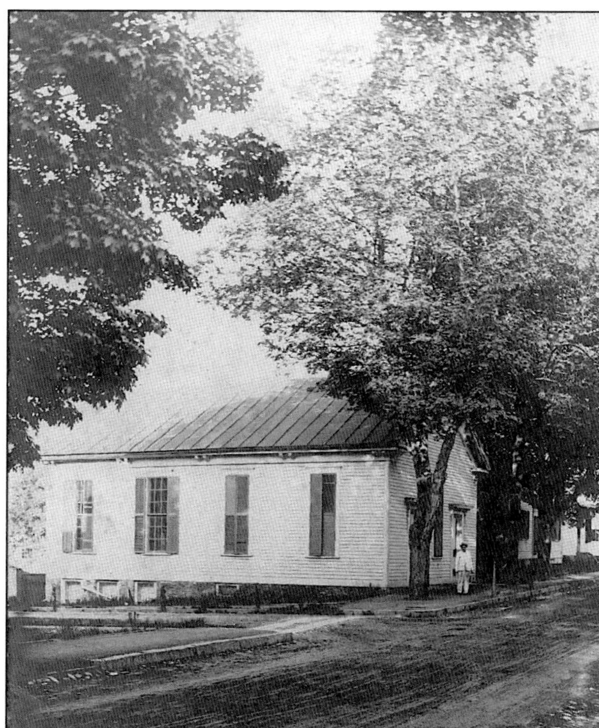

The Advent Christian Church. The Second Advent Chapel was constructed on the corner of Academy and School Streets in 1927. Organized in 1858, the church built its first chapel on Winter Street. That building was purchased in 1864 by the Rev. James Quinn and was eventually converted to the first Catholic church in Killingly. The Academy Street building later became Cliff Smith's Garage.

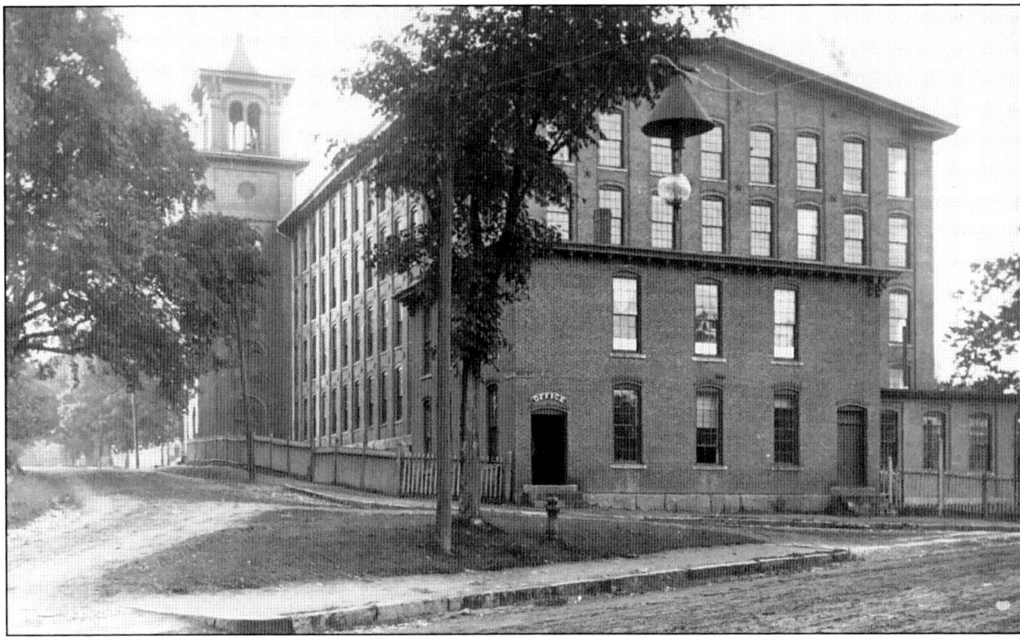

THE DANIELSON COTTON MILL, 1868. Daniel G. Sherman erected a brick mill on the corner of Main and Maple Streets. The brick mill replaced a frame cotton mill and two stone mills, which have since been destroyed. Shirting and sheeting were manufactured here. In 1925, Powdrell & Alexander took over and used the plant for bleaching and weaving. Nearly 160 years of continuous textile production ended in 1964, when the dyeing company expired.

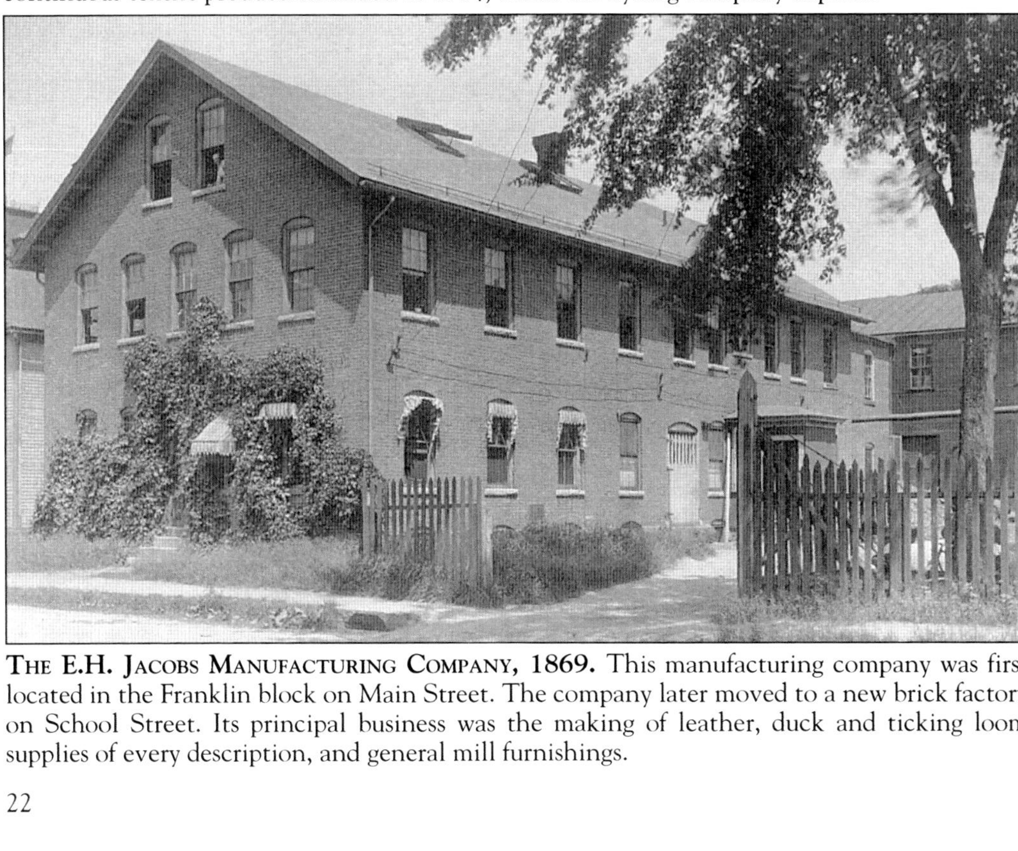

THE E.H. JACOBS MANUFACTURING COMPANY, 1869. This manufacturing company was first located in the Franklin block on Main Street. The company later moved to a new brick factory on School Street. Its principal business was the making of leather, duck and ticking loom supplies of every description, and general mill furnishings.

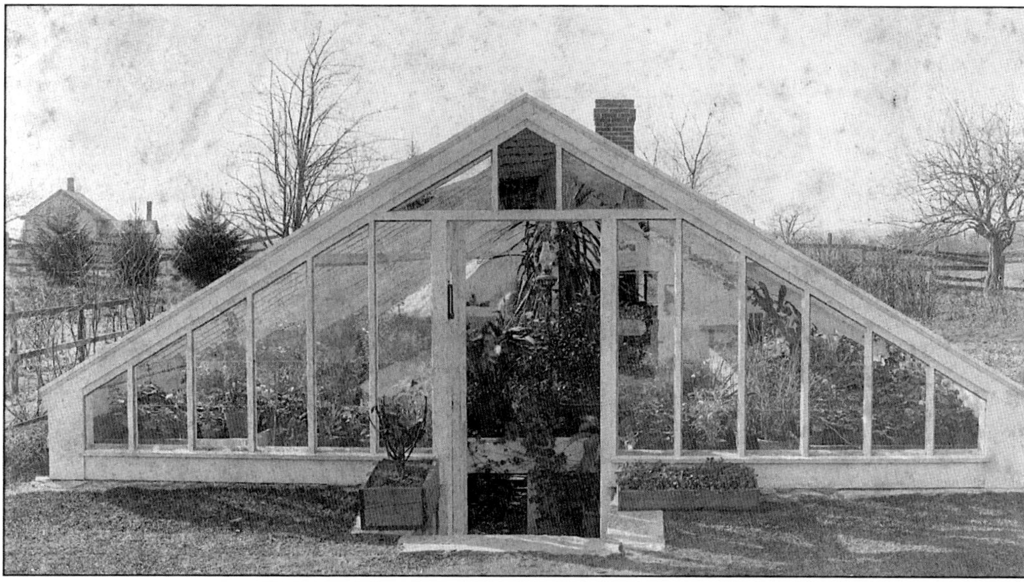

LOGEE GREENHOUSES. This greenhouse is one of Danielson's oldest continuously operated businesses. John Mahr, a sexton of Westfield Cemetery, started the greenhouse *c.* 1870 to grow plants for the cemetery. Mahr's son-in-law, William Logee, continued the plant business and expanded it into a commercial florist operation. The business remains with his descendants today and is known to plant enthusiasts around the world. This photograph, *c.* 1892, shows the original greenhouse.

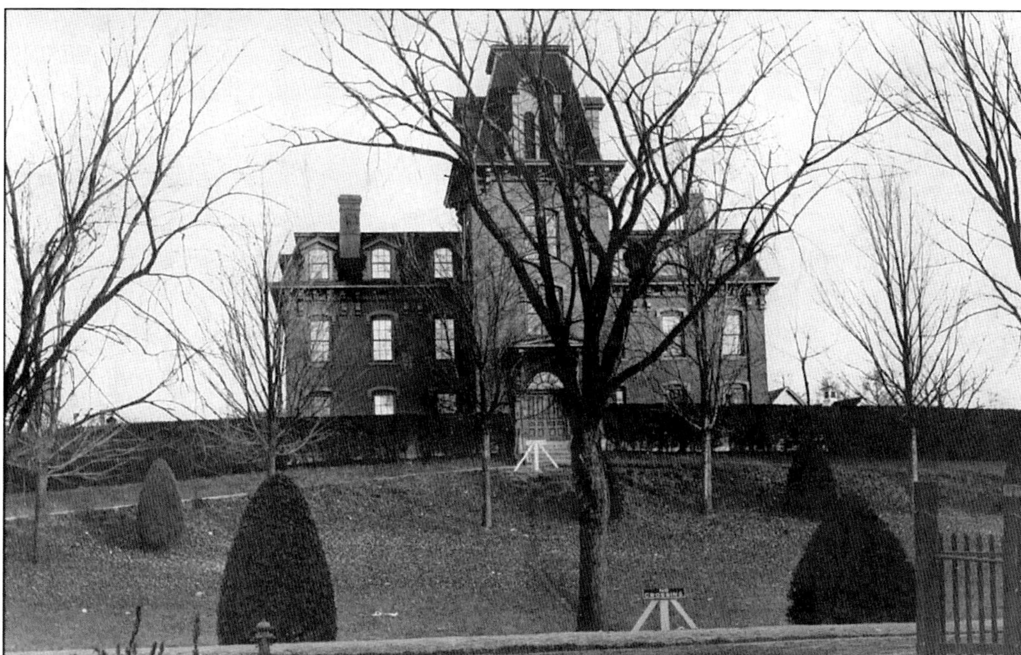

KILLINGLY HIGH SCHOOL, 1871. A public school was built in the borough of Danielson to house borough children in the lower eight grades and to provide a secondary education for all children in town. When the new high school was built in 1908, this building remained a grammar school until the Killingly Memorial School replaced it in 1952.

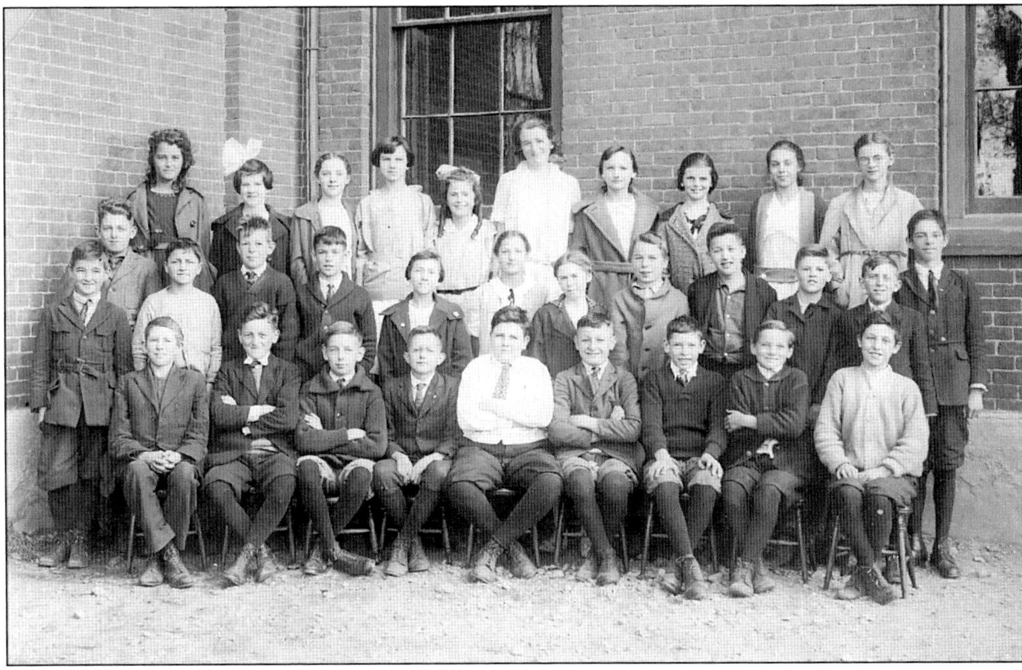

A Danielson Grammar School Class. The only identification on this photograph is a note that states this was a sixth grade class. Note that most of the boys wore knickers.

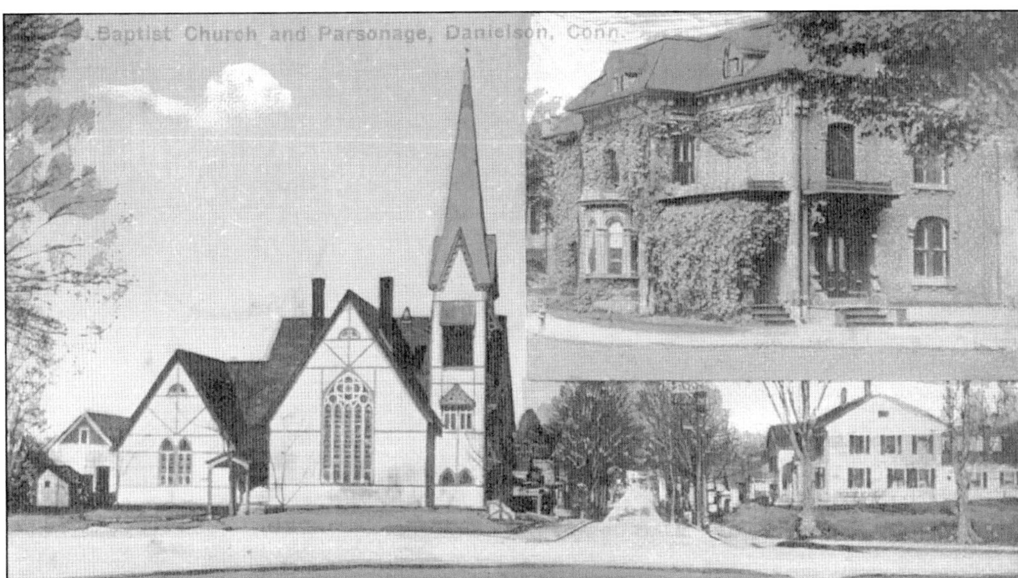

The Danielson Baptist Church and Parsonage, 1879. The first Baptist church was organized on February 5, 1874. The church was built on the corner of Broad and Academy Streets in 1879 and served the members for more than 85 years. In 1966, the building was demolished and replaced by a modern church. The first parsonage, located on the corner of Broad and Reynolds Streets, is now an undertaking establishment.

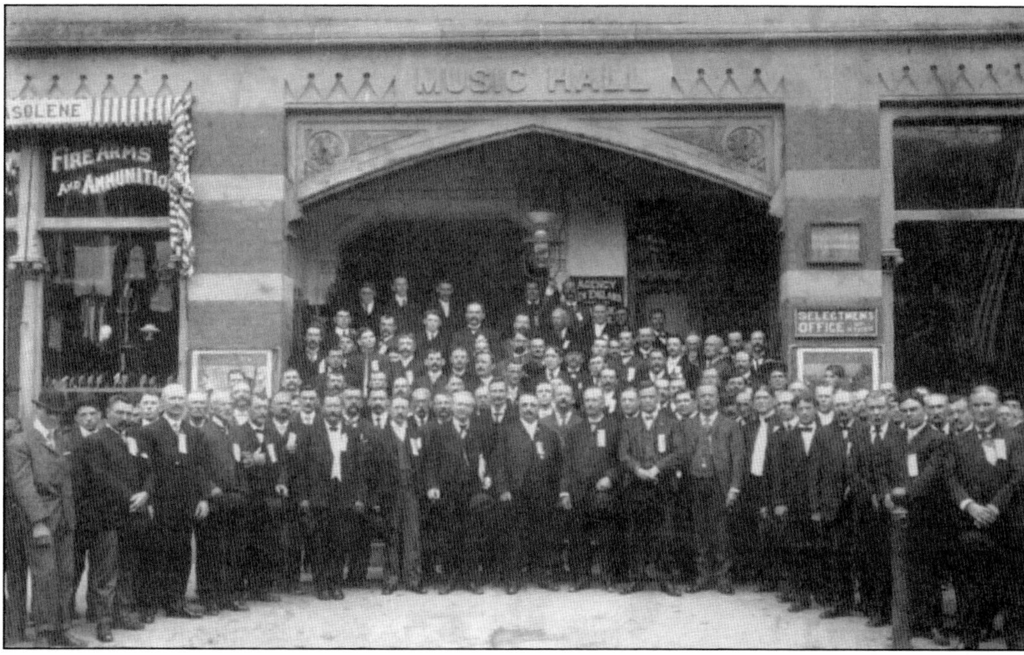

Gentlemen in Front of the Music Hall. The Music Hall was one of the finest buildings for public entertainment in all of Windham County. The 800-seat auditorium had a stage and gallery. A store and post office occupied the front of the building on the ground floor, the Killingly National Bank was on the second floor, Armory Hall was on the third floor, and Grand Army Hall was on the fourth floor.

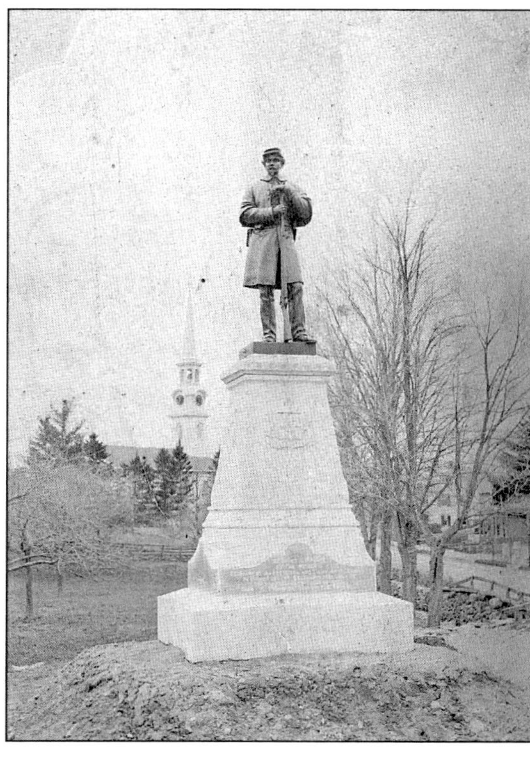

The Soldiers' Monument, 1878. Erected in memory of the soldiers and sailors who served in the Civil War, this monument was the only outdoor sculpture in town. The women of Killingly raised half the money to pay for the monument and the Town paid the balance. A little later, a cannon and a pyramid of cannonballs were placed in front of the figure of the Civil War soldier in uniform holding a musket.

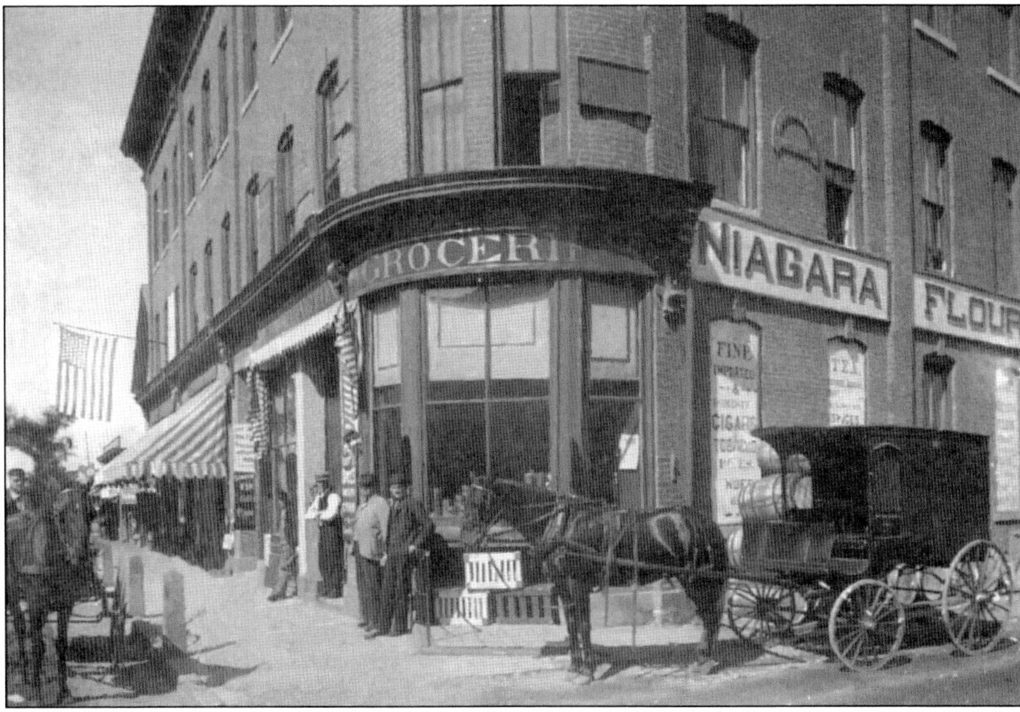

THE ARMINGTON GROCERY STORE. An 1882 Danielsonville business directory lists A.H. Armington as selling "Fruits, Ice Cream, and Oysters." The corner store was on the first floor of the Exchange block, at Main and Central Streets. After the owner's death in 1924, his son, Frederick Armington, carried on the business for a couple of years. Then, in 1926, W.T. Grant opened here.

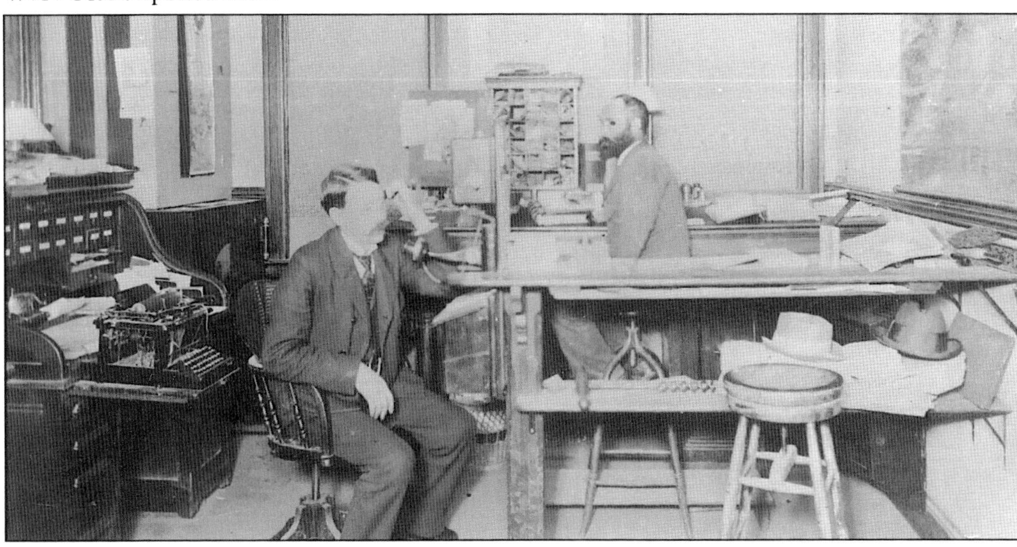

THE FIRST TELEPHONE IN DANIELSONVILLE, 1882. The Connecticut Telephone Company installed the first telephone in the residence of E.H. Jacobs in May 1882. The company office was located in M.P. Dowe's store. By October 1882, there were 40 subscribers in Killingly. The first intercity telephone cable for the Danielson area was installed in 1882–83, linking Hartford, Willimantic, Danielson, and Providence. Most of the telephones served industry.

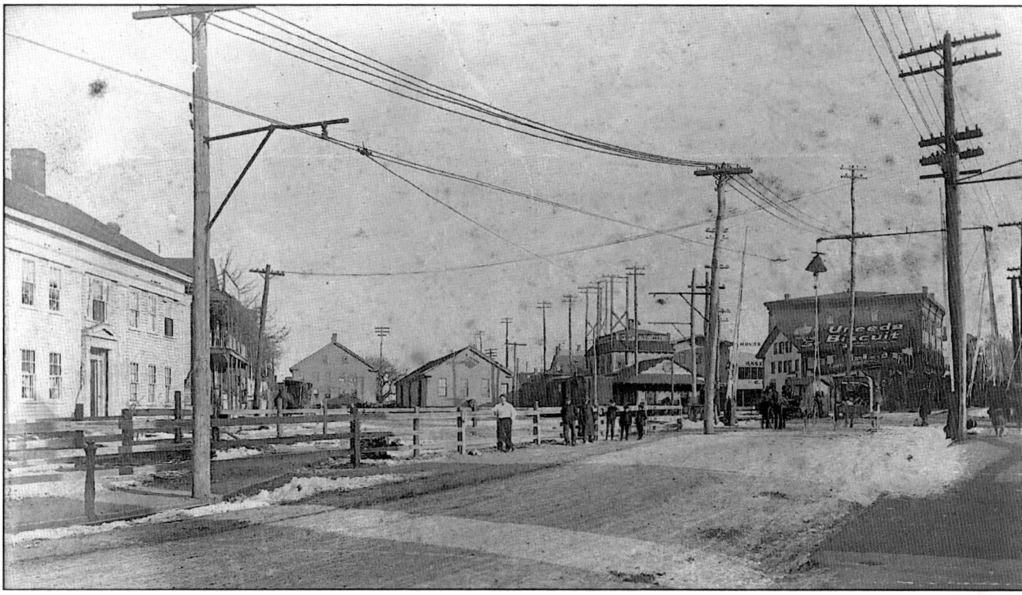

Streetlights, 1882. The Borough of Danielson bought gas streetlights. There were 100 lamps and posts. The lamps were lighted for 6¢ per burner per night for 20 nights every month. The lamplighter was a Mr. Wetherall. On each of those 20 nights, lamplighter Wetherall went from post to post in his horse-drawn wagon, which carried a short ladder. He climbed the ladder and lit the street lamp with a torch. This photograph by photographer S.A. Davis shows the area called Depot Village, where Commerce Avenue is now located.

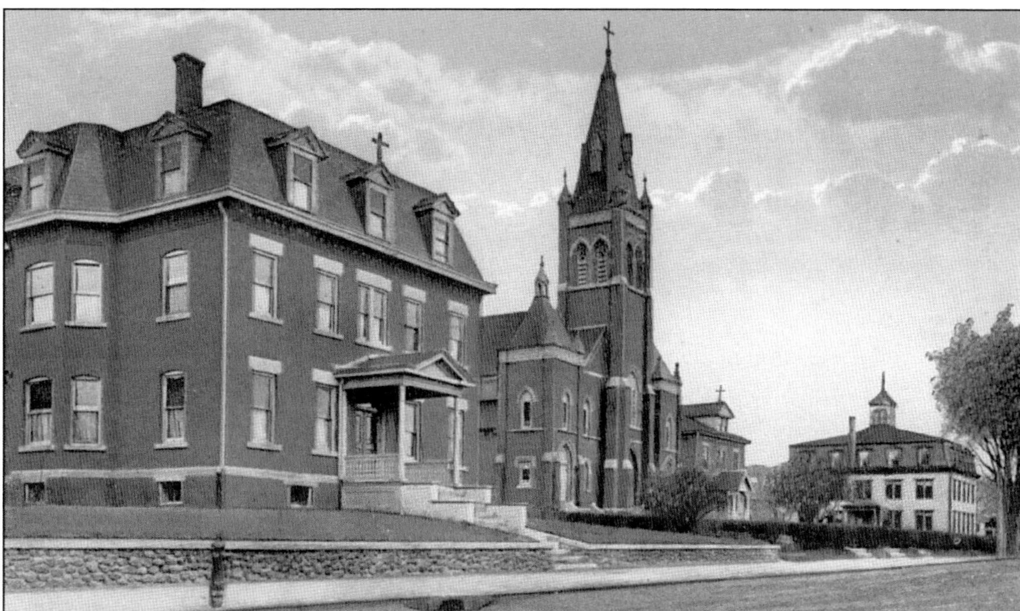

St. James Church and Old Parochial School, 1889. The parochial school opened on Franklin Street in 1889, the new St. James Church in 1900, and the new rectory in 1901. Late in the 1940s, St. James Hall was constructed beneath the church. The Sisters of St. Joseph occupied the old rectory on Franklin Street in 1909. The architecture of the church is attributed to Joseph Jackson of Waterbury.

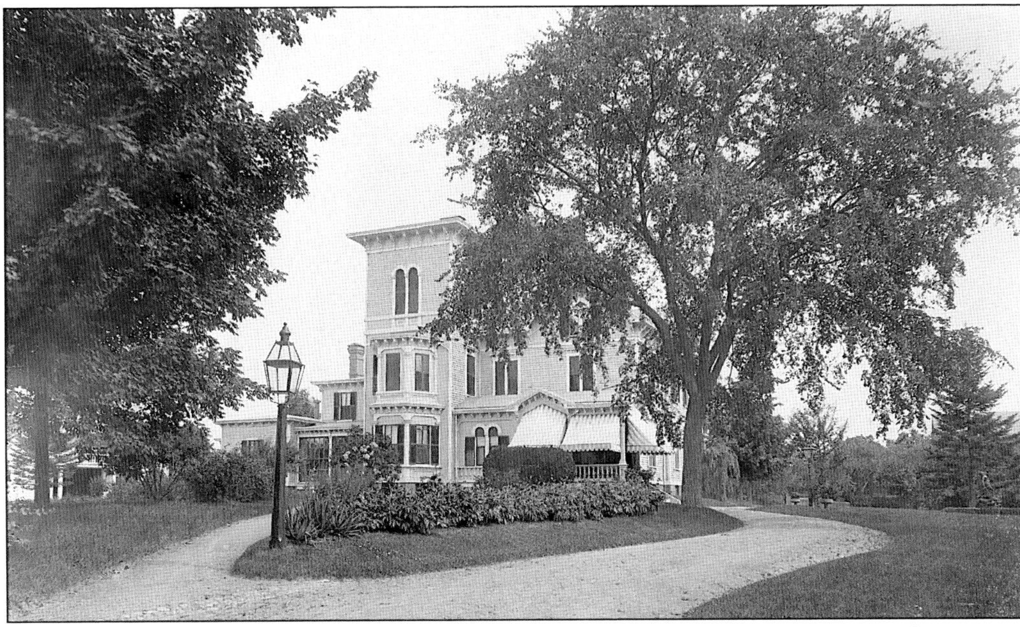

The Home of Timothy E. Hopkins. This beautiful home stood on the corner of Main and Hutchins Streets, where Killingly Memorial School is now located. In the mid-1930s, it was known as the Kingswood Inn. In earlier days, this was the site of Dr. Penuel Hutchins' home, which was later moved to another location on Hutchins Street.

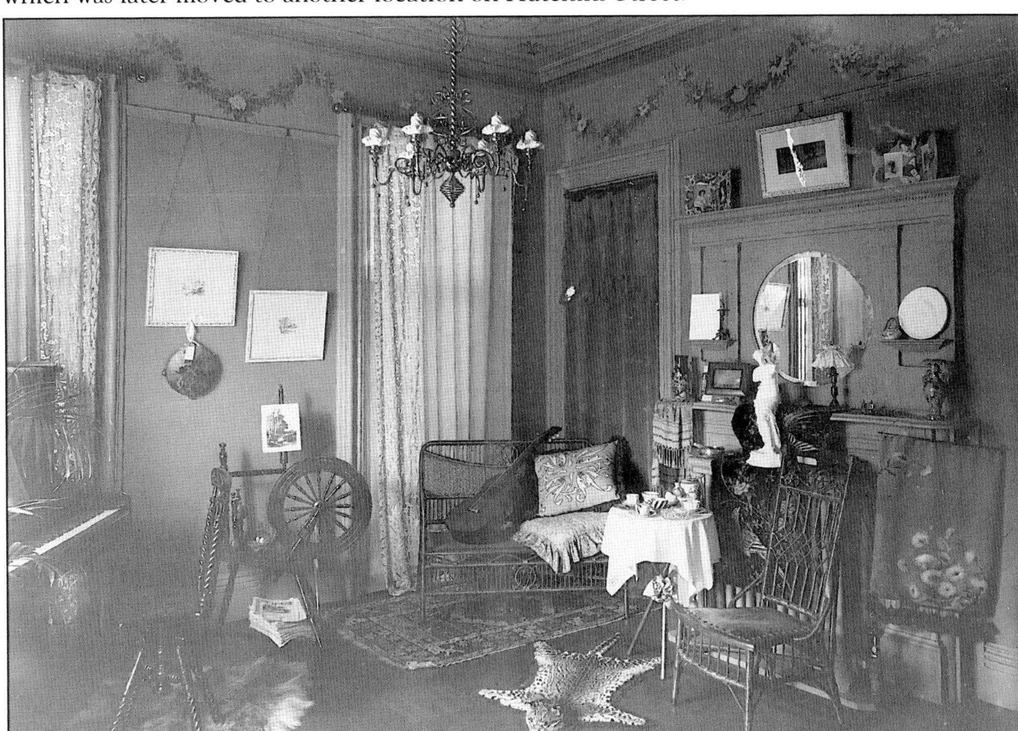

The Music Room. It is interesting to see how the T.E. Hopkins family decorated one of the rooms in their elegant home. The furnishings ranged from the utilitarian to the exotic.

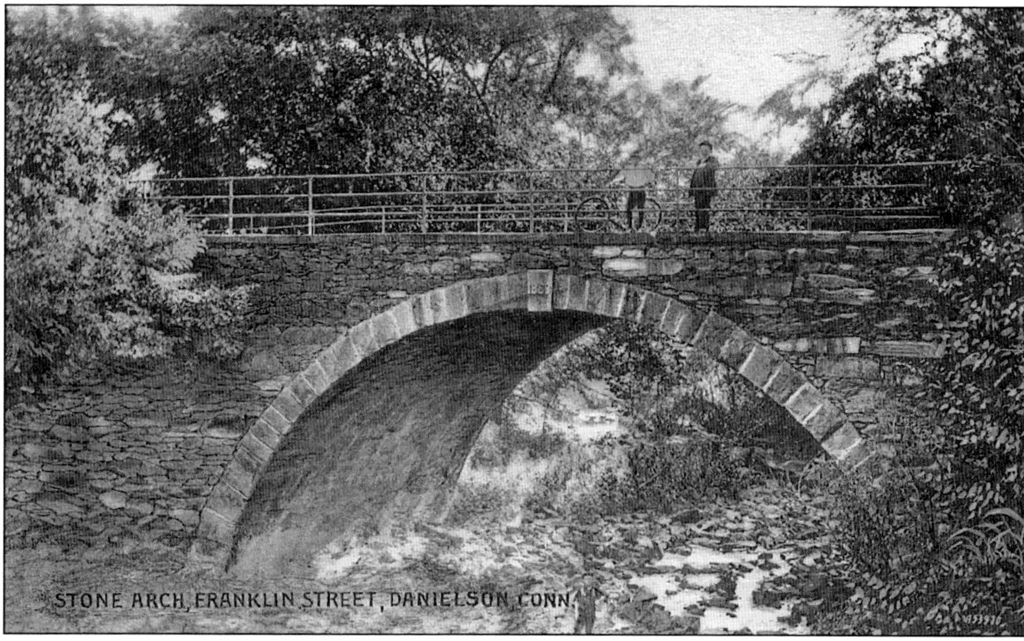

THE STONE ARCH BRIDGE ON FRANKLIN STREET, 1889. Stonemason Thomas Bradford built this handsomely crafted bridge at a cost of $5,000. Bradford had many talents. He was also a wagon maker, a machinist, and a steam heater salesman. The bridge formerly carried Franklin Street across the Five Mile River. It was demolished in 1957 when the rotary was constructed.

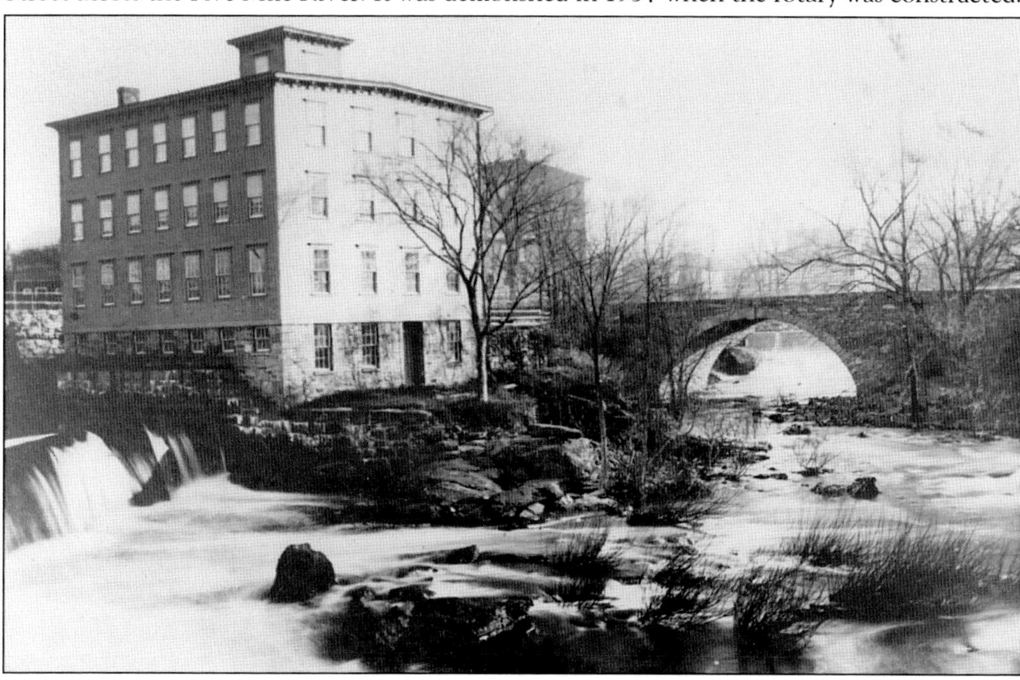

A GRISTMILL AND THE FRANKLIN STREET BRIDGE, LATE 1800S. This mill, located on the corner of Franklin and Main Streets, was used as a grain mill during the late 1800s. William Gleason, Benjamin Burlingham, and others served as millers there. Both the bridge and the mill were removed in 1957 to make way for a new traffic circle.

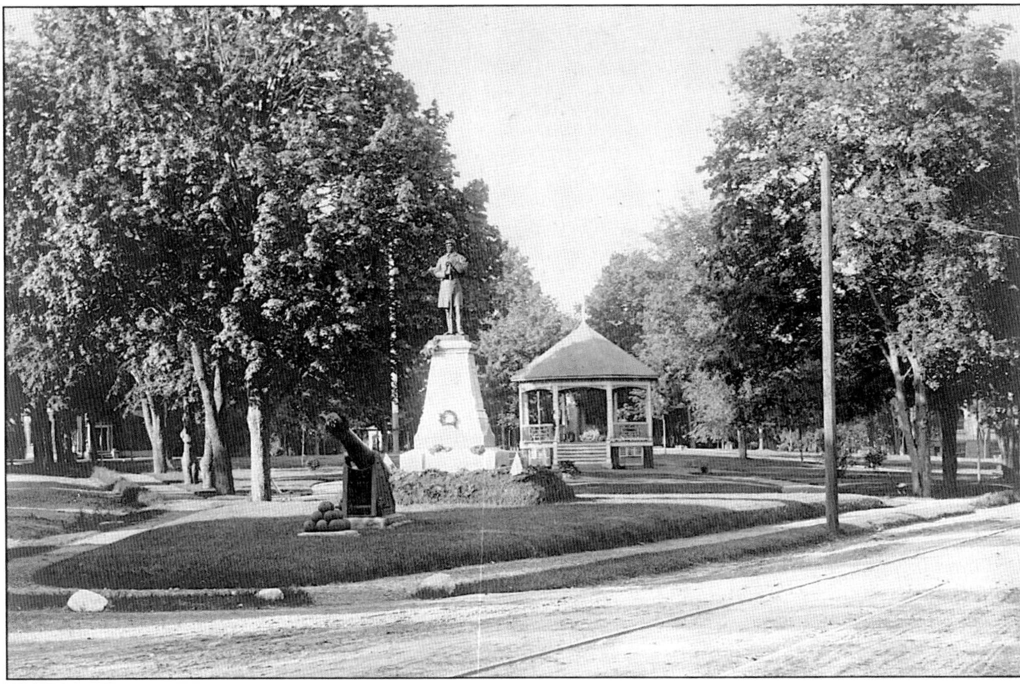

DAVIS PARK, 1890. Mr. J.Q.A. Stone, editor of the *Windham County Transcript,* spearheaded a movement to raise money to buy land from the estate of Capt. Samuel Reynolds for a park. Altogether, $6,000 was raised. The largest individual gift was from Edwin W. Davis, a former resident of Danielson. Davis requested that the park be named in memory of his father and mother, Randall and Philia Kies Davis.

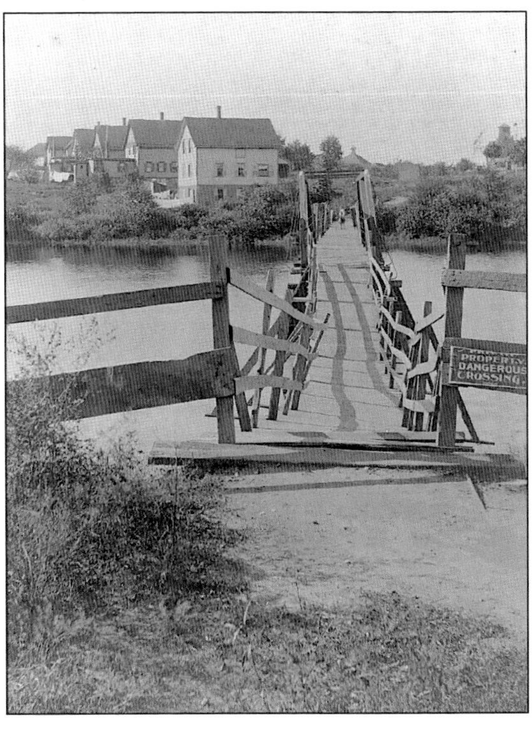

THE FIVE MILE RIVER FOOTBRIDGE. The first footbridge was built *c.* 1850 by Dr. Stephen C. Griggs, at his own expense, as a shortcut to his home on Maple Street. It was nearly opposite the end of Union Street. The next bridge was erected *c.* 1890 by the proprietors of the Riverview Association. In 1902, a bridge was laid out by the selectmen "to be a wooden structure with gravel and stone." This bridge was replaced in the 1930s.

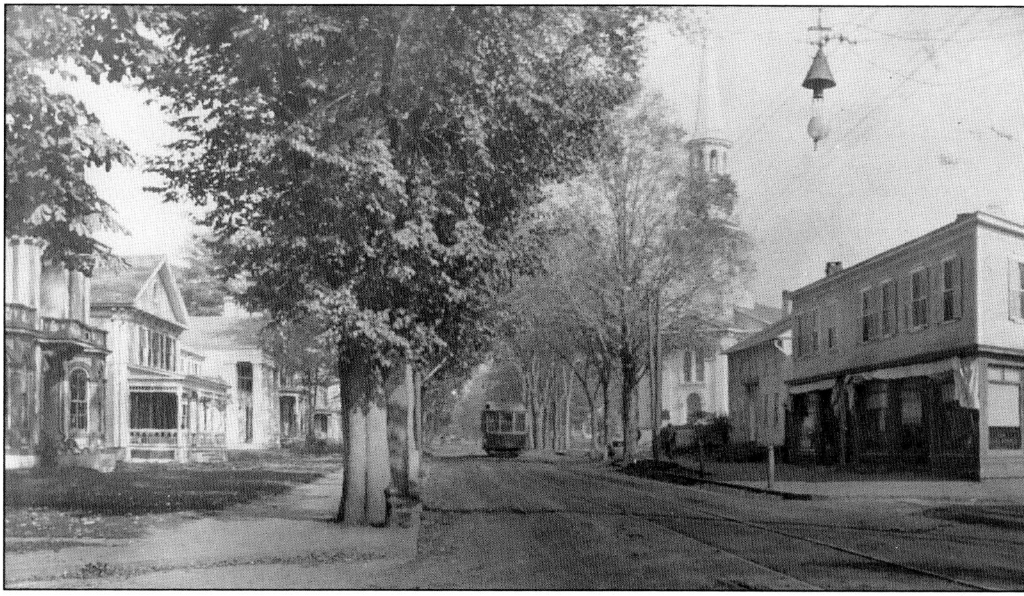

Electricity, 1893. Killingly's first electricity was provided by the People's Light and Power Company. Lines were extended later to Plainfield and Brooklyn. This view shows Main Street where it crosses Academy Street. On the far right is D.P. Burlingham's Store. Next to that is the Dimmick house, where the Killingly Historical Society Library and Museum is now located. Except for the church, all the buildings in this picture are now gone.

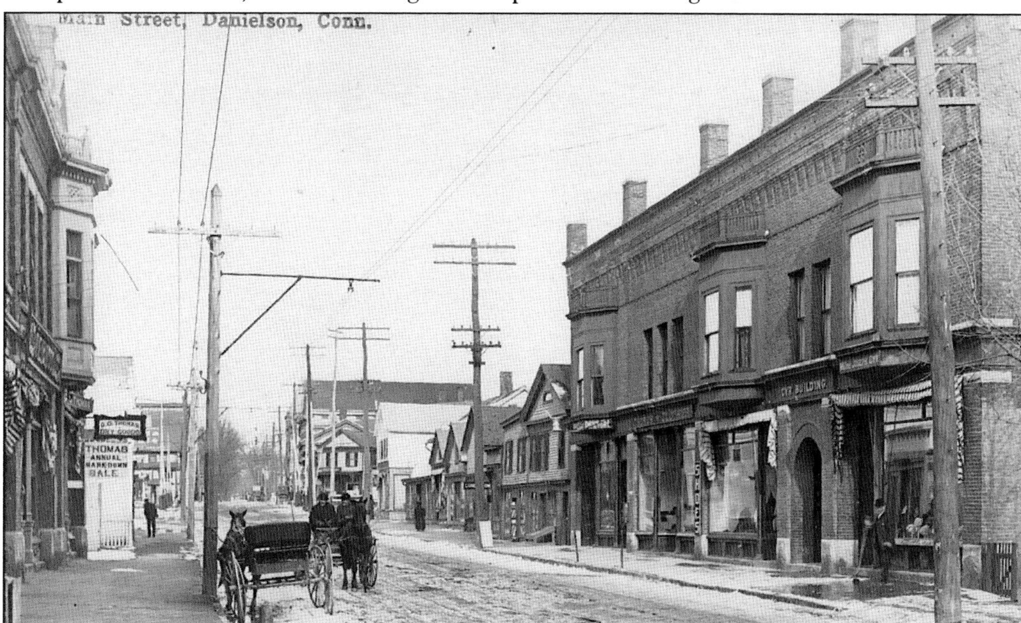

The Cyr Building, 1893. This building is of historical interest because it reflects the accomplishments of Danielson's leading woman entrepreneur of the 19th century. Valerie M. Cyr was a successful milliner, one of the few opportunities open to women in that period. She started her business in 1876. By 1893, she had prospered sufficiently to build this large block, which accommodated her shop, a clothing store, and doctors' offices on the upper floor.

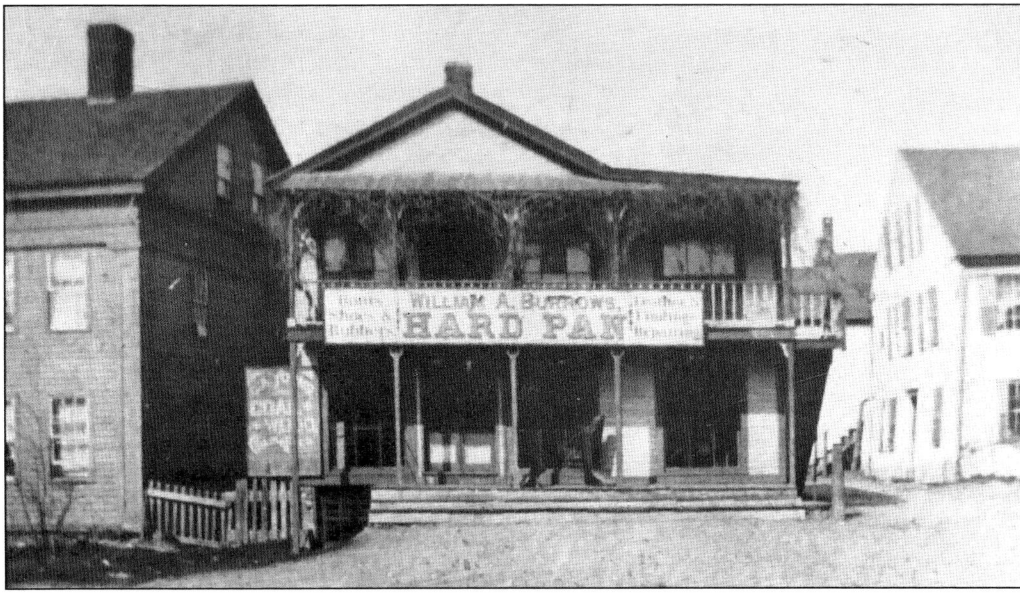

The Hard Pan, 1894. The Hard Pan Boot and Shoe Store of William A. Burrows Sr. was established on Railroad Street (now Commerce Avenue) in 1850. In those times and for several decades to come, men and boys wore boots more often than shoes. The store remained here well into the early 1900s and is remembered by old-timers for the giant boot standing out front. The building was taken down in 1950.

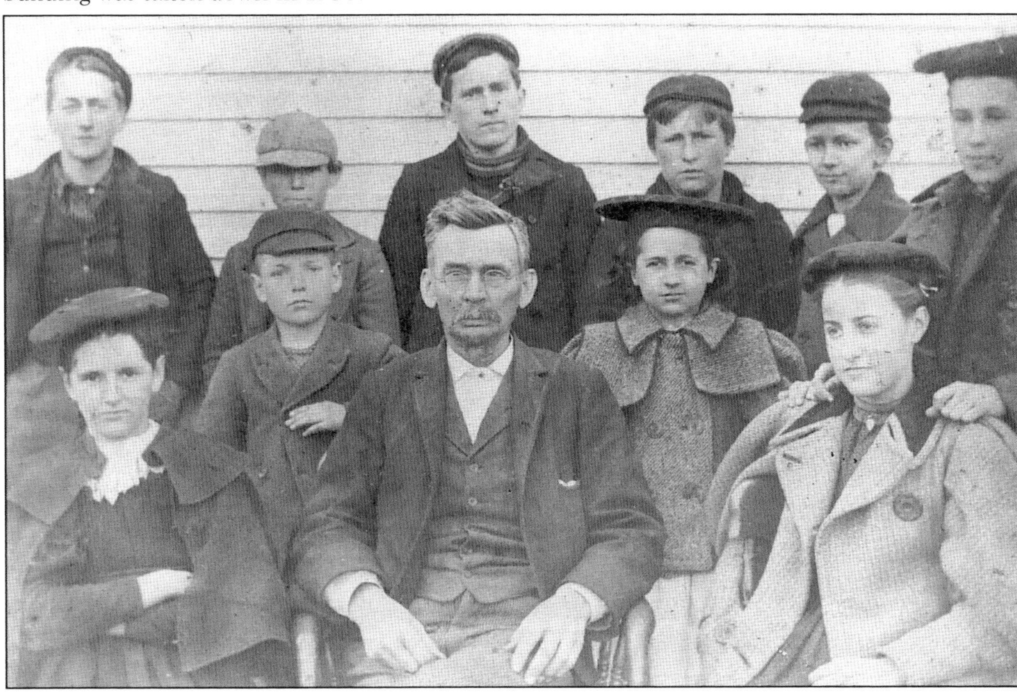

The Lysander Warren School, c. late 1800s. This school was on Green Hollow Road across from the Ernest Warren Farm, near Shepherd Hill Road. The teacher in the photograph was Nehemiah Wood. The students were from the Bassett, Jordan, and Bailey families. The school closed in 1898.

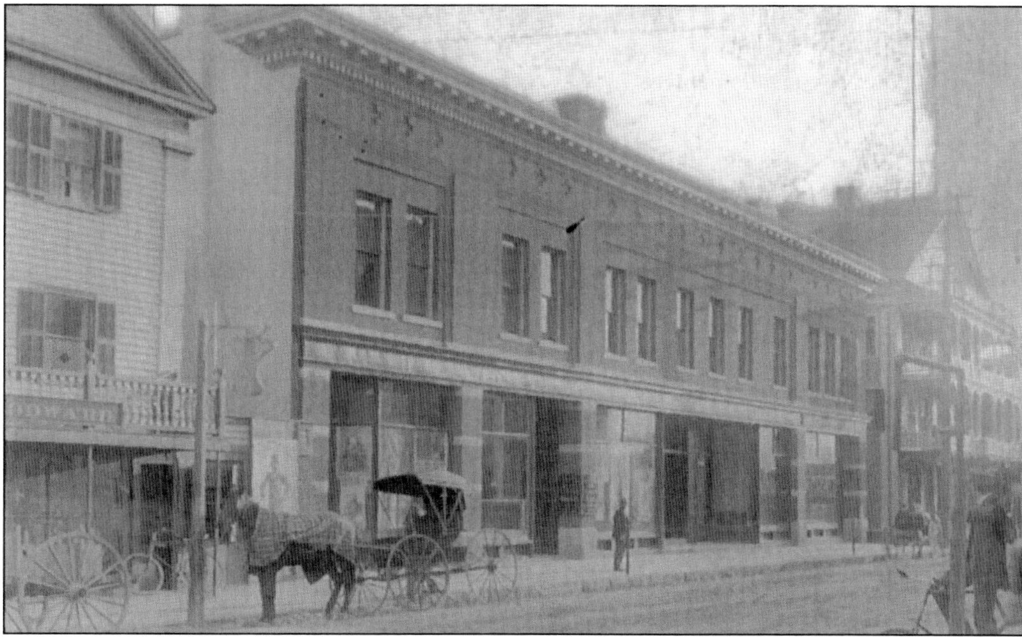

The Phoenix Block on Main Street, c. late 1800s. It is hard to imagine Main Street without an automobile in sight. Hitching posts were used to tie up the horses. Note the gentleman on the bicycle. Woodward's Drug Store was on the corner of Center Street and had been operating there since 1868. The store's advertising mentioned varnish and paint, as well as medicines, tobacco, and confectioneries.

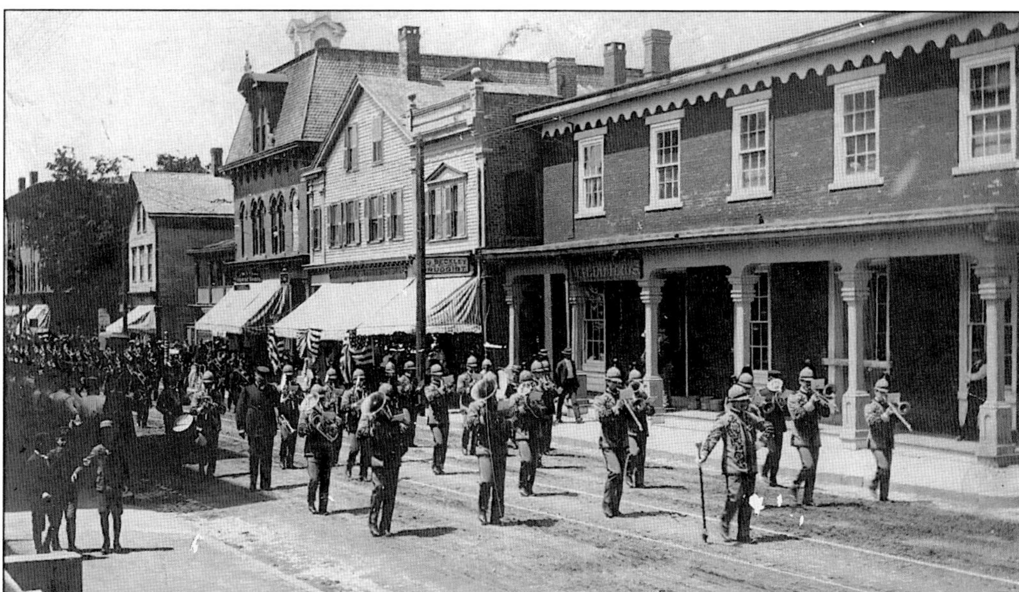

The Mechanics Band, June 20, 1902. The band marched smartly down Main Street in this parade. On the right was the Waldo block. Located on the corner of Academy Street, it was later known as the Gallup block. Next, was A.G. Beckley, Druggist. Note the spire of the old Danielson Methodist Church in the background. It was on the corner of Central and Main Streets.

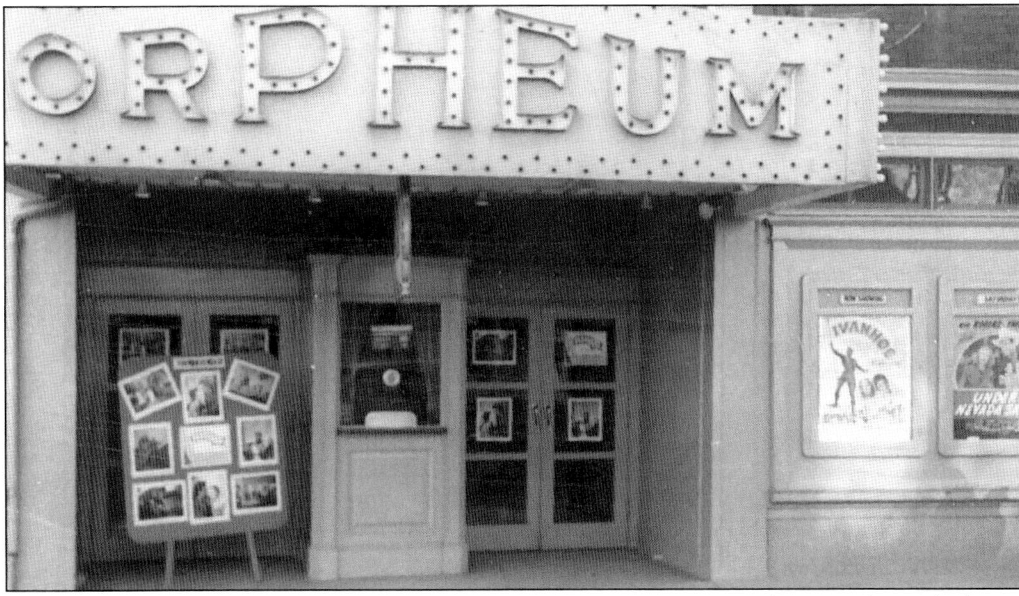

THE ORPHEUM THEATRE. From 1900 to 1921, this theater was known as the Danielson Playhouse. It then became the Orpheum Theatre, where over the years entertainment ranged from silent films with piano or organ music to vaudeville acts to talking pictures. Henry Johnson was the manager for many years. Henry Mazzarella purchased the theater in 1954 and changed its name to the Danielson Cinema. The building burned in 1978.

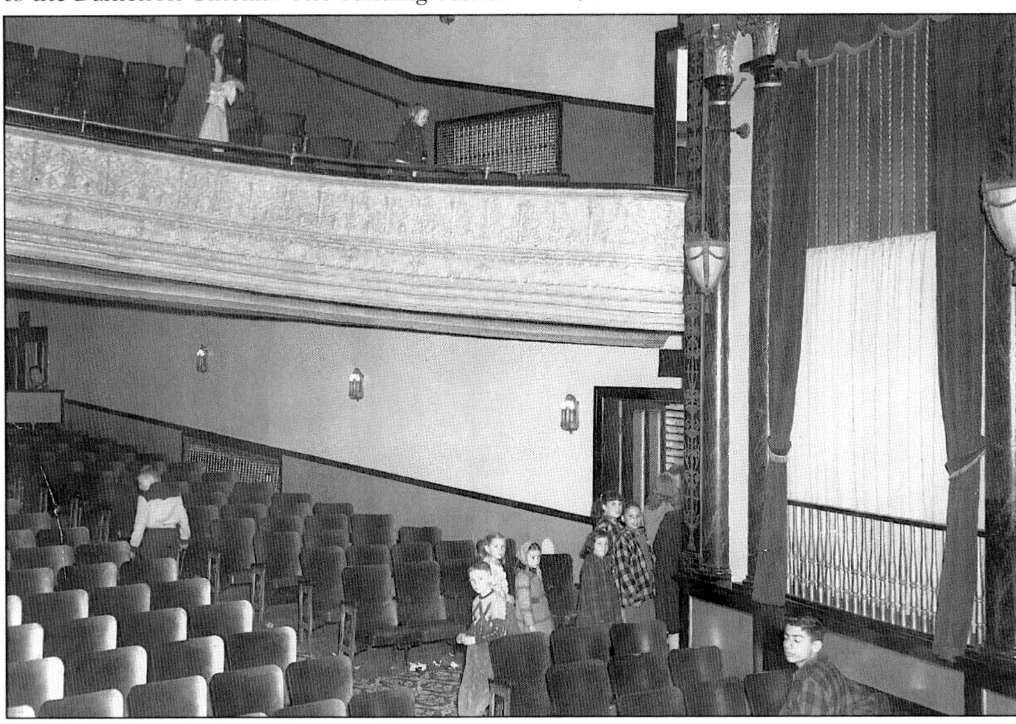

THE INTERIOR OF THE ORPHEUM THEATRE, C. 1941. Even in its later years, the theater retained the ornate style of the original Orpheum. The original stage and orchestra pit remained, along with the balcony, pillars, moldings, and ceiling.

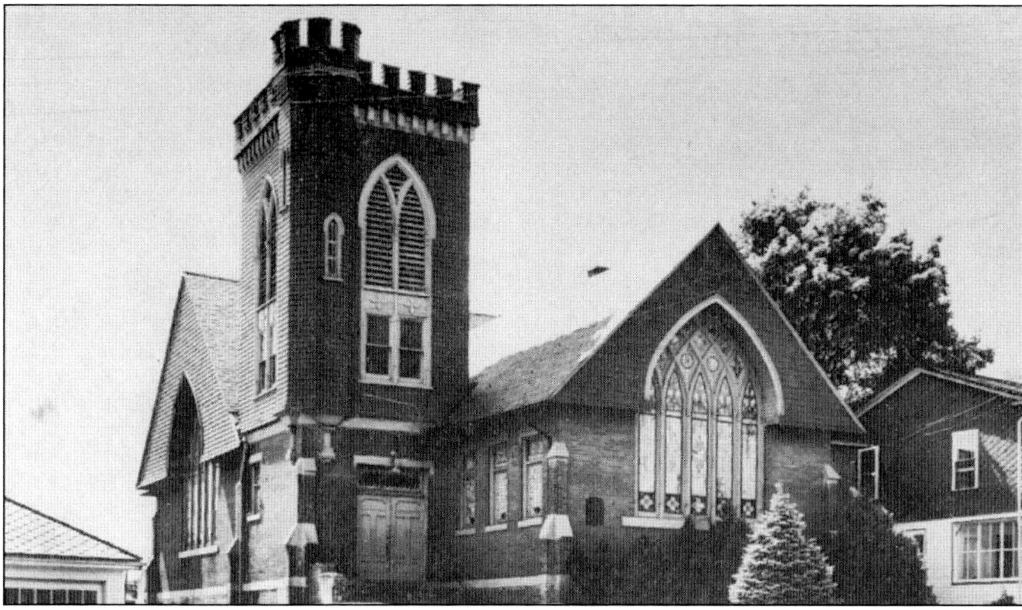

The New Methodist Church, 1902. Some 100,000 bricks were used in the building of this Methodist church. Sidney S. Stone was in charge of the construction work. A parsonage was dedicated in 1941 on the corner of Broad and Cottage Streets. A new parsonage was built on Dorrance Street, *c.* 1960.

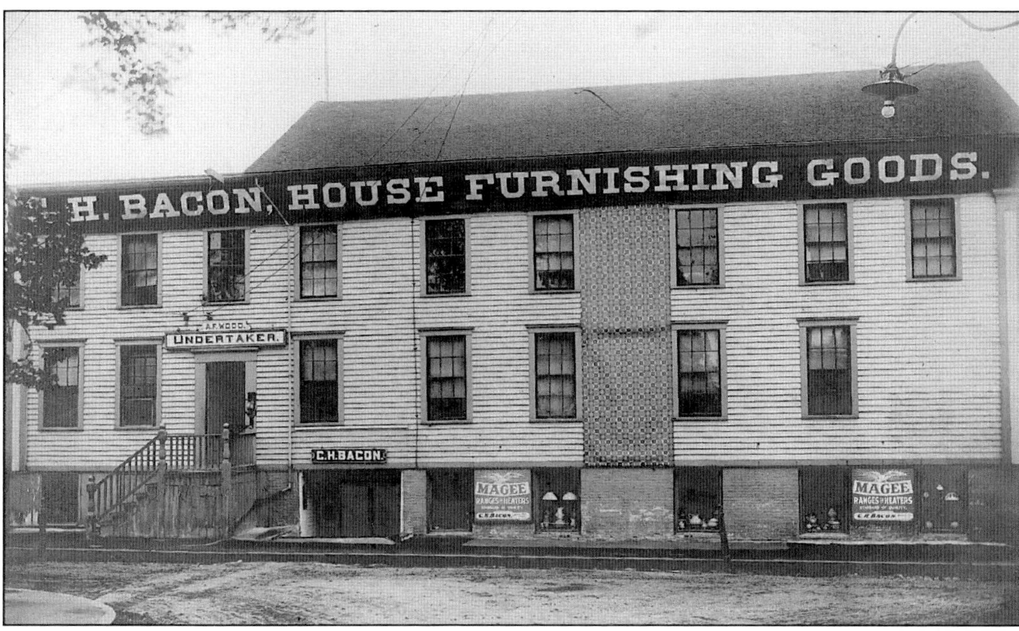

C.H. Bacon. In April 1903, C.H. Bacon purchased the old Methodist church building on the corner of Main and Central Streets and had it moved to face Railroad Square. Bacon then remodeled it into a business block, featuring house furnishings. A.F. Wood's undertaking establishment was also in the building.

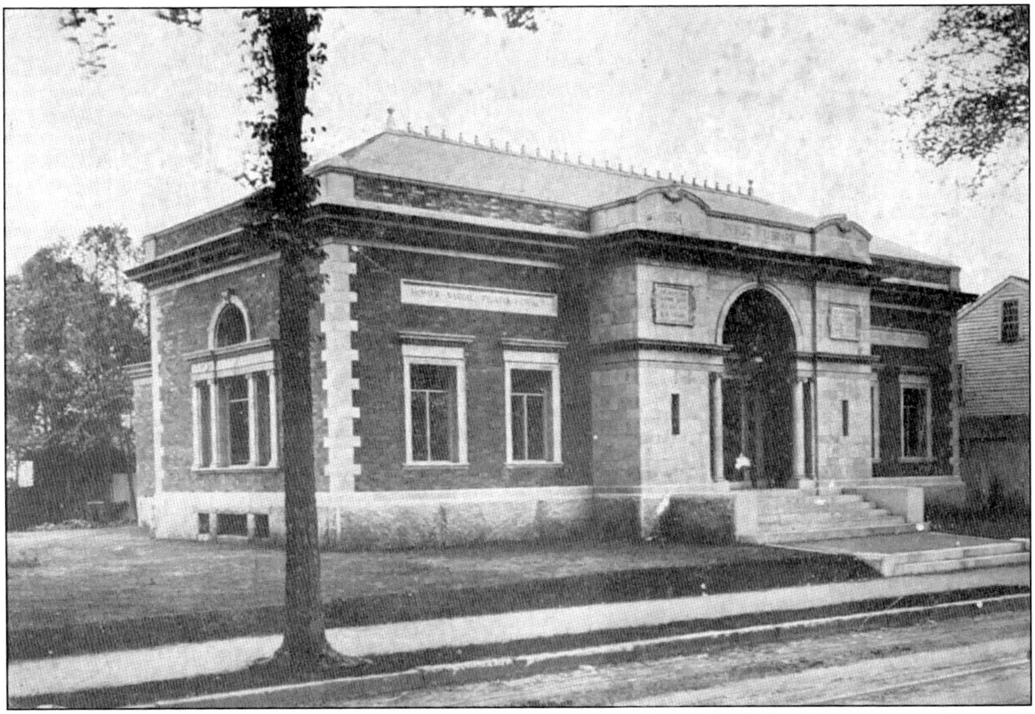

The Bugbee Memorial Library, 1903. An architectural jewel of the Renaissance Revival style, this building was constructed with a $15,000 bequest from Edwin Holmes Bugbee. Bugbee built it to house his collection of books and to serve as a library for the community. The building now serves as the Killingly Historical & Genealogical Society's Library and Museum.

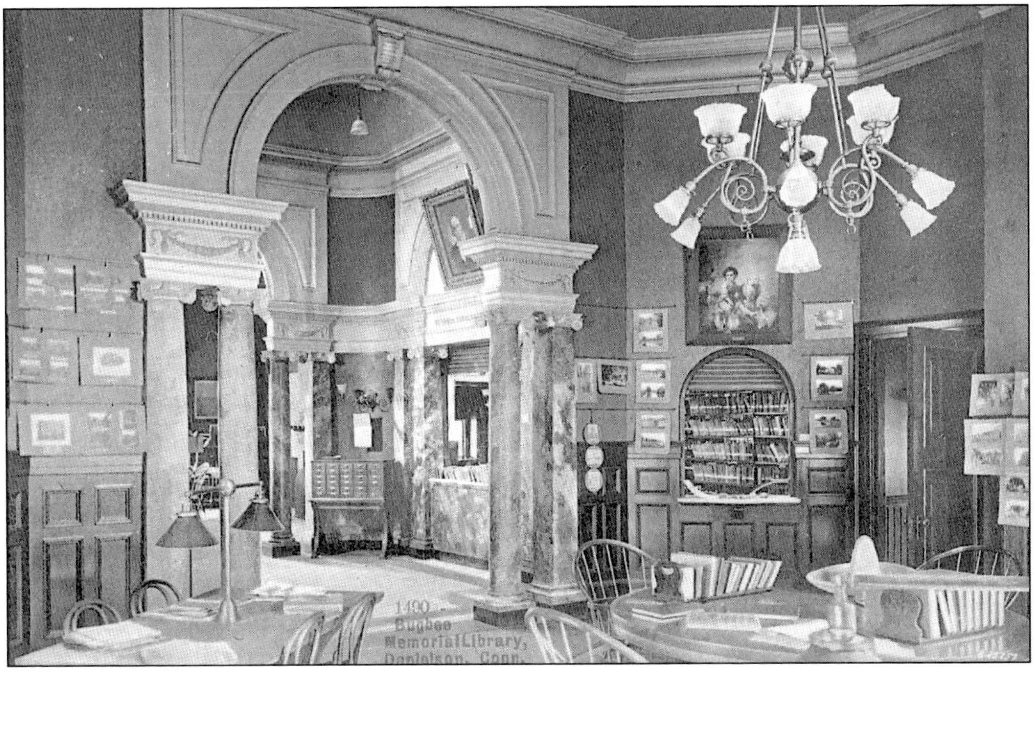

TOWN HALL. On November 17, 1906, the Town of Killingly voted to spend $20,000 to purchase the Music Hall block for use as the town hall. In later years, the first floor was used as a high school gymnasium. The building is a fine example of High Victorian Gothic architecture. An addition was constructed at the rear of the building.

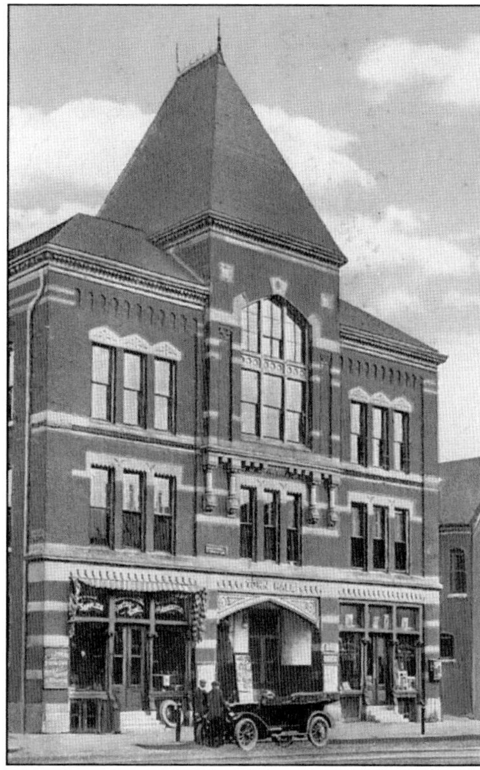

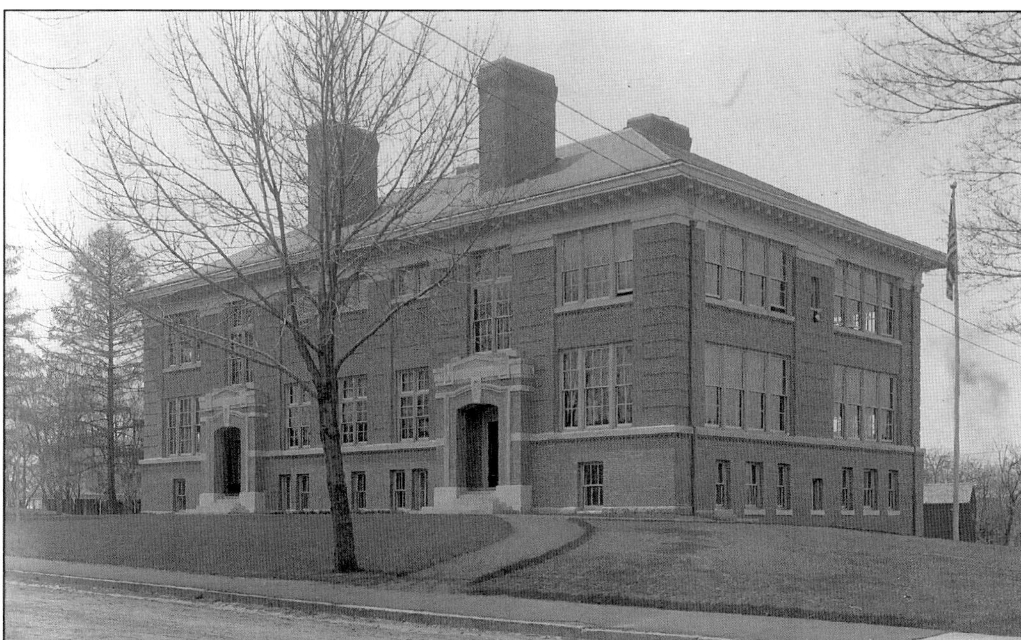

KILLINGLY HIGH SCHOOL, 1908. The bicentennial celebration of the Town of Killingly included the dedication of the new high school on Broad Street. The school was built on property donated by John W. Danielson. The principal of the new high school was Charles T. Stone. In 1927, an addition to the school was formally opened.

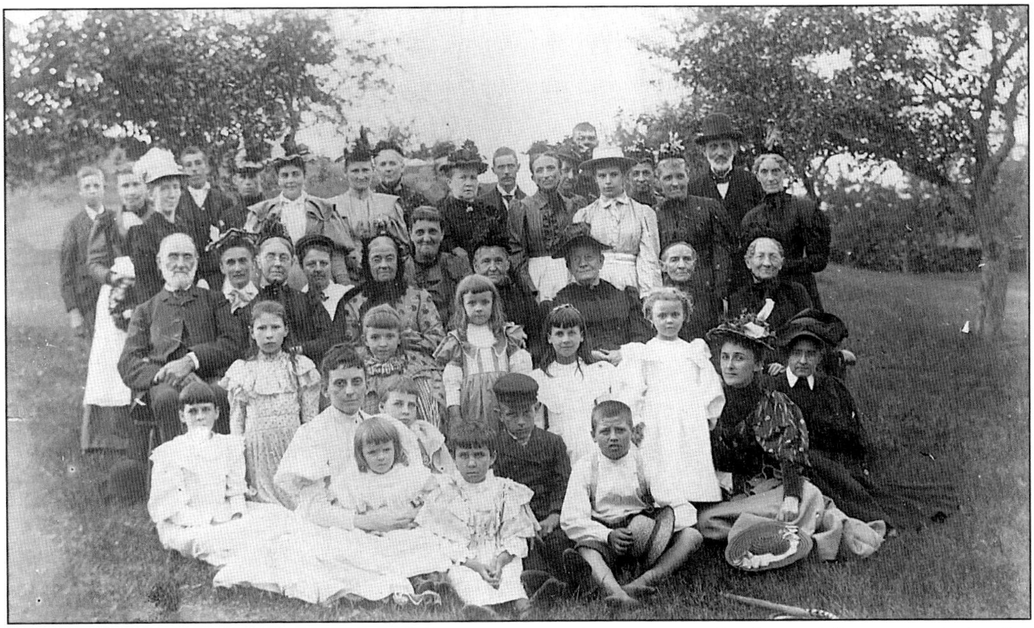

A Picnic in the late 1800s. It is fun to compare the way people dressed for a picnic in the 1800s with how they dress today. This photograph was found in the home of Susan M. Stone on September 1, 1916, and was part of Agnes Jacobs's collection.

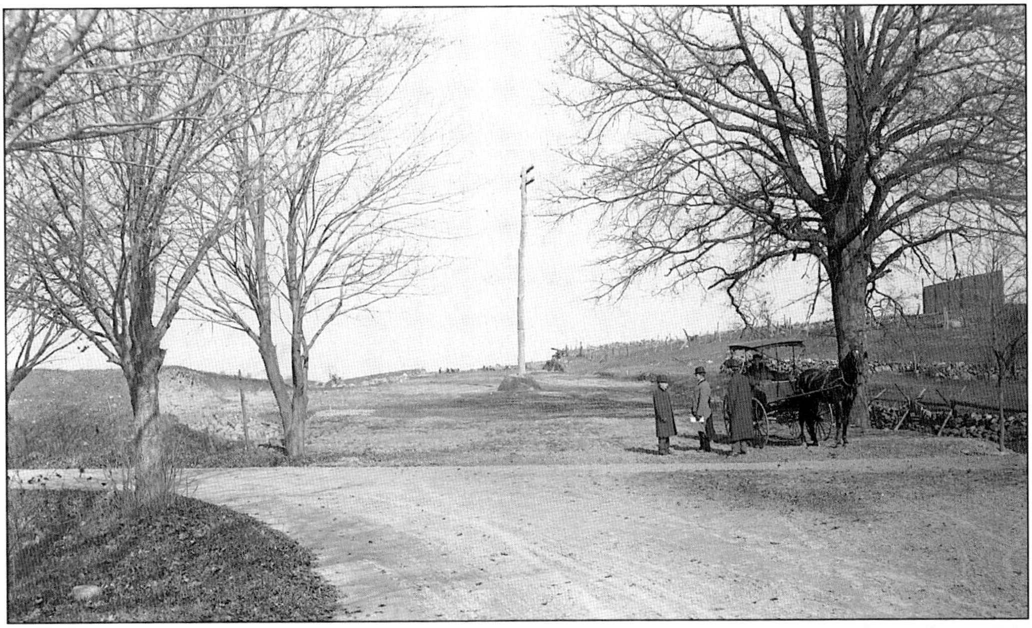

Industrial Place, 1906. Two New Britain entrepreneurs, doing business as the Industrial & Manufacturing Company, bought a vast tract of land north of the built-up part of Danielson. They advertised the tract as Industrial Place. Two large factory buildings were erected and rented out to manufacturers. Within a short time, the company became insolvent. Photographer A.A. Dean took this early photograph.

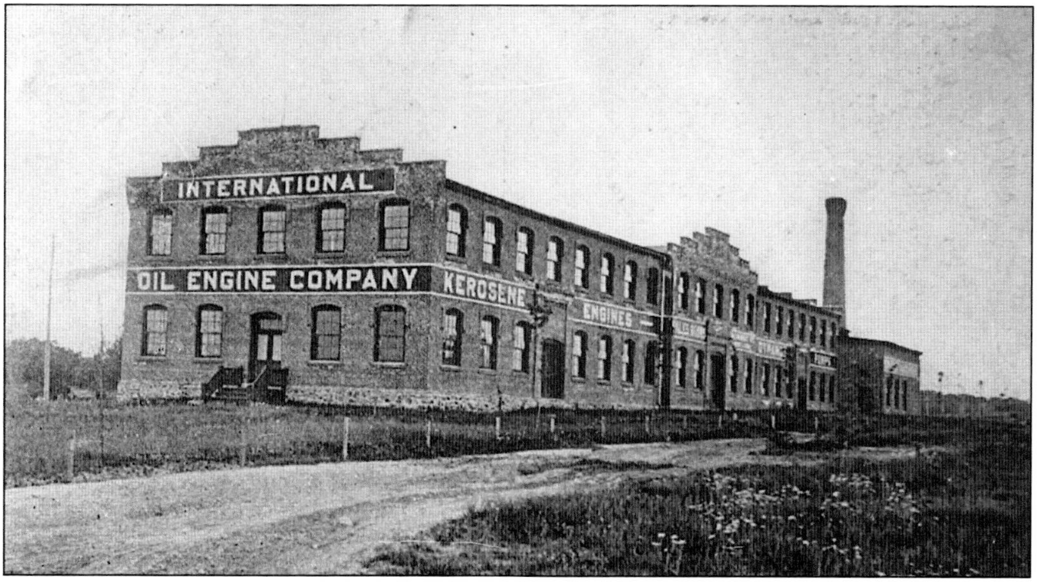

The Industrial Oil Engine Company, 1907. The owners of this company, located on Connecticut Mills Avenue, were attracted to Danielson through the efforts of the local board of trade. By 1908, the company had produced a kerosene-driven car, as well as kerosene oil engines. As automobiles became a favorite means of transportation, Killingly's industry diversified accordingly.

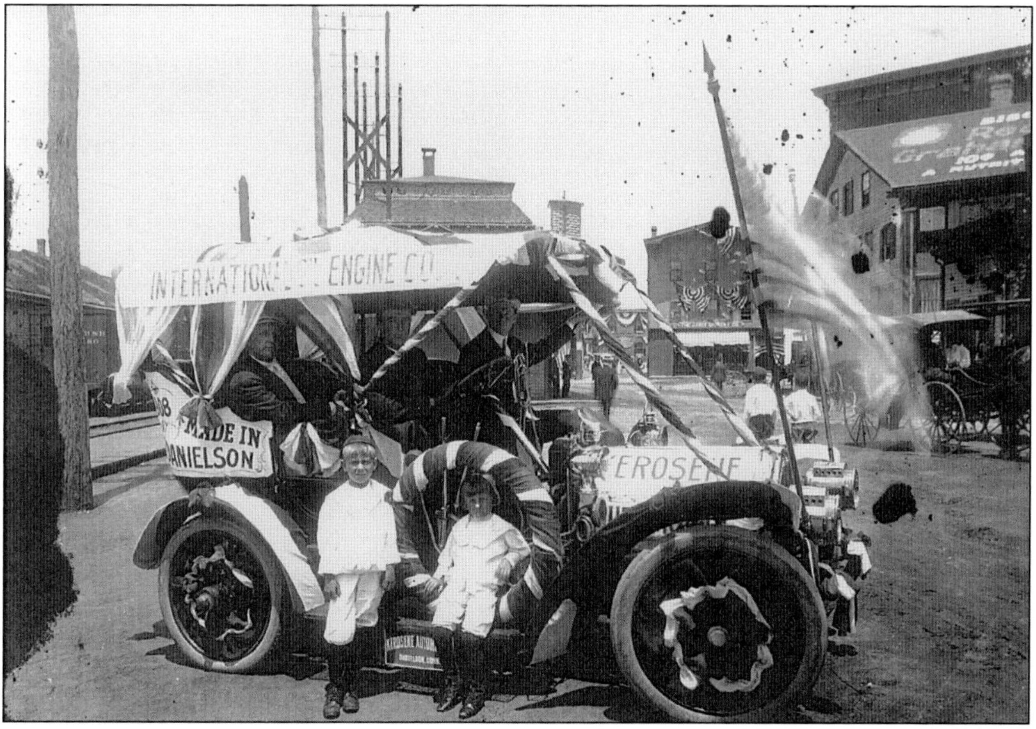

Made in Danielson, 1908. One of the entries in the 1908 Bicentennial Parade was this kerosene-driven automobile, manufactured by the International Oil Engine Company. This photograph was taken in Railroad Square, near the depot.

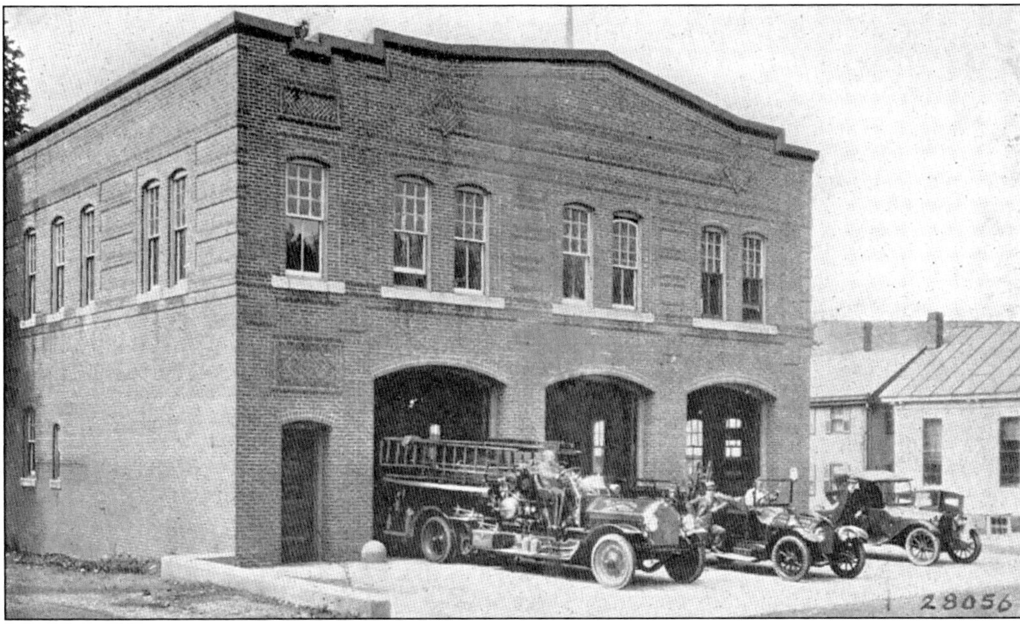

THE DANIELSON FIREHOUSE, 1908. In 1908, the fire station on the corner of School and Academy Streets was completed and all equipment was moved from Boro Hall on Water Street. A fire alarm system was installed. In 1910, the fire department purchased a horse-drawn supply wagon.

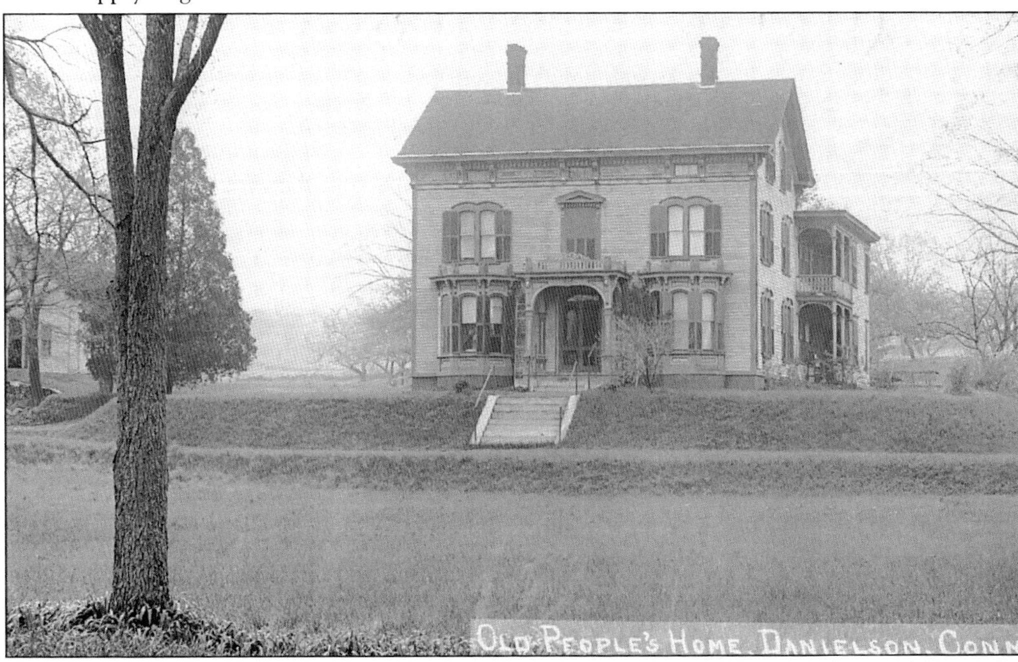

THE WESTCOTT-WILCOX OLD PEOPLE'S HOME, 1904 AND 1909. The Wilcox Old People's Home was incorporated in 1904. Betsey Wilcox, who said she would endow the home, left a substantial sum from her estate in 1939. Elmira E. Westcott promised to donate her dwelling to the corporation on condition that the home's name be changed to Westcott and Wilcox Old People's Home. This was done on January 18, 1909.

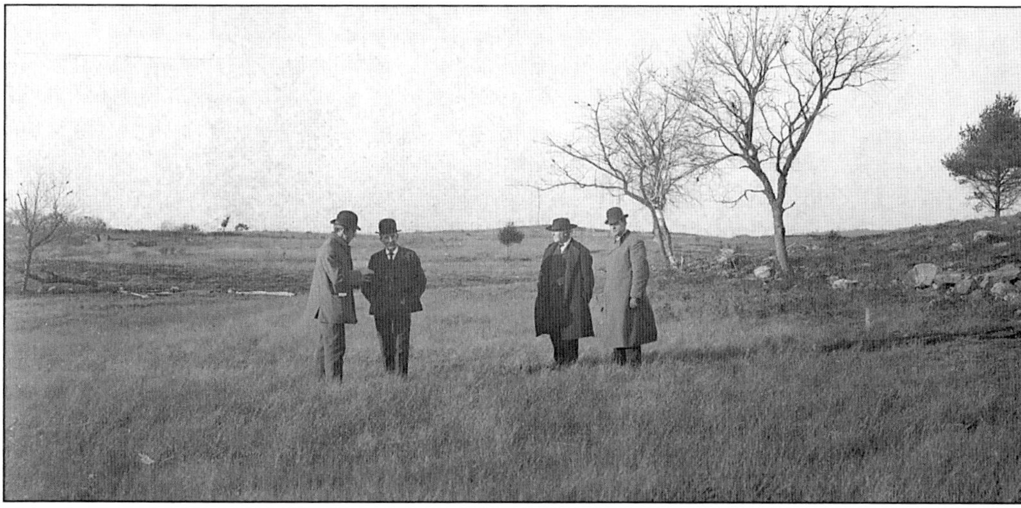

THE CONNECTICUT MILLS CONSTRUCTION SITE, 1909. A.A. Dean took a series of photographs detailing the construction progress of this important project. Members of the Pike family were involved in surveying in this community for three generations: George W. Pike was engaged in that profession from 1868 to 1900; his son, William K. Pike (third from the left), continued the business until his death in 1950; and William K.'s son, William W. Pike, then carried on the family tradition.

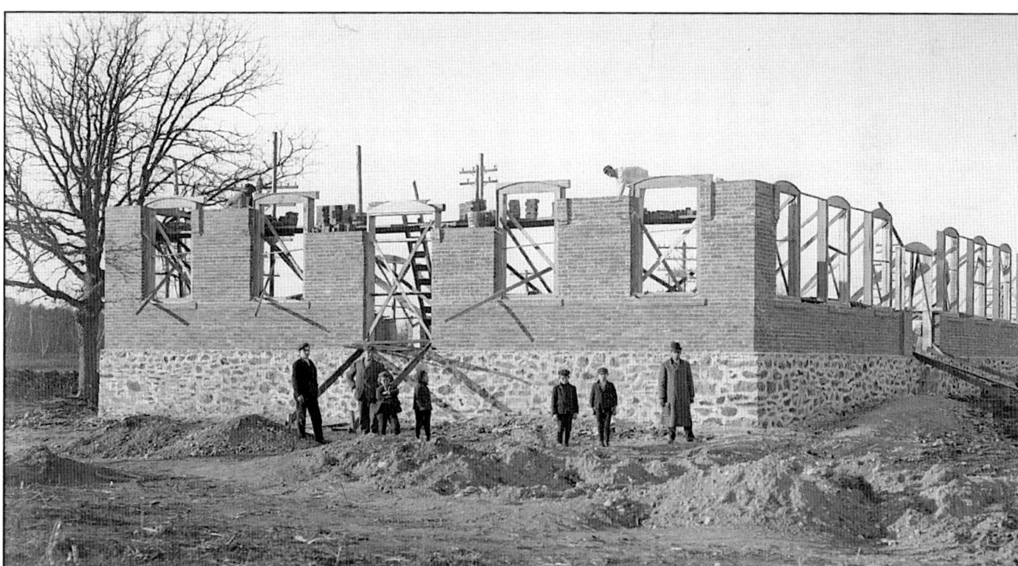

THE CONNECTICUT MILLS COMPANY, 1909. The Connecticut Mills Company, one of the tenants of Industrial Place, manufactured canvas for tire belting. The company acquired the factories and most of the Industrial Place land, including several houses. It never used waterpower but relied on steam. It was located next to the Norwich & Worcester Railroad, one mile north of the center of Danielson. In 1926, the company moved production south and sold off its holdings.

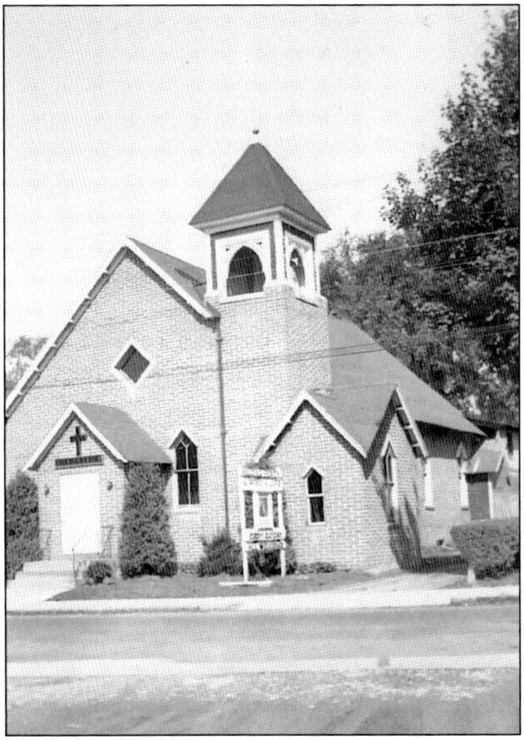

The Church of the Nazarene, 1912. In 1897, a Holiness convention was held in the Danielson Advent Church, resulting in the organization of a Holiness Gospel Mission. The mission rented a hall in the Perkins block on Main Street for nearly two years. Later, the mission used rooms in the Advent Church and the vestry of the old Methodist church. In 1912, this church building on the north side of Academy Street was dedicated.

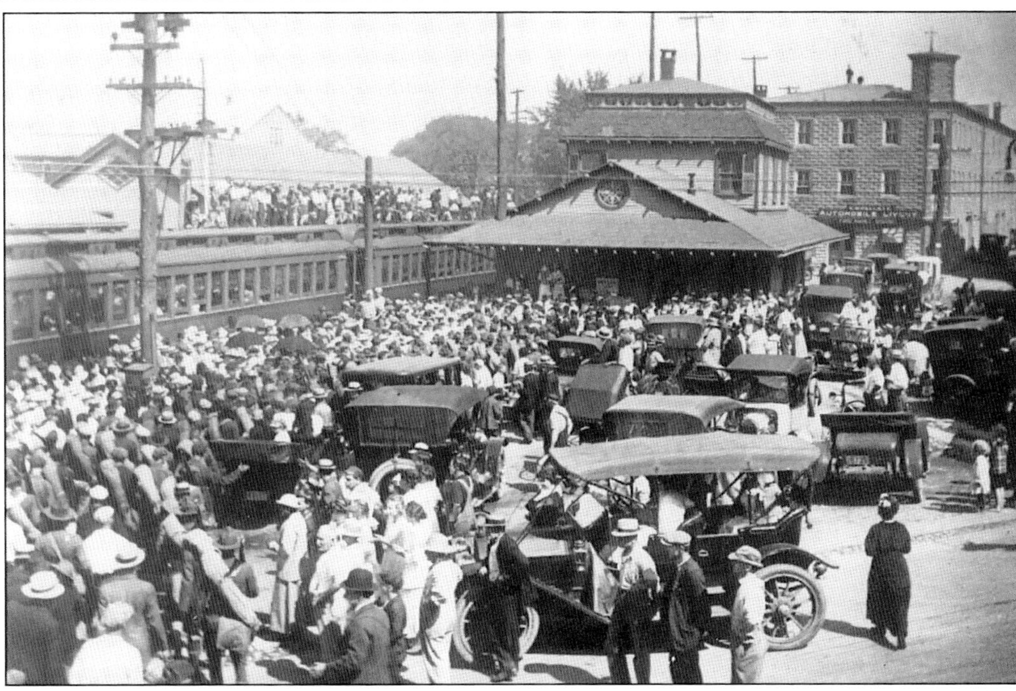

Seeing the Boys off for World War I. The railroad station was located on the east side of the tracks, behind the bank, on the current site of the municipal parking lot. The station closed in 1938, after passenger service was discontinued. Before being demolished, the building was used as a feed and grain store and later as a barbershop.

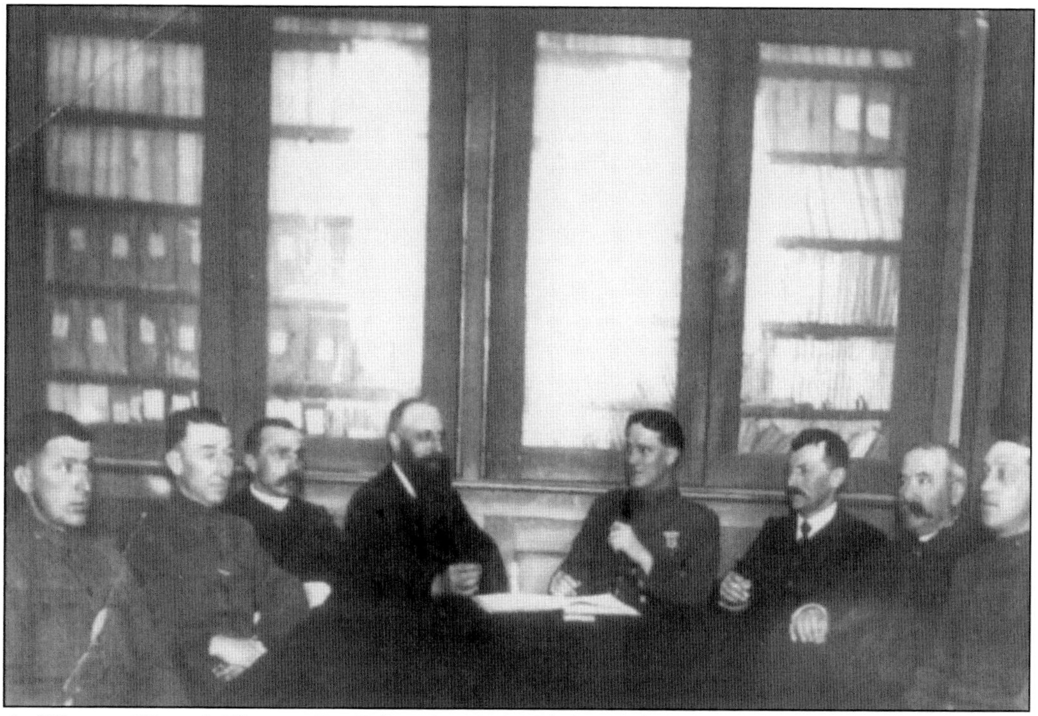

A World War I Hero. On July 18, 1918, Philip Roberge of Dyer Street, a private in Company D, 103rd Machine Gun Battalion, was awarded the Distinguished Service Cross for "extraordinary heroism in action" and the Croix de Guerre. He is pictured here, second from left, at the signing of the Treaty of Versailles, along with Gen. John Pershing, fifth from left.

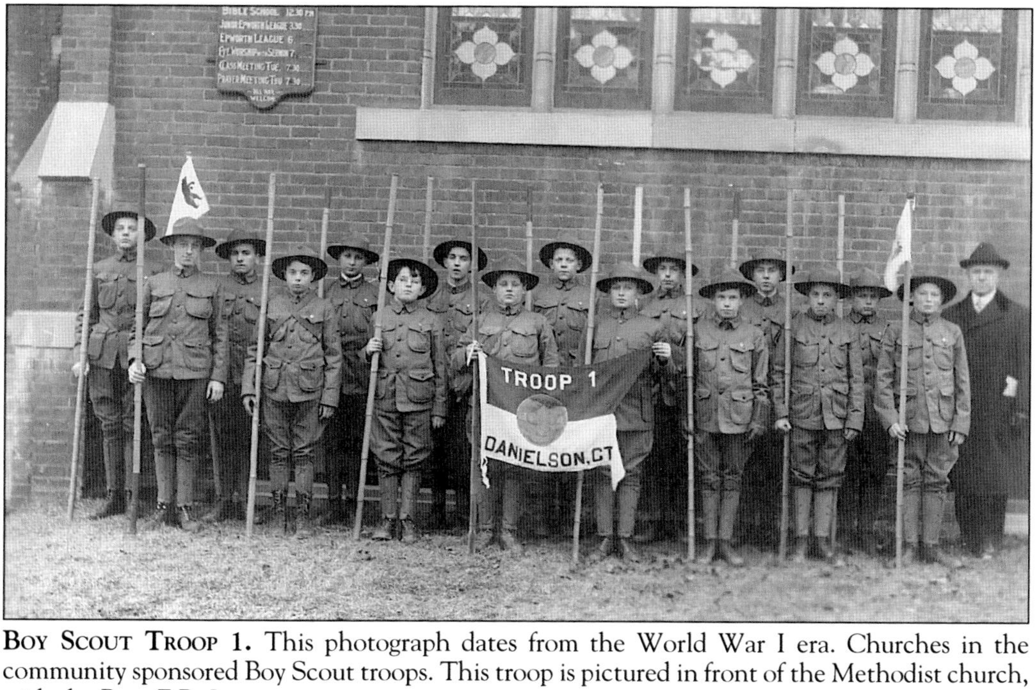

Boy Scout Troop 1. This photograph dates from the World War I era. Churches in the community sponsored Boy Scout troops. This troop is pictured in front of the Methodist church, with the Rev. E.R. Legg, pastor.

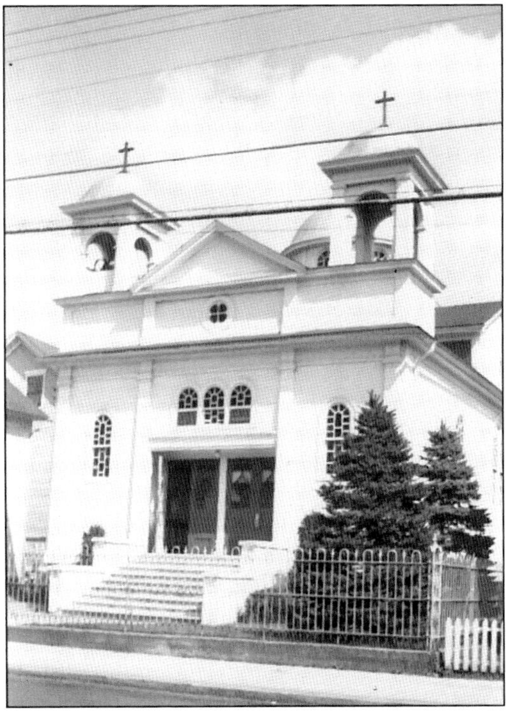

HOLY TRINITY GREEK ORTHODOX CHURCH, 1918. Residents of Greek descent held their first service in a small hall on Elm Street, East Brooklyn, in 1916. The following year they purchased land on Water Street from the Taunton Cotton Mills Company and built a house of worship. Members attended the first Divine Liturgy in the new church on February 8, 1918.

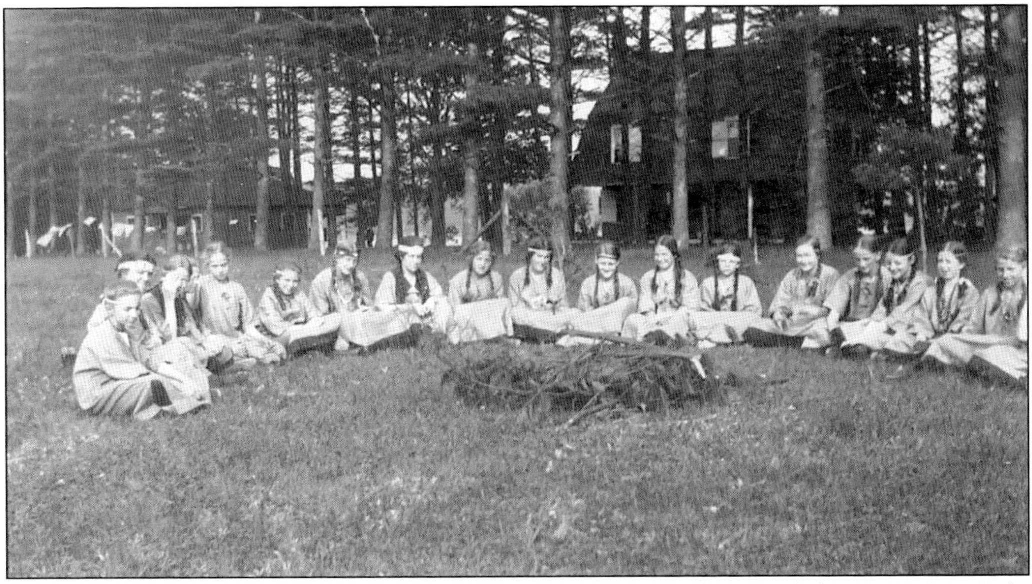

CAMPFIRE GIRLS, 1918. Members of the Ihacanyuha Council Fire of the Campfire Girls, sponsored by the Danielson Methodist Church, are shown at camp. Viola (Long) Langevin was among these girls, dressed in uniforms that they made themselves. Viola's dress, decorated with acorn beading for fringe, is on display at the Killingly Historical Society.

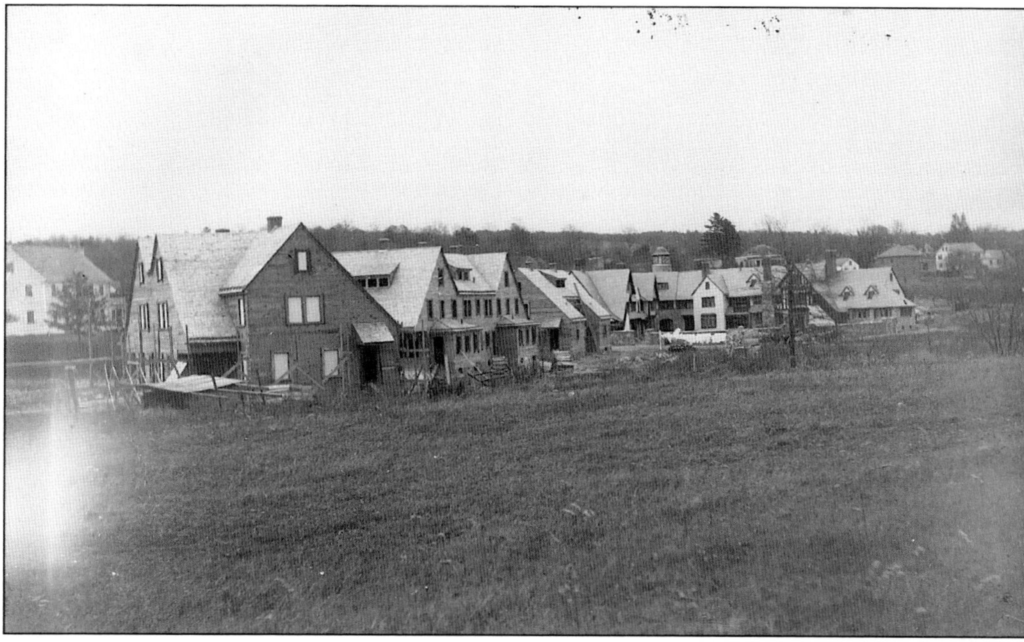

The Gables, 1917. The Connecticut Mills Company engaged Danielson contractor Damase Boulais to build this centerpiece of its Tudor and Colonial Revival-style housing on Morin Avenue. This housing was a major example of 20th-century industrial paternalism. A domed clock tower rises at the junction of two sections of the multi-apartment building. A plaque in the archway proclaims "Connecticut Gables—A Forward Step in Good Housing for Working People." Photographer Herb Grube took this photograph.

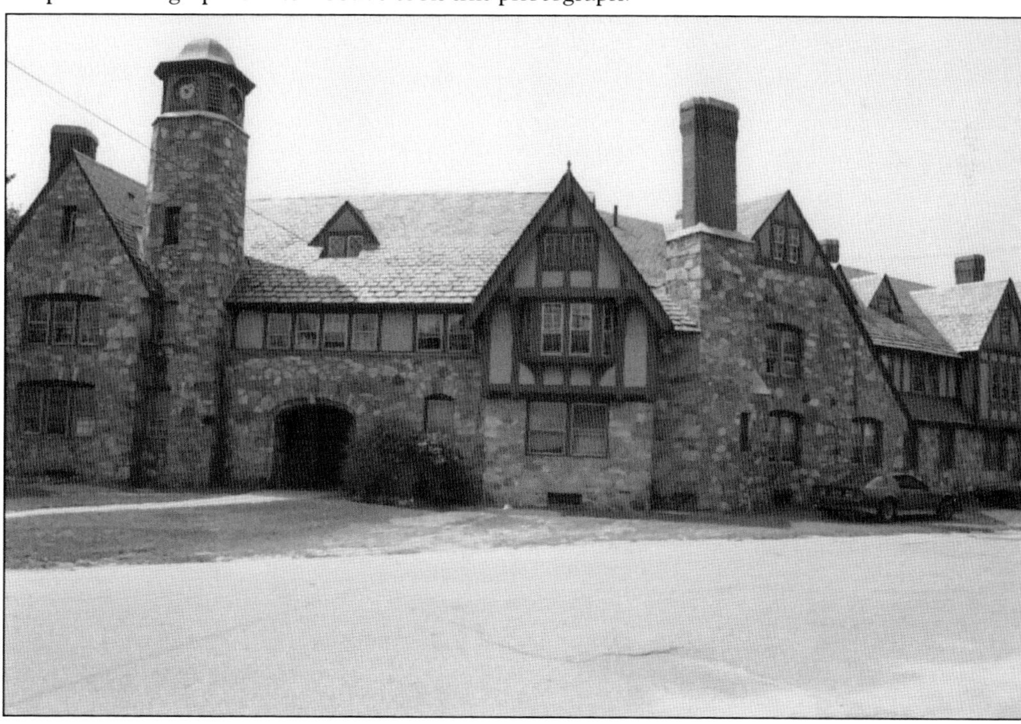

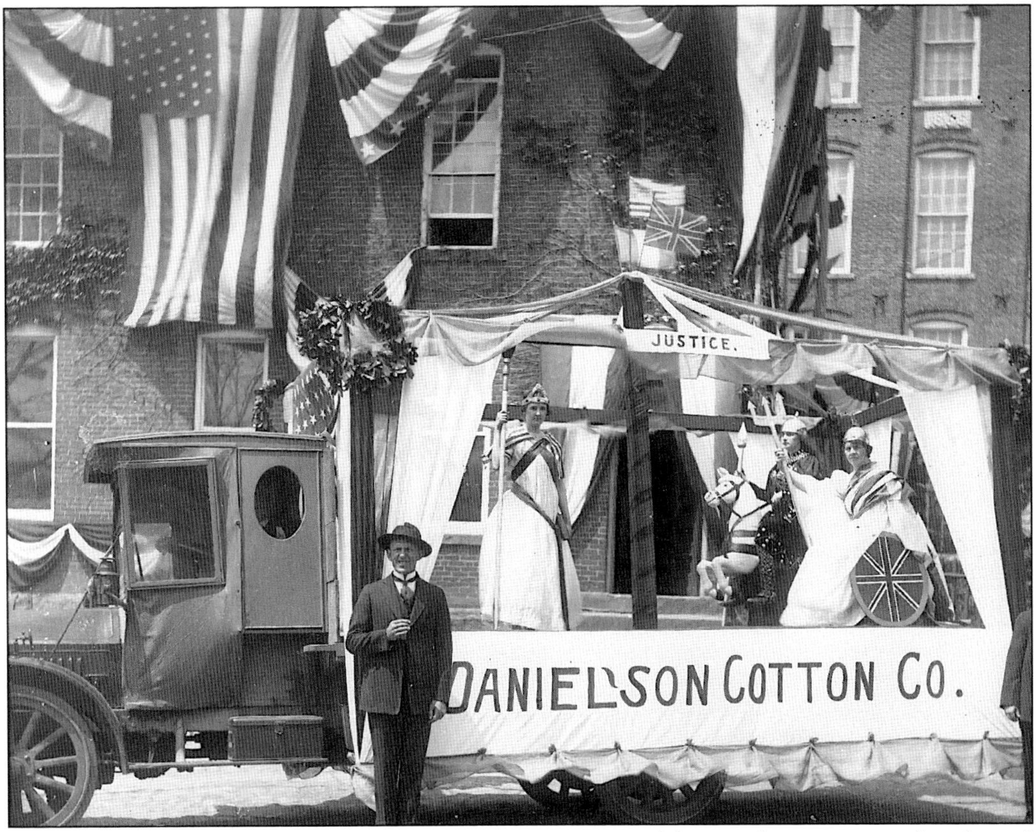

A Danielson Cotton Company Float, 1919. One unit of the ten divisions, nine bands, and drum corps took part in the Welcome Home Day Parade. The people of Killingly organized the parade to honor all the town residents who served during World War I. Local photographer Herb Grube recorded most of the floats and marching units of this gigantic celebration, held May 15, 1919.

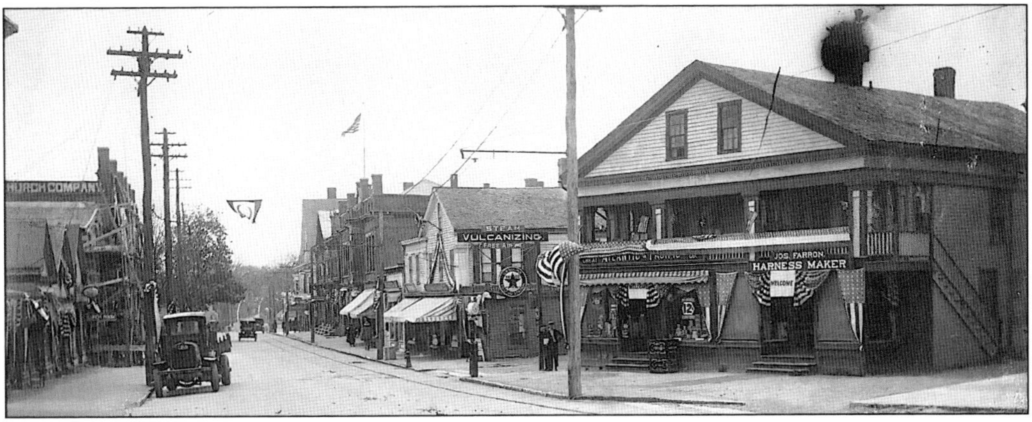

The A&P, c. 1920. Located on the corner of Main and Union Streets in the Day Building, the Atlantic & Pacific Tea Company was one of the main grocery stores in town. Unlike the supermarkets of today, clerks had to get every item for a customer, write the price on the side of a brown paper bag, and then add the total amount without the help of a cash register or calculator.

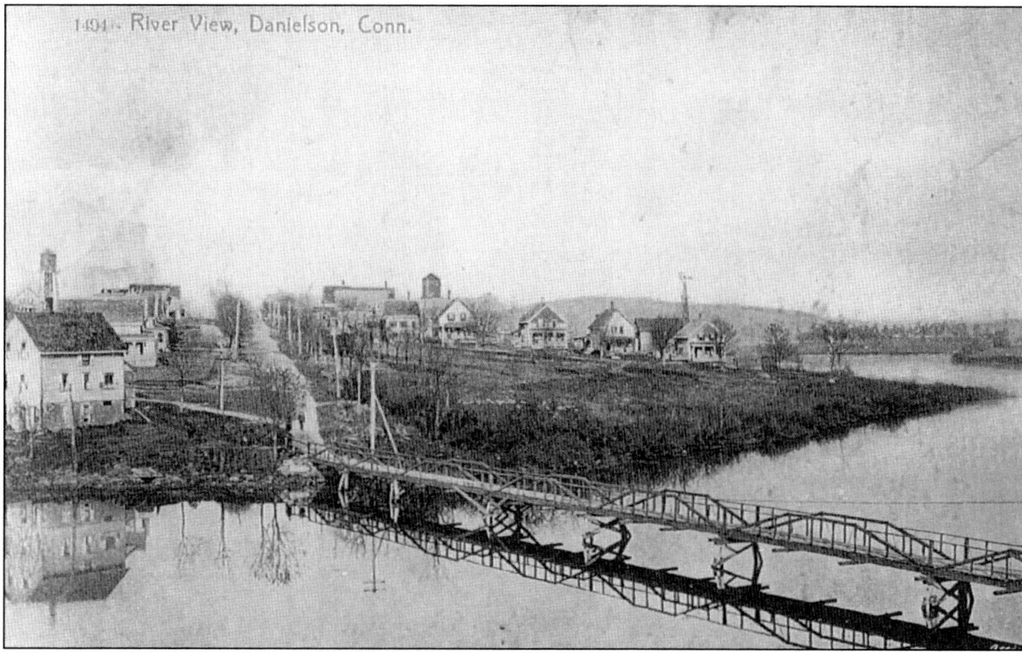

The Danielson Footbridge, c. 1920. This bridge is a 20th-century replacement for an earlier multispan bridge that crossed between the downtown and the Riverview housing development. The earlier bridge was erected *c.* 1890 by the proprietors of the Riverview Association, who wanted to make their house lots more accessible. The Warren truss design of this bridge makes it typical of standard 20th-century truss engineering. The earlier bridge was still in place in 1913.

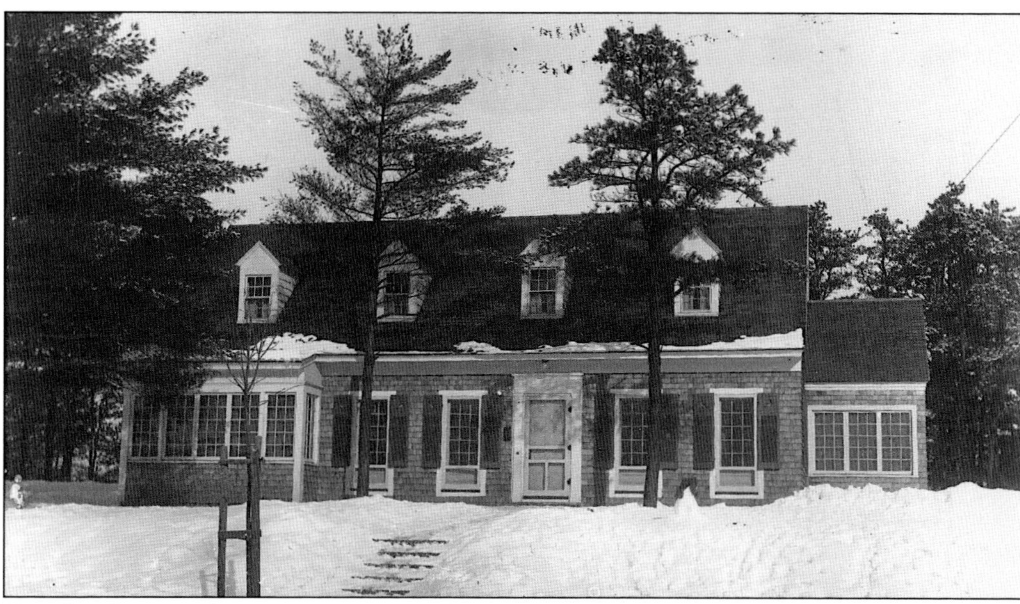

The St. James's Connecticut Mills School. In 1926, a large house and several lots on the north side of Lewis Boulevard were purchased as a supplementary annex to the Franklin Street parochial school. The school was set up for the convenience of the children from the Connecticut Mills section of Danielson. It was used until 1956.

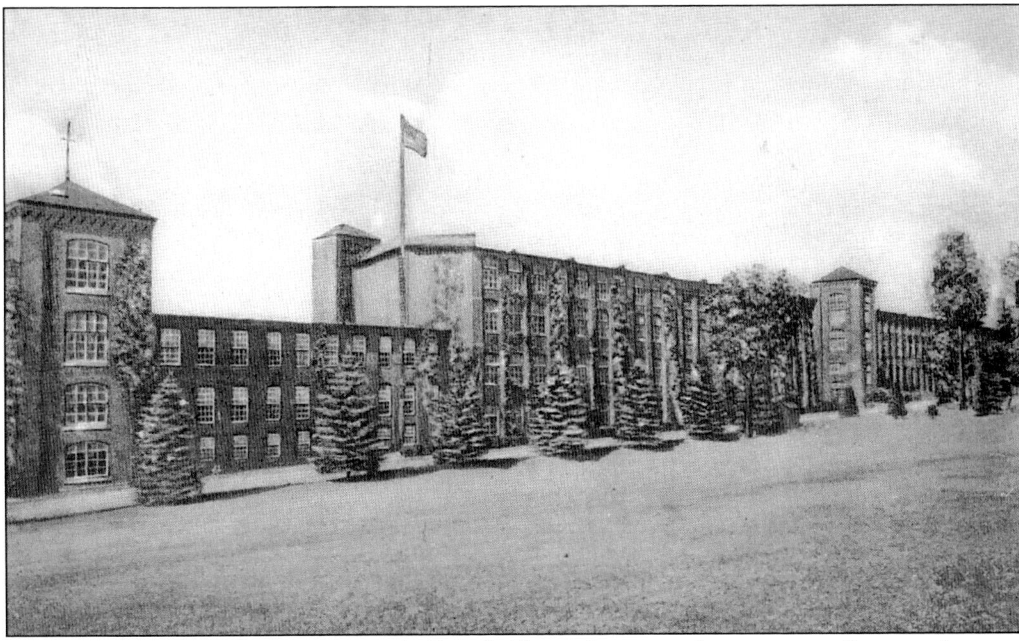

CONNECTICUT MILLS. In 1929, Powdrell and Alexander opened executive offices in the main plant on Connecticut Mills Avenue. In the ten years since its beginning, the company had risen to the peak of the industry. Danielson became known as "Curtaintown, USA."

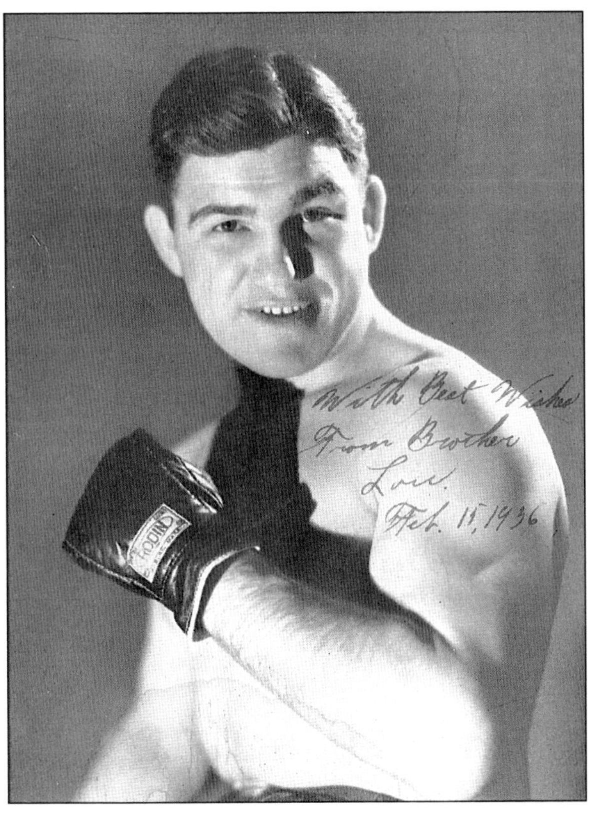

BOXING CHAMPION LOU BROUILLARD. When Lou Brouillard won his first world title as welterweight champion in 1931, the town of Danielson went wild. Sirens and mill whistles howled the news. A short time later, the town held a huge parade for its adopted son. Two years later, Brouillard captured the middleweight championship. He hung up his gloves in 1941. Four years after his death in 1984, Brouillard was inducted into the World Boxing Hall of Fame.

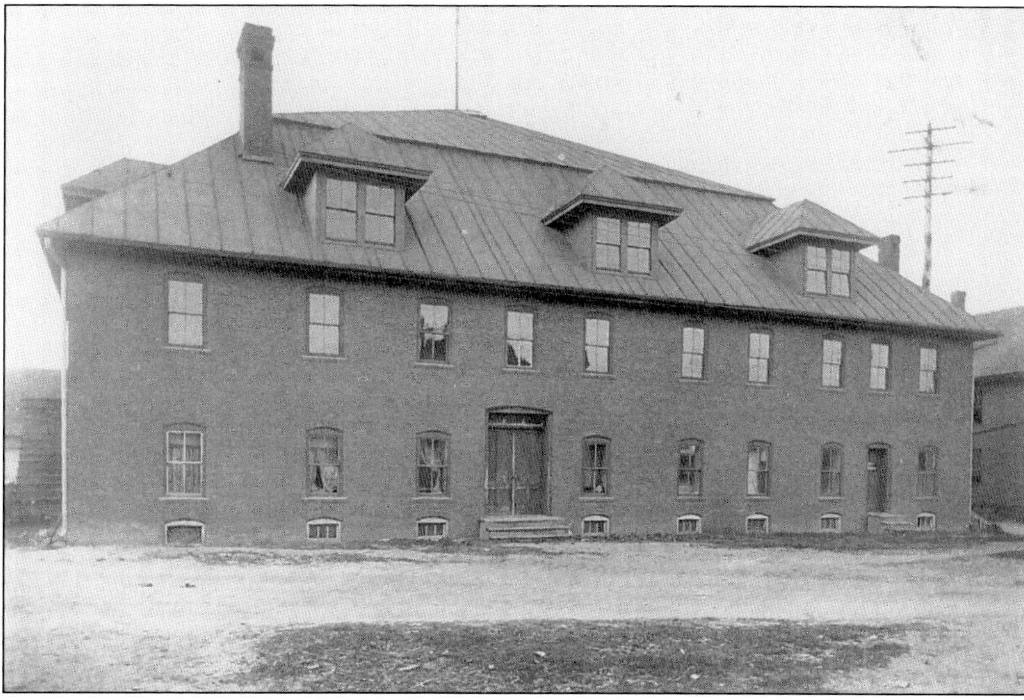

THE OLD ARMORY. Located on Railroad Street, but facing the road leading to the footbridge, was the old Armory. It burned on December 25, 1931. The loss was estimated at $43,650.

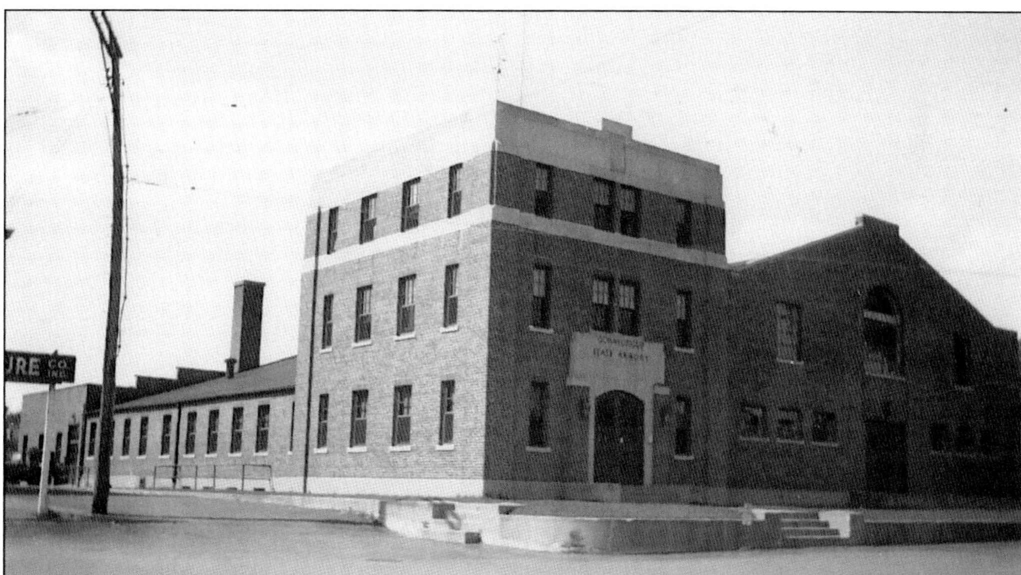

THE STATE ARMORY, 1932. The new Armory was built on the site of the old one that burned. It is an important local example of military architecture, designed by Payne and O'Keefe of New London. It was the home of the Connecticut National Guard 250th Engineer Company until 1992, when it closed.

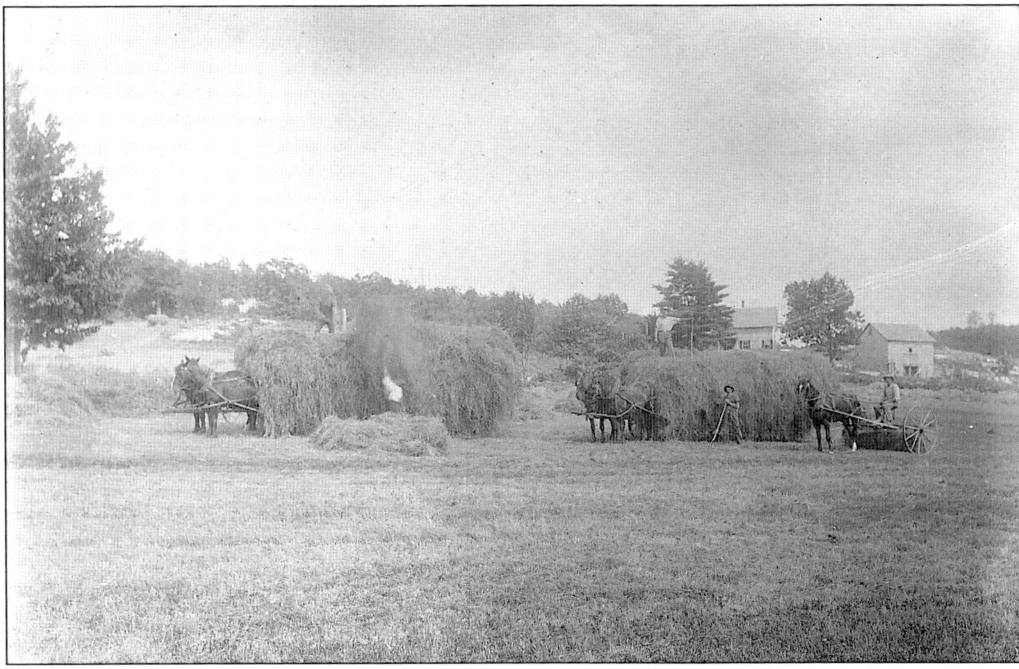

HAYING ON EAST FRANKLIN STREET. Long before there were tractors and balers, this was the way the farmers had to get in their hay. There was an art to loading hay on a wagon and to making a haystack that would shed water. In this photograph, the Jordans showed how it was done.

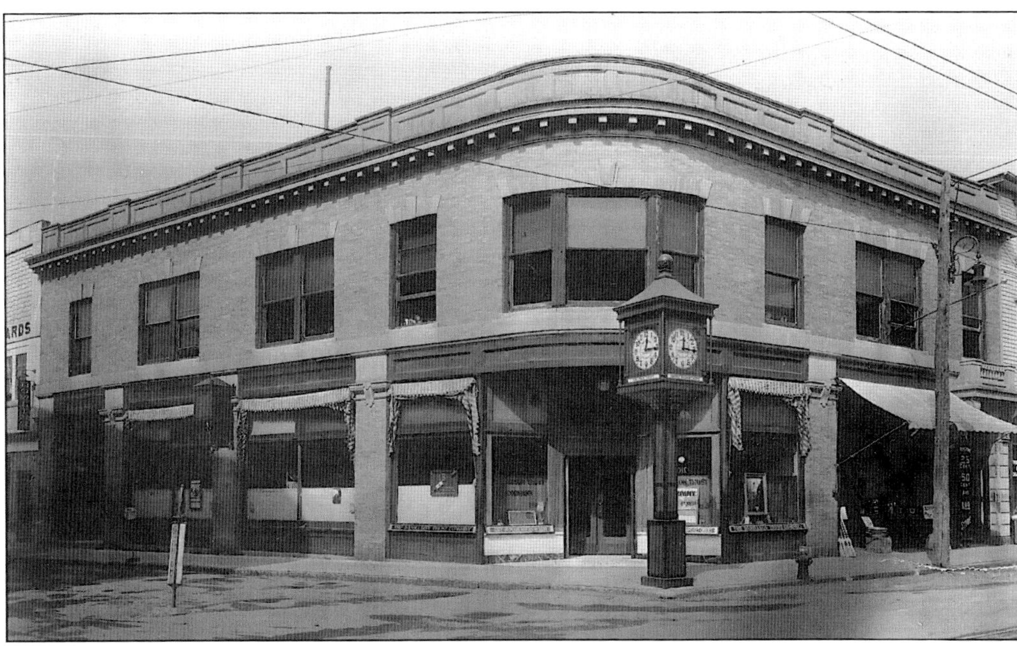

THE TOWN CLOCK. In the early 1930s, this clock was placed in front of the Danielson Trust Company, on the corner of Main and Central Streets. It became known as the Town Clock. When the Rexall store moved into the building, the advertising on the clock changed, too. The clock was removed in the mid-1900s.

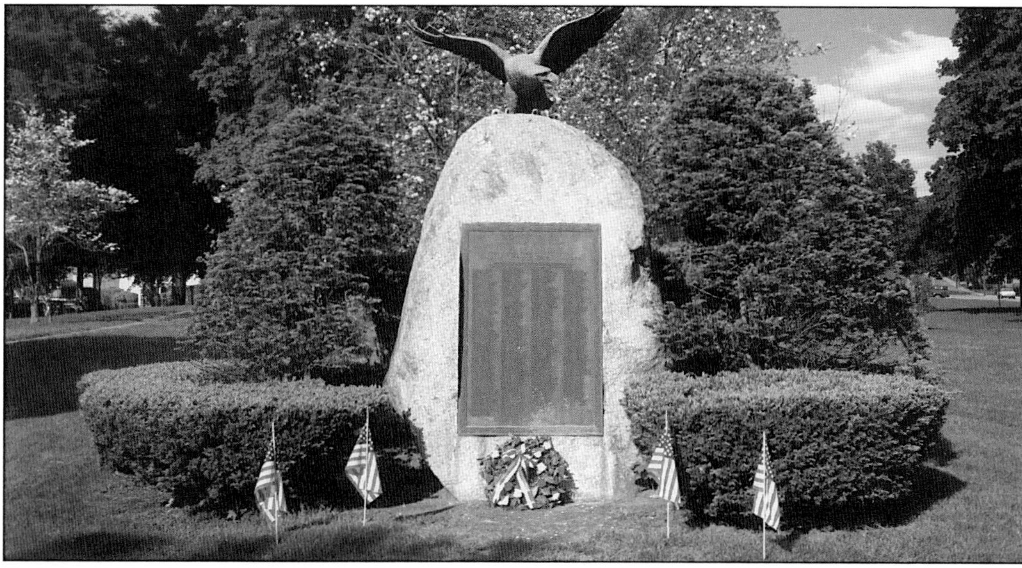

The World War I Memorial Boulder, 1933. The Veterans of Foreign Wars, under their first commander, Henry A. Myers, erected a permanent memorial to replace the wooden one put up in 1919 to honor local residents who served in World War I. The huge boulder came from the backyard of Charles Dixon, on North Main Street, and was transported on a low carrier by Clifford Davis. An eagle with spread wings tops the boulder.

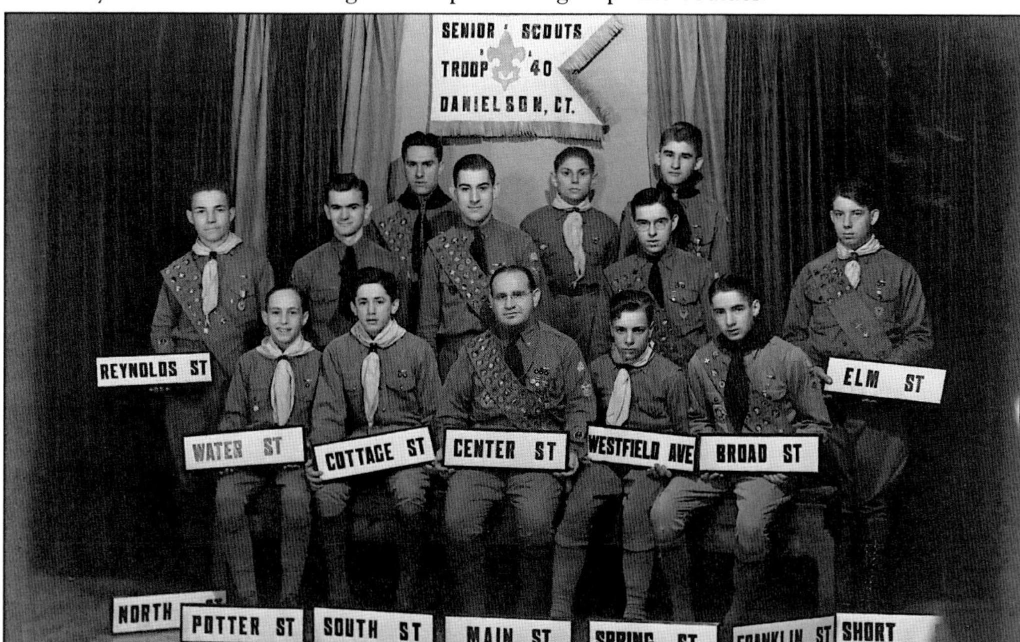

Senior Scouts, Troop 40, 1936. These Boy Scouts made 120 street signs to replace the deteriorating signs in the borough at no expense to the community. It was a job well done—except that the signs were nailed to electric light poles, which was against the safety rules of the Public Utilities Commission. Some of the young men, photographed by Pappajion Studio, were from the following families: Heneault, Berthiaume, Gendreau, Marland, Legault, Bedard, and McGinty.

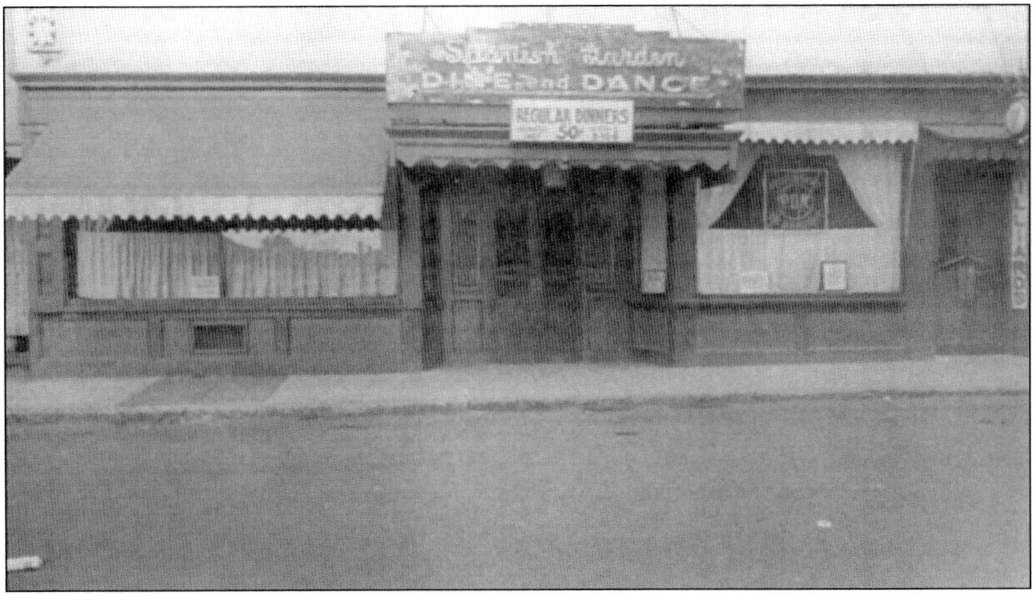

The Spanish Garden Dine and Dance, c. 1935. This restaurant was located in the former C.H. Bacon Furniture Store on Central Street from 1933 to 1937. Frank Barber and his two partners operated it. A businessman's dinner cost 45¢. The building was called the Casino Amusement Center. It had facilities for bowling, roller-skating, and boxing.

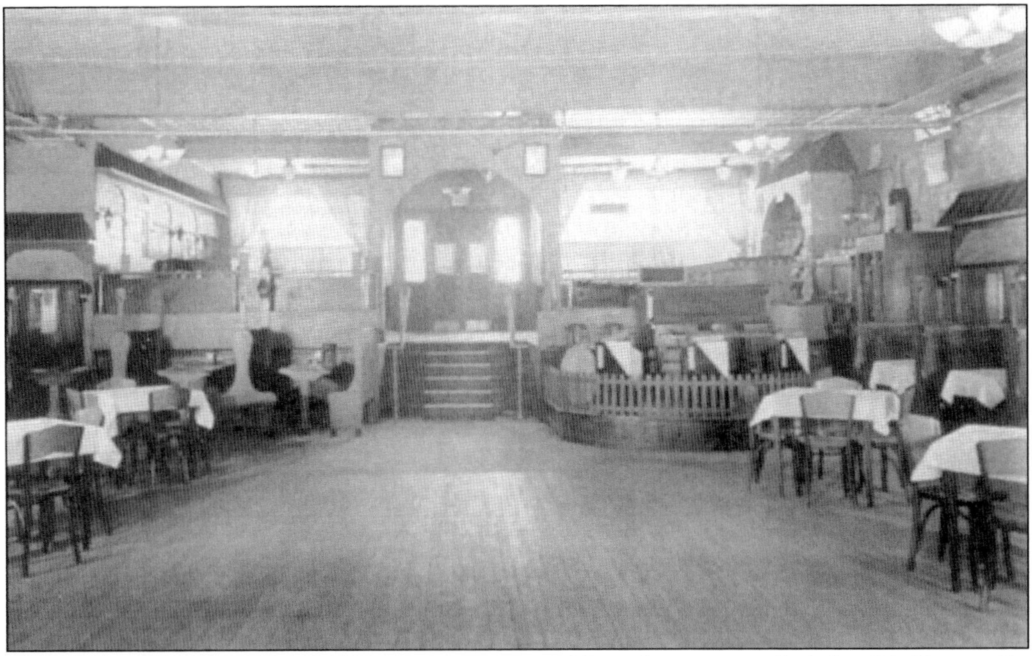

The Interior of the Spanish Garden, c. 1935. The advertising called this "A Tavern Fit for a King." There was a special floor show and an orchestra on Thursday, Friday, and Saturday. When the restaurant closed, the building was taken over by the French Club.

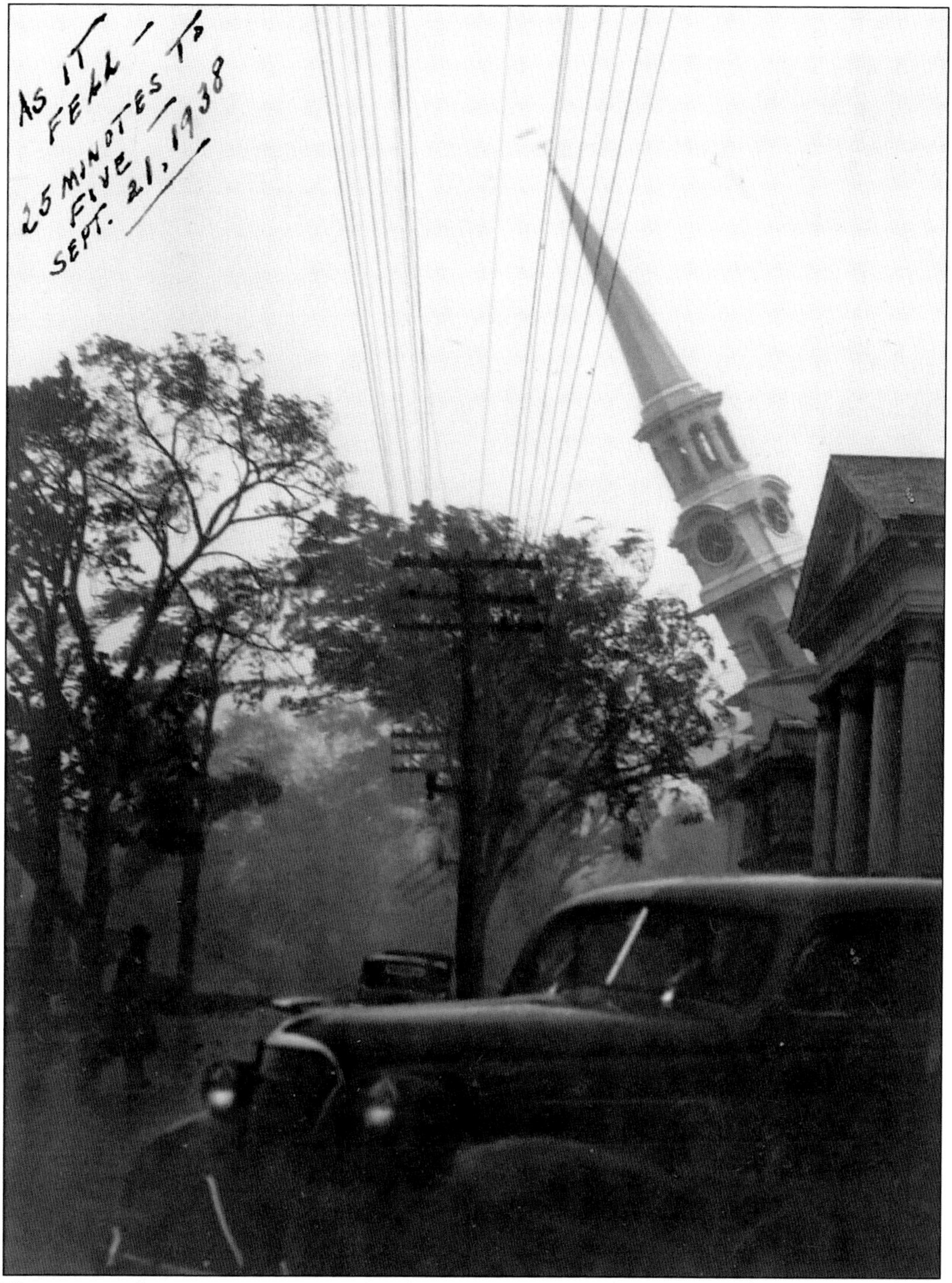

HURRICANE, SEPTEMBER 21, 1938. Residents were caught unprepared for the devastation that struck that day. The hurricane took its toll on the steeple, clock, and bell of the Westfield Congregational Church at Main and Reynolds Streets. The historical spire was toppled earlier in its life by a severe storm in 1877. The building was first used on July 1, 1855, to replace the original church, erected farther north on Main Street in 1796.

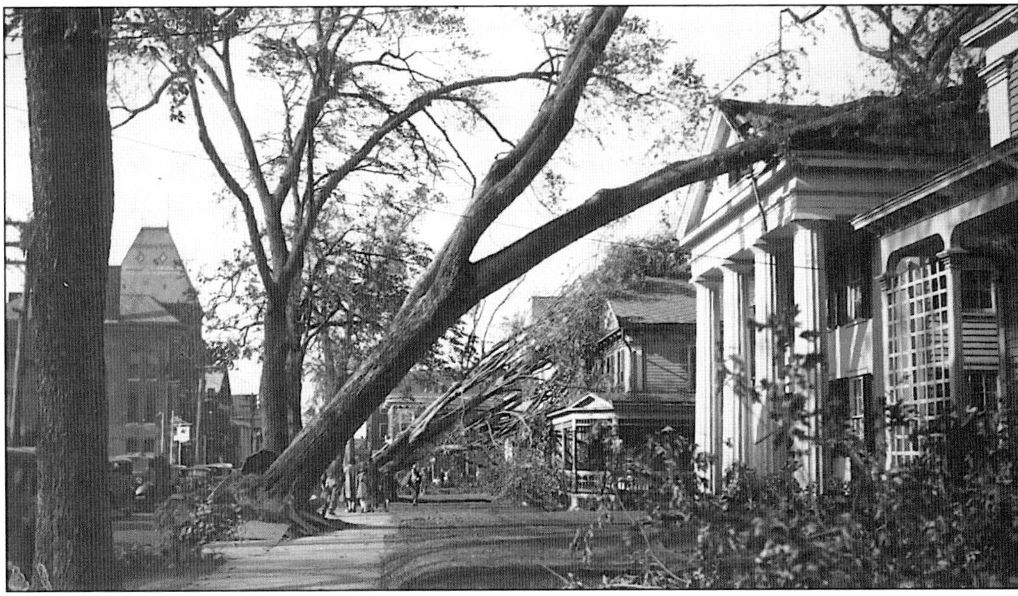

DAMAGE FROM THE 1938 HURRICANE. Enormous trees were easily uprooted by the lash of winds up to 100 miles per hour. Shingles and entire roofs were ripped off buildings. The force of the wind was so strong that a salt residue was left on the houses, although the ocean was miles away. Falling trees and wires created havoc. Scores of men worked to clear debris, open streets blocked by fallen trees, and restore electricity and telephone service. The demand for carpenters, masons, and glaziers was so great it took men away from performing emergency work.

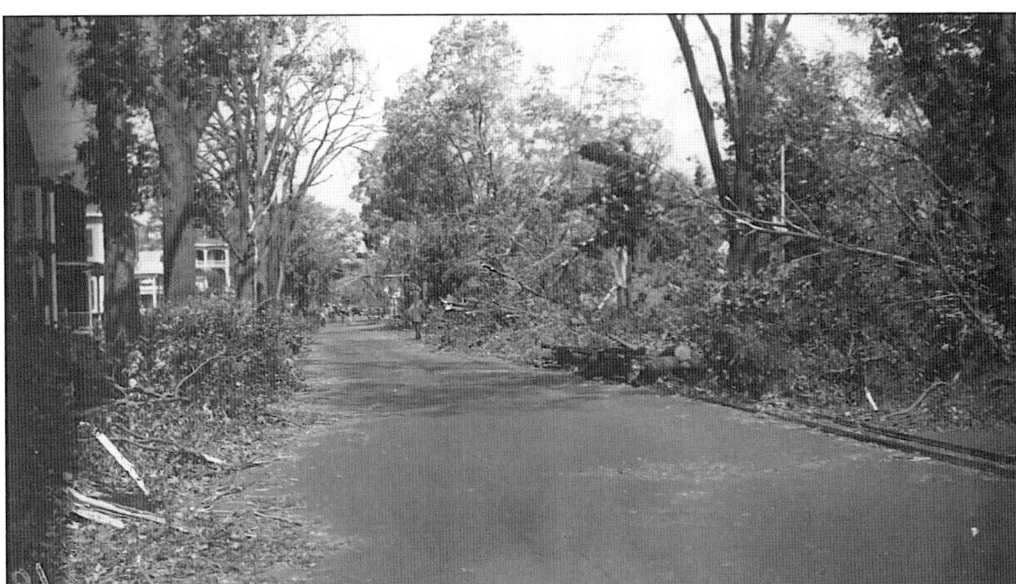

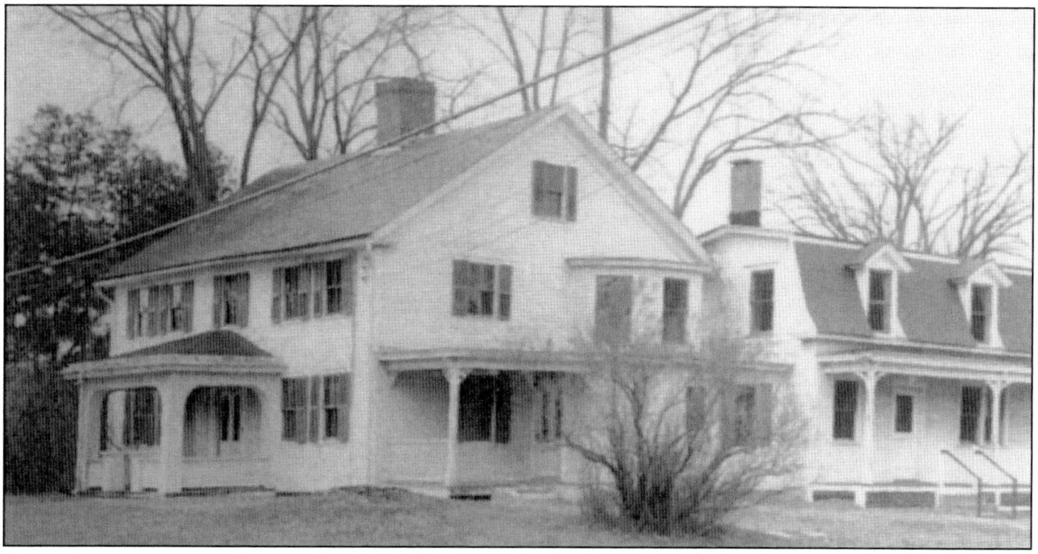

The Connecticut State Police Barracks, Troop D. The local headquarters for the Connecticut State Police was originally the home of Charles A. Tillinghast, located on the east side of North Main Street, near Benny's store, less than a mile from the junction of Routes 12 and 6. The Davis family built the house *c.* 1800.

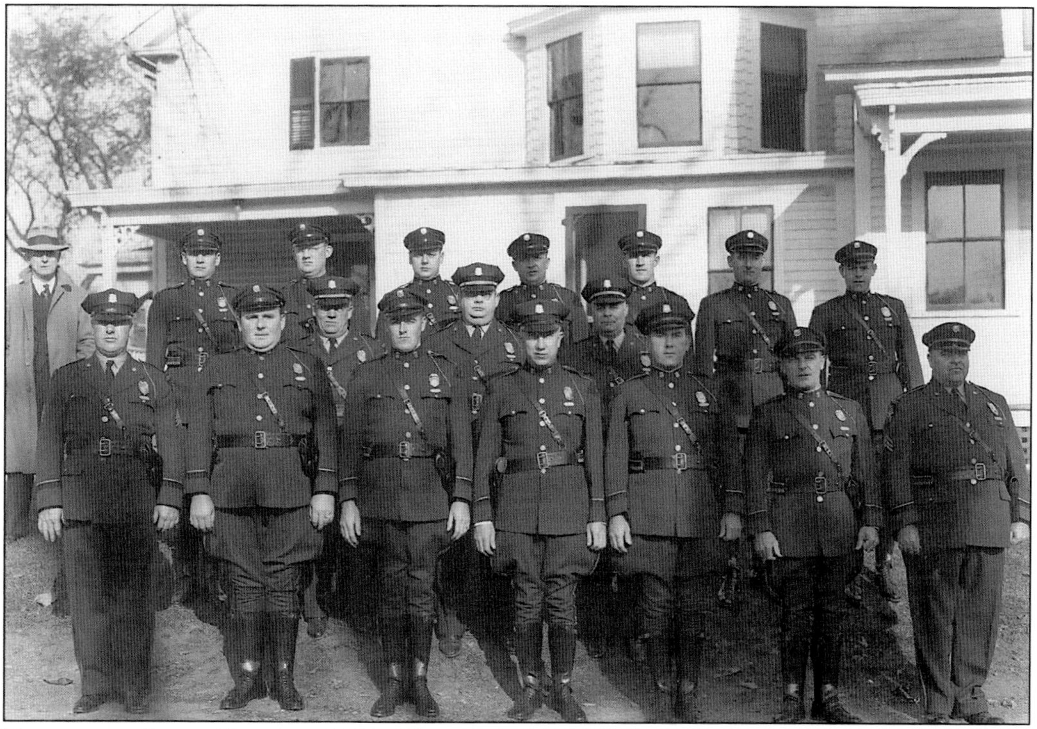

Danielson State Police, 1938. Shown in front of the State Police Barracks on North Main Street are, from left to right: (front row) Sergeant Lowery, Officers Martin, Reardon, J.T. Murphy, Kearney, and Nolan, and Sergeant Scranton; (middle row) Lieutenants Pettigill, Urquhart, and Bushy; (back row) Major Nichols and Officers Gowdy, Delaney, Myers, Powell, and J.B. Murphy.

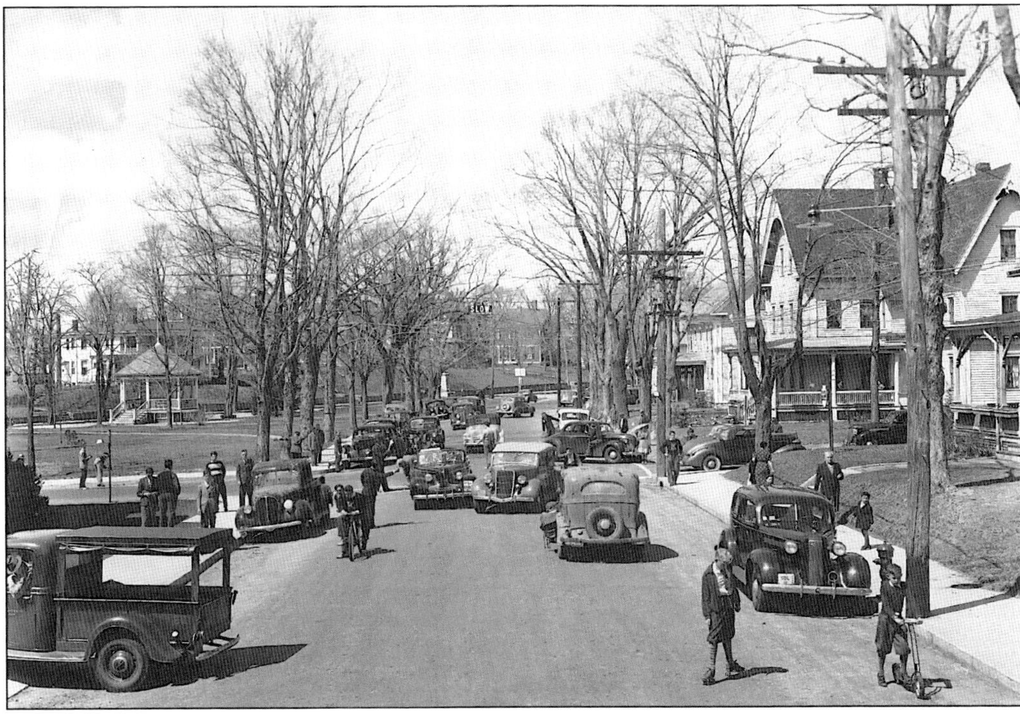

HIGH SCHOOL SAFETY PICTURE, 1939. This picture was set up for a Killingly High School safety test, sponsored by the Connecticut State Police and the Killingly Board of Education. A copy was distributed to each class, and students were asked to point out all the safety hazards. How many can you find?

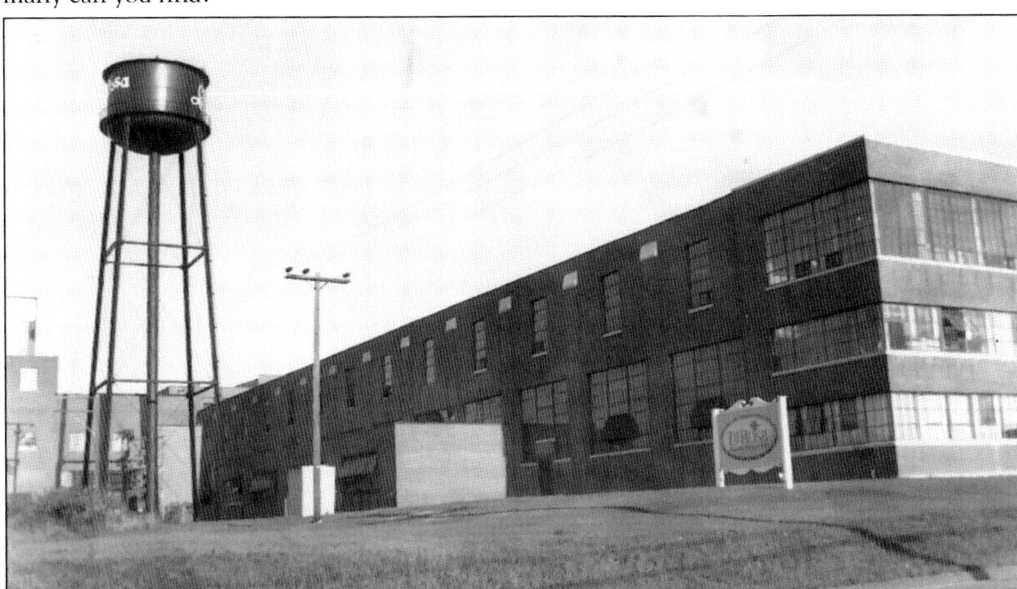

V. LAROSA & SONS, 1939. Vincent LaRosa and his sons began manufacturing macaroni products in a plant on the Wauregan Road. The plant reflected a great improvement over 19th-century architecture and was a relatively rare style in eastern Connecticut. In the 1970s, in what was a unique turnaround for this area, the plant was converted to textile production.

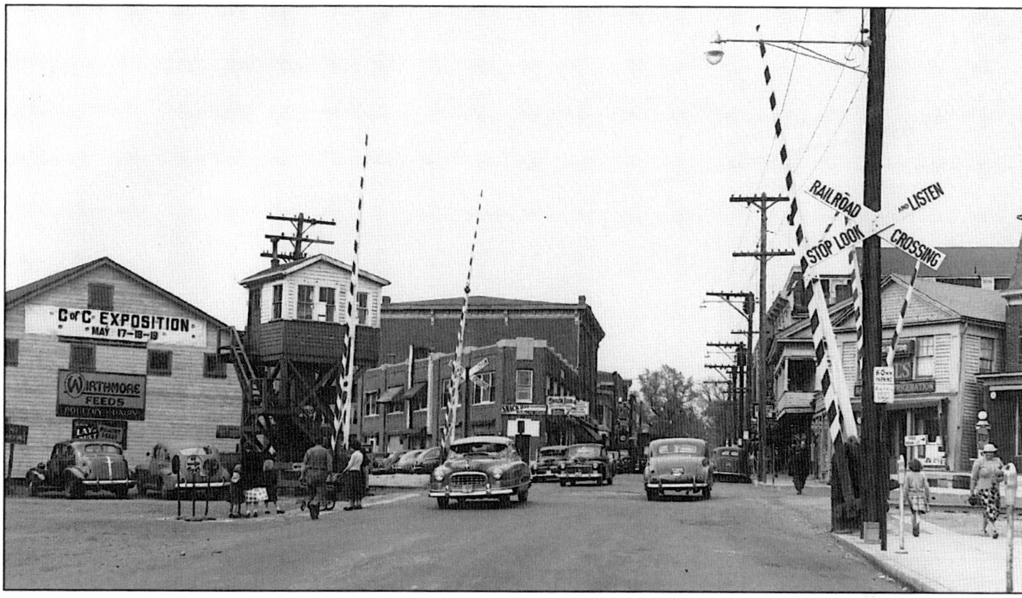

THE RAILROAD GATE TOWER, 1940. A gate tender tower was built for the Main Street railroad crossing in Danielson. One of the grain sheds is pictured on the left. A corner of the Danielson Inn is visible on the far right, next to Phil's Radio & Refrigeration.

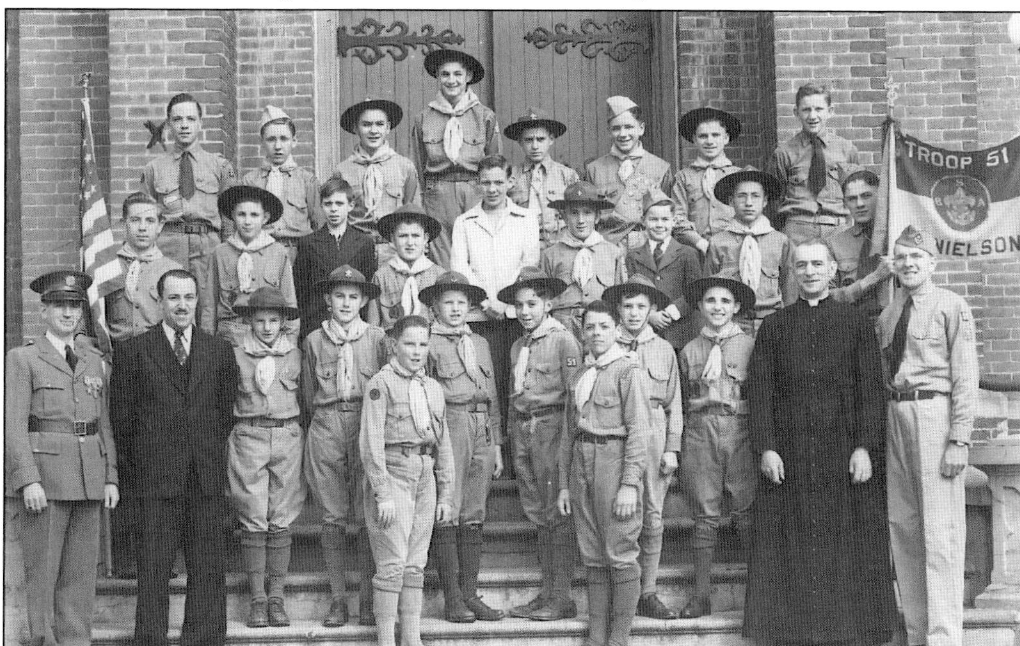

BOY SCOUT TROOP 51, C. 1944. The Boy Scout troops were led by fathers and other men in the community. Leading this troop were, front row, far left, John Ramsey Sr. and Paul Pelletier and, far right, Father Morin and Mr. Gileau. Boys were from the following local families: Hubert, Paquin, Mosher, Page, Thomas, Bernier, Winchell, Racicot, Comire, Brousseau, Madon, Gauthier, Bachand, Berthiaume, Leclaire, Grenon, Giguere, Dupont, Curran, LaPrade, Derosier, and Barrette.

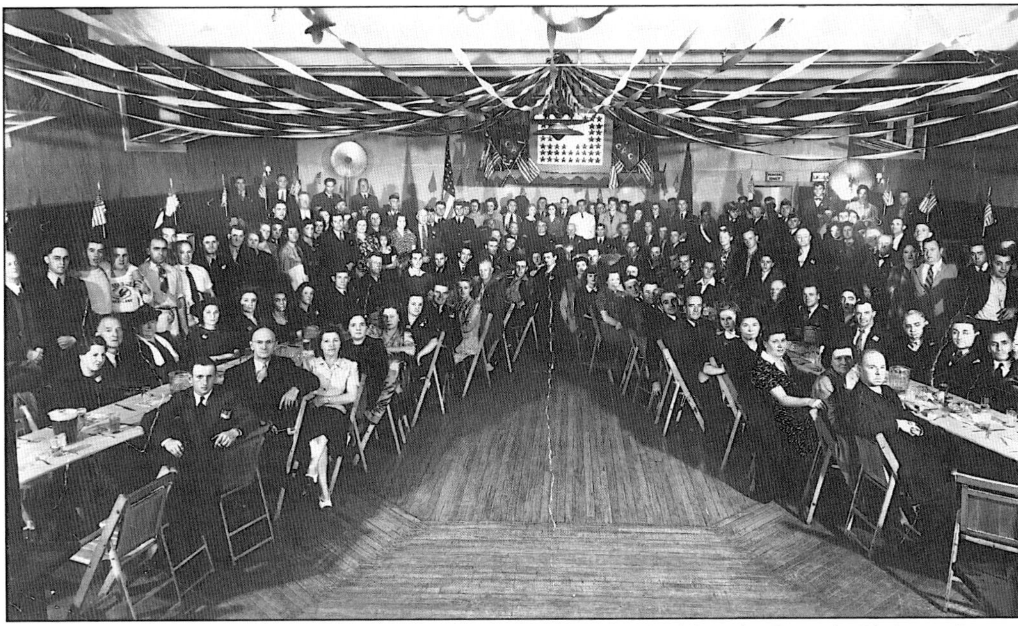

A World War II Victory Dance. A gala celebration was held at the French Club on Central Street after the end of World War II. The event was a very happy, well-attended affair.

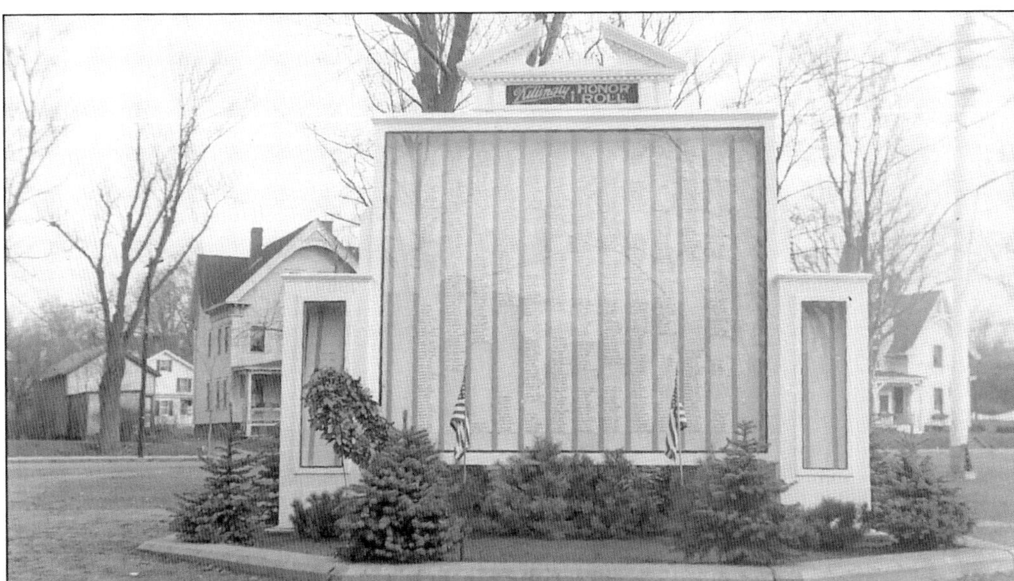

The World War II Honor Roll, 1946. An honor roll was placed in the fountain basin in Davis Park, surrounded by shrubs. The center section contained the names of all the local residents who served in World War II. In the two smaller sections on each side, all under glass, were the names of those who had given their lives. In 1964, a permanent monument replaced this temporary memorial.

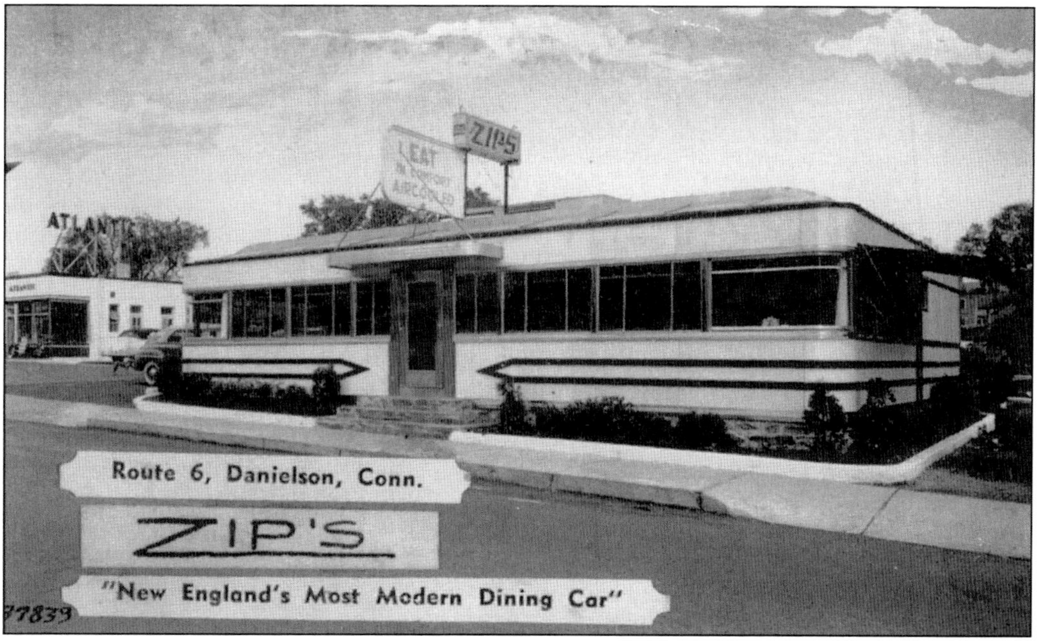

ZIP'S CURTAINTOWN DINER, OCTOBER 1946. Henry "Zip" Zehrer, a former semi-professional football player and Connecticut state policeman, opened this diner in 1946 near the junction of Main and Maple Streets. When the traffic circle for Routes 6 and 12 was built, the diner was moved to the city of New London, across from the Gold Star Bridge.

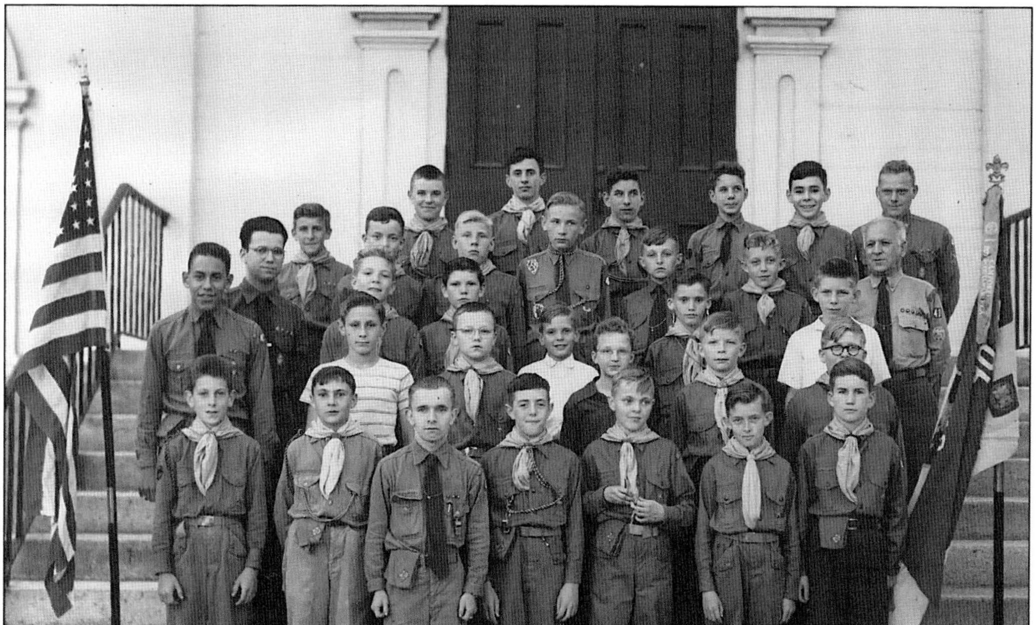

BOY SCOUT TROOP 43, C. 1949. This group of the town's future citizens and businessmen were led by William Vett, in the fourth row at the far right. Included are young men from the following families: Brunell, Sasse, Boston, Tillinghast, Burton, Carr, Cunneen, Cowles, Leire, Gould, Wold, Smith, Kirkconnell, Chase, Craig, Wells, Etheridge, and Eyers.

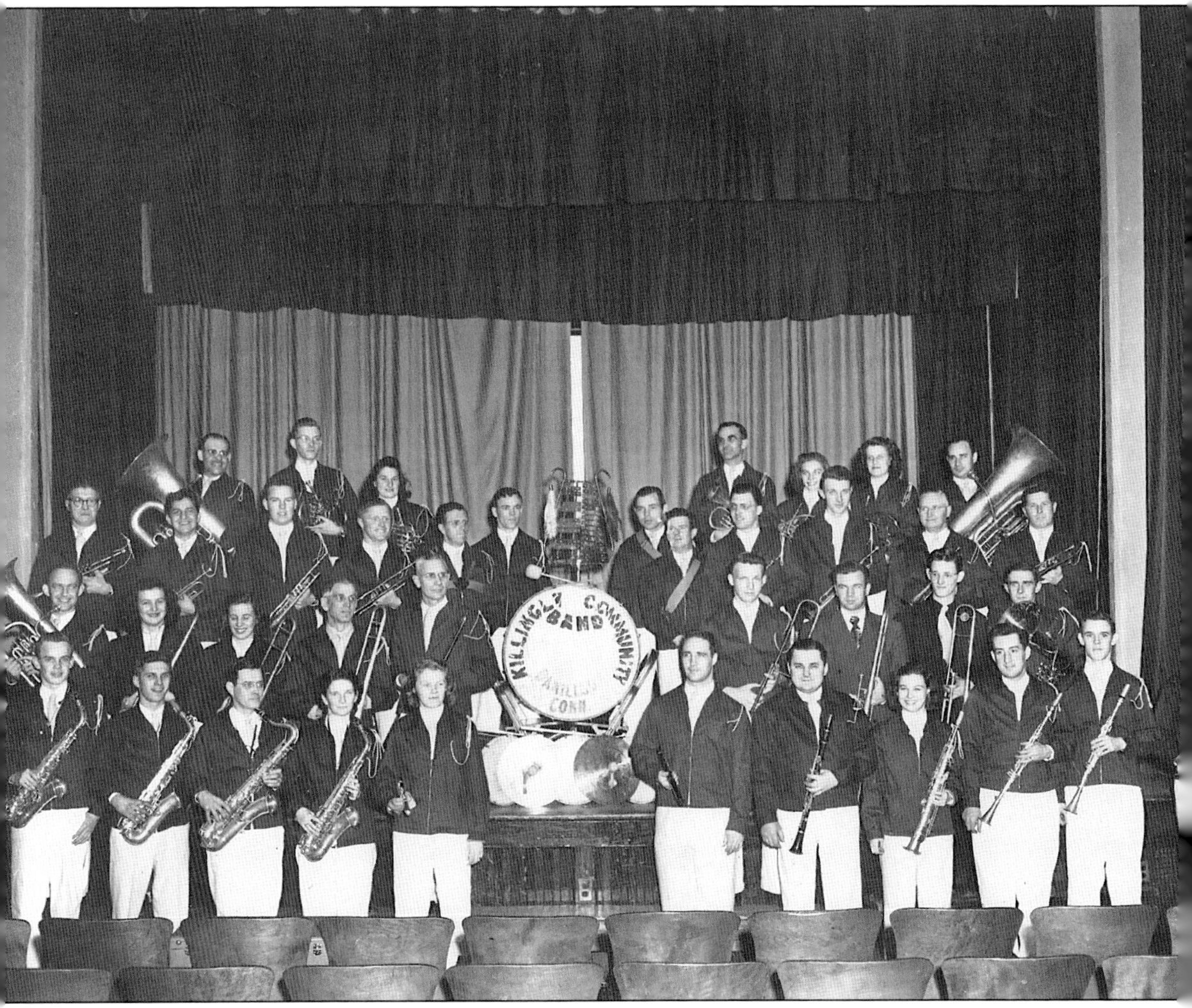

THE KILLINGLY COMMUNITY BAND, C. 1950. The Killingly Community Band was exactly what its name implied—community. Band members were all ages and came from all walks of life. They included a barber, garage mechanic, jeweler, monument maker, and high school student. Under the direction of Mr. Wylie, they were an enthusiastic group who provided good music for the enjoyment of the community.

Two

ATTAWAUGAN:

ASPINOCK AND NORTH KILLINGLY

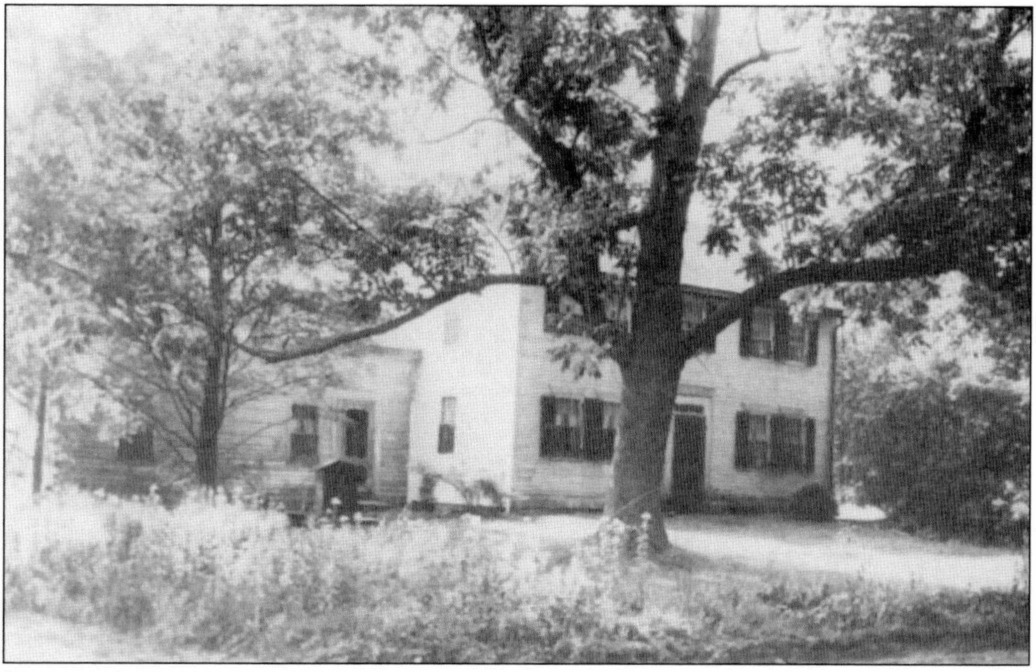

KILLINGLY'S OLDEST HOUSE, 1726. This house was designated by the Celebrate Connecticut 350 Committee as the oldest house in Killingly. A portion of this Route 21 home was built in 1726 by Jabez Allyn, one of Killingly's original proprietors. In the 1740s, the property was deeded to James Adams of Barrington, Rhode Island, whose family retained ownership for over 200 years. The present owners are local historians Margaret and Charles Weaver.

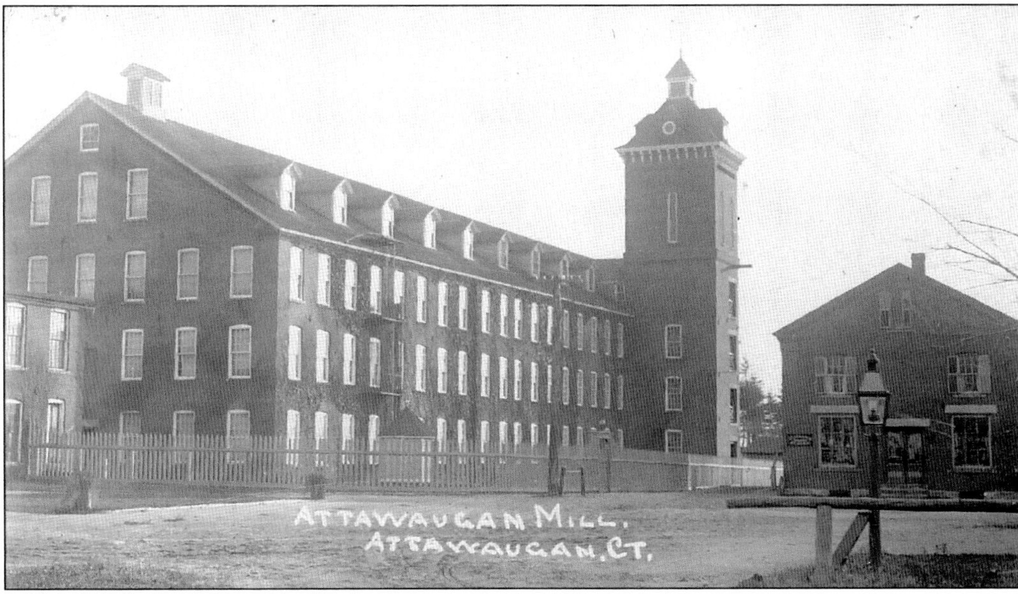

THE ATTAWAUGAN COMPANY. Constructed alongside George Weatherhead's "Fine Sheeting" factory, the Attawaugan mill was built in 1860 and was known as the Attawaugan Company. Mule teams carried bricks from the brickyard near Ralph Tracy's home to build the mill. The mill was enlarged several times and was purchased by Powdrell & Alexander in 1927. It operated as a curtain-making firm until the early 1950s.

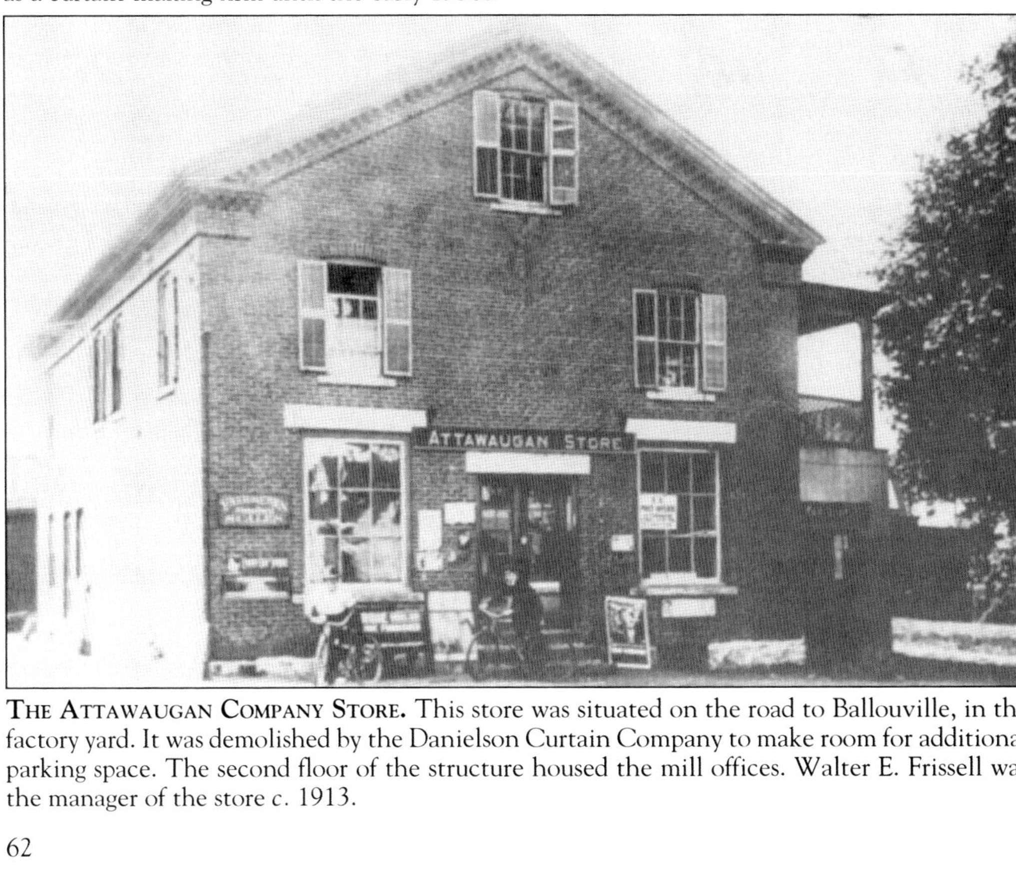

THE ATTAWAUGAN COMPANY STORE. This store was situated on the road to Ballouville, in the factory yard. It was demolished by the Danielson Curtain Company to make room for additional parking space. The second floor of the structure housed the mill offices. Walter E. Frissell was the manager of the store c. 1913.

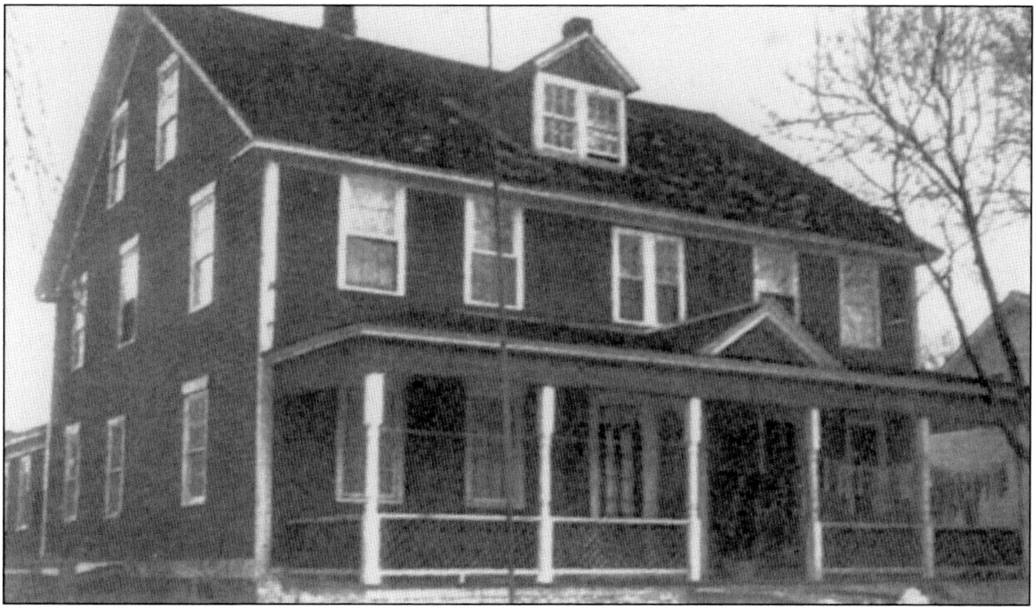

THE ATTAWAUGAN BOARDINGHOUSE, C. 1865. Unmarried workers, who were often transients, lived here. Michael H. Grimshaw and his wife, Mary, took charge of the boardinghouse for the mills. Grimshaw worked here until his death in 1918. Mrs. Grimshaw carried on for a number of years after that.

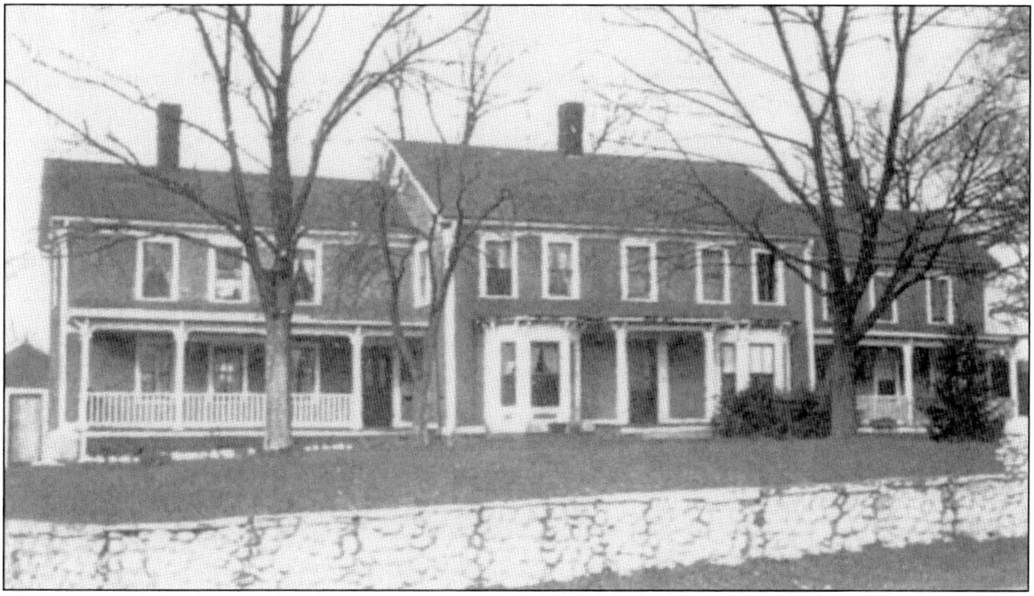

THE ATTAWAUGAN HOTEL. Although area residents often refer to the structure as the Attawaugan Hotel or the Inn, the need for such lodging here is obscure. In the late 19th century, the road that runs in front of the building, Route 12, was a major north-south road. So, the hotel may have accommodated travelers, or the absentee mill owners could have used it on their visits to the mill villages on the Five Mile River.

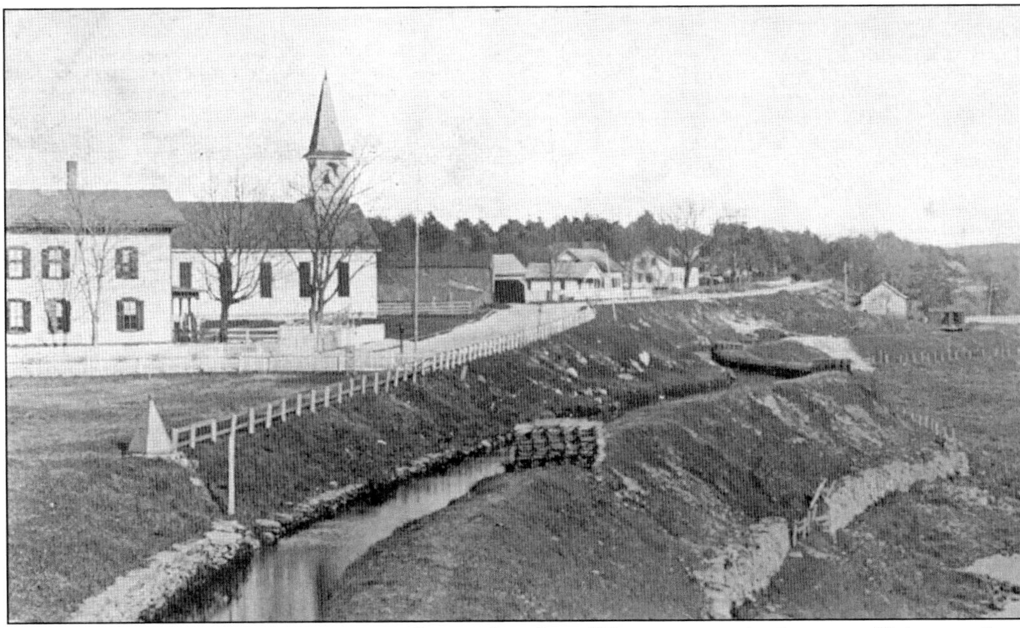

ATTAWAUGAN STREETS. Some 30 small, two-family mill houses were built in parallel rows along Mill Road, Church Street, and Attawaugan-Ballouville Road, along with other mill houses on Route 12. Some of the houses date from 1865. In 1933, when Powdrell & Alexander put them up for sale, many were bought by the workers who were living in them.

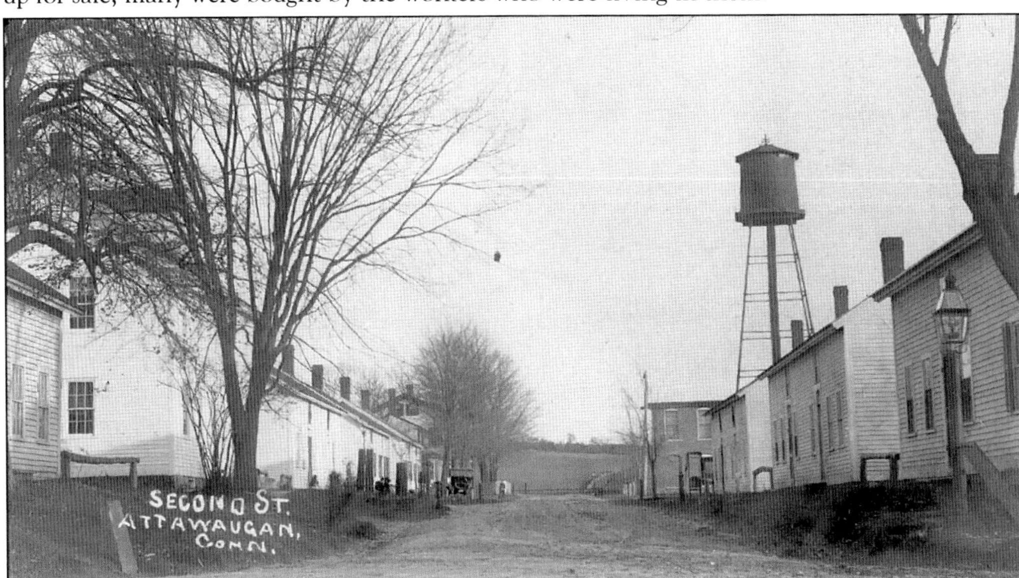

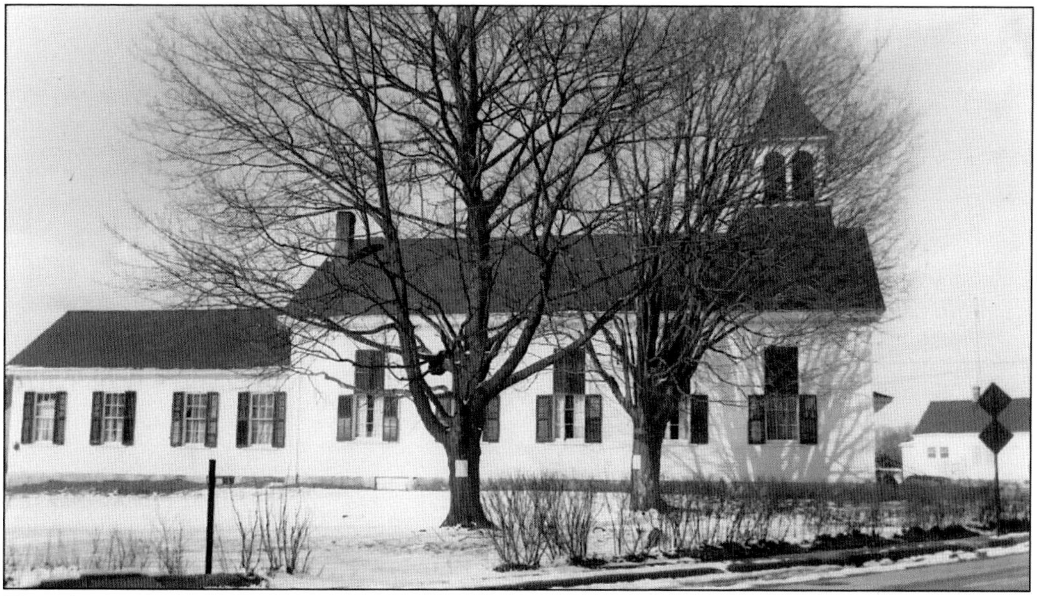

The Attawaugan Methodist Church, 1870. The Attawaugan Company established a non-denominational church for its workers in 1870. At that time, the Methodist sect enjoyed considerable popularity among Protestant mill workers, in part because of its democratic theology. In 1872, the Attawaugan church voted to join the Methodists.

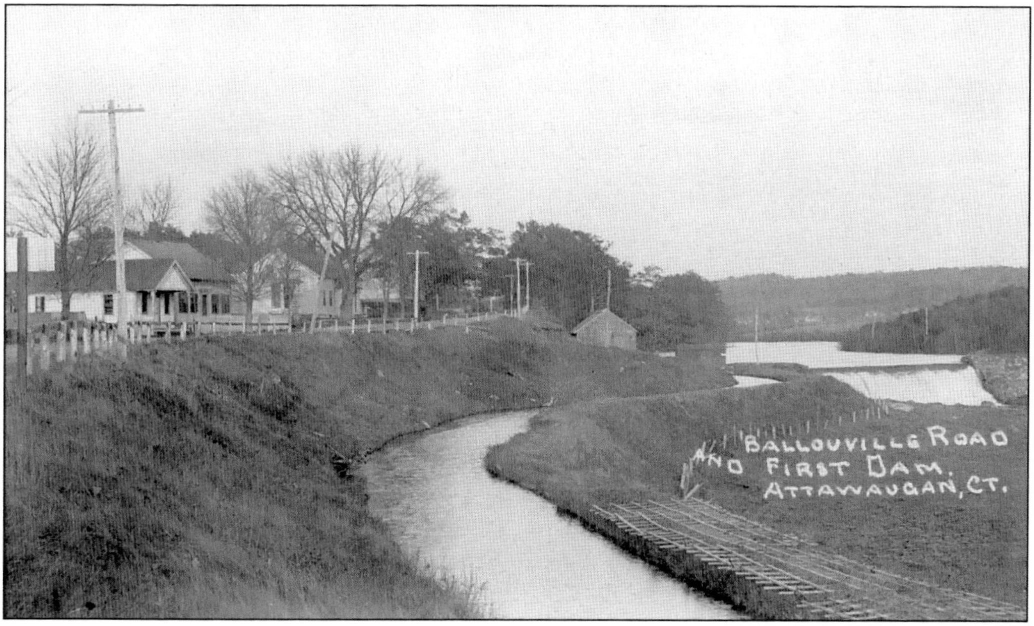

The Attawaugan-Ballouville Road. This view shows the Attawaugan Methodist Church and the Attawaugan Dam on the Five Mile River.

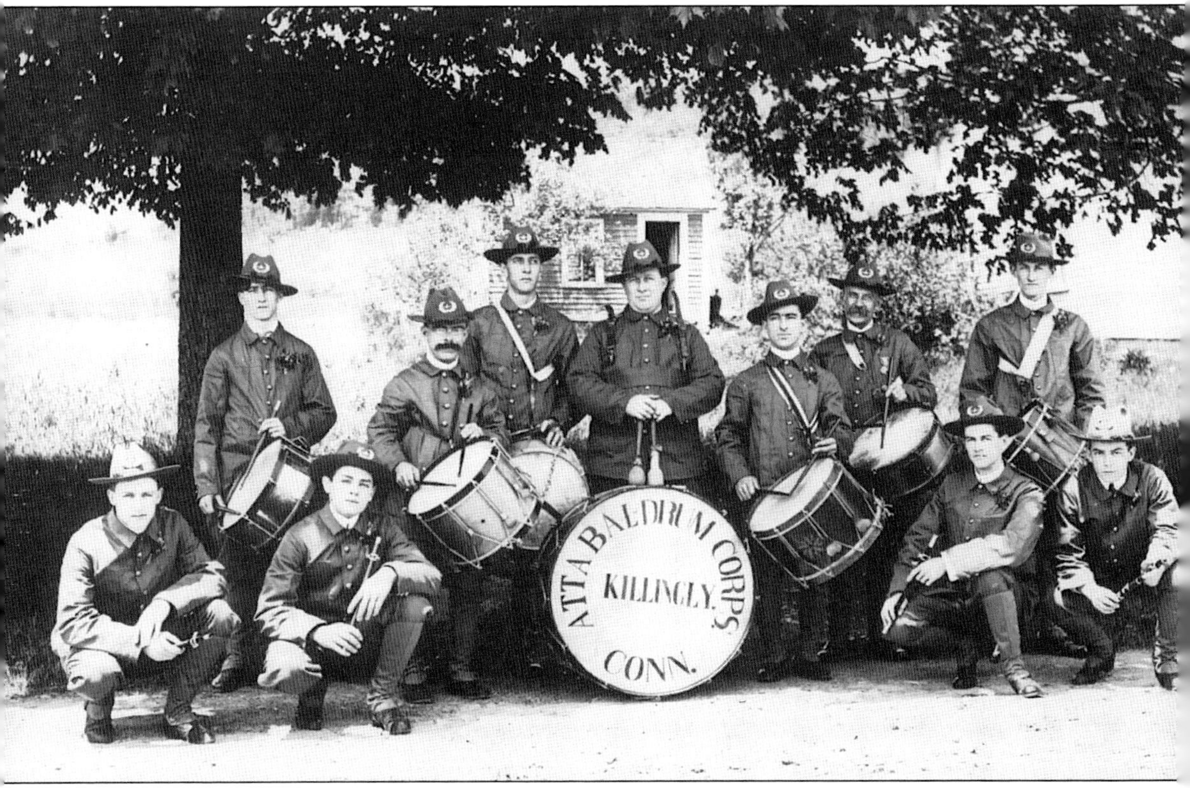

THE ATTAWAUGAN-BALLOUVILLE DRUM CORPS. All the members of the drum corps were residents of the two villages. Attawaugan and Ballouville often joined for various activities. The group shown here marched in the local parades that featured veterans of the Civil War and the Spanish-American War.

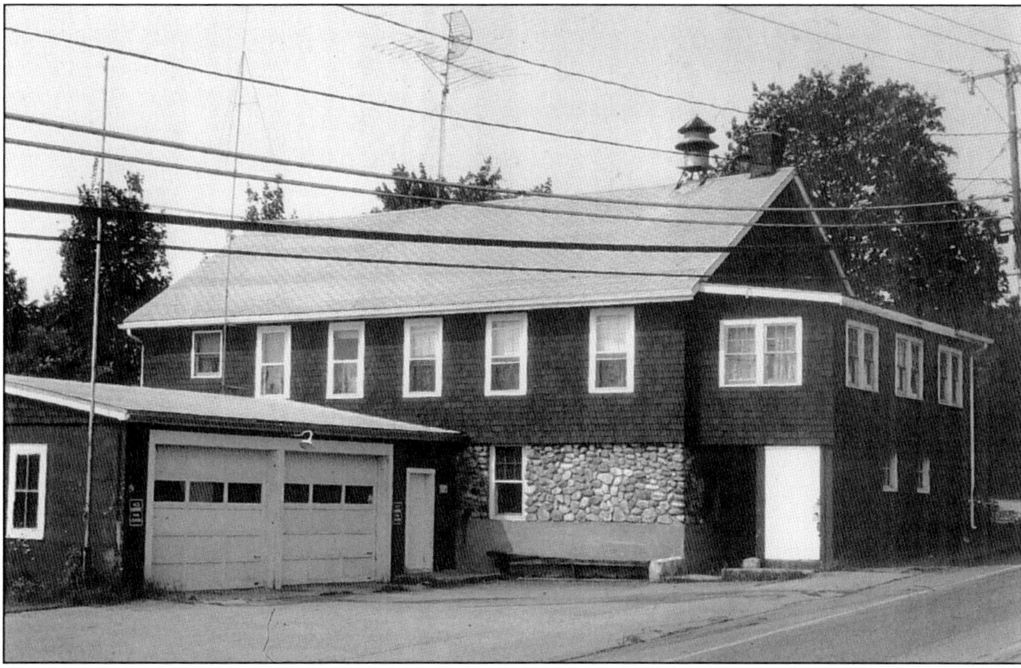

The Attawaugan Social Club, c. 1910. This building was an important component of the mill village. Erected by the Attawaugan Company, it was formerly named Blackstone Hall after one of the founders of the company. The mill workers held social functions here, and the club included a baseball team. In January 1917, the Attawaugan Clubhouse was formally opened. It later years, it was occupied by the Attawaugan Fire Department.

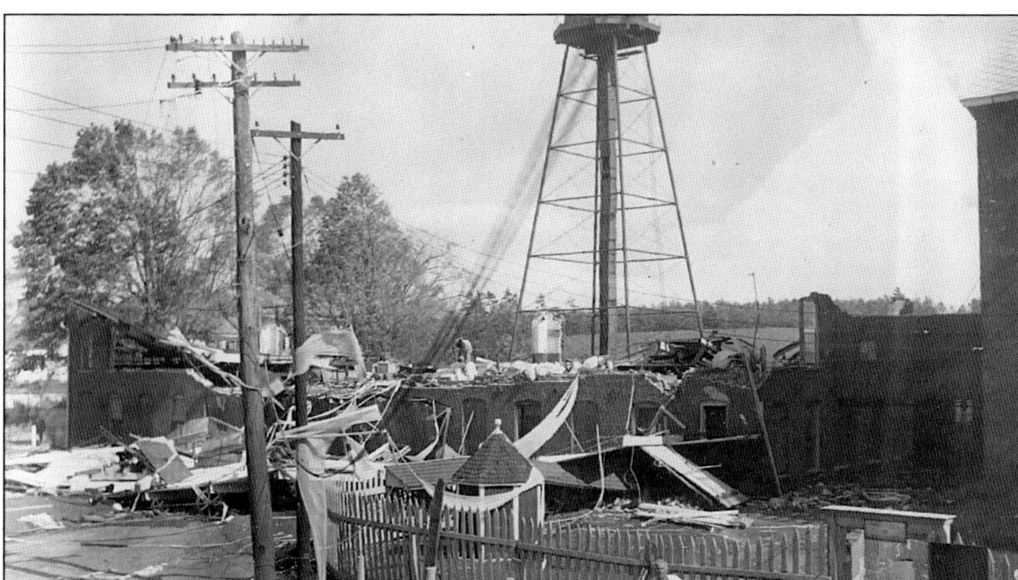

The 1938 Hurricane. The Attawaugan plant of Powdrell & Alexander sustained much damage from this powerful hurricane. No village in Killingly escaped the wrath of the winds.

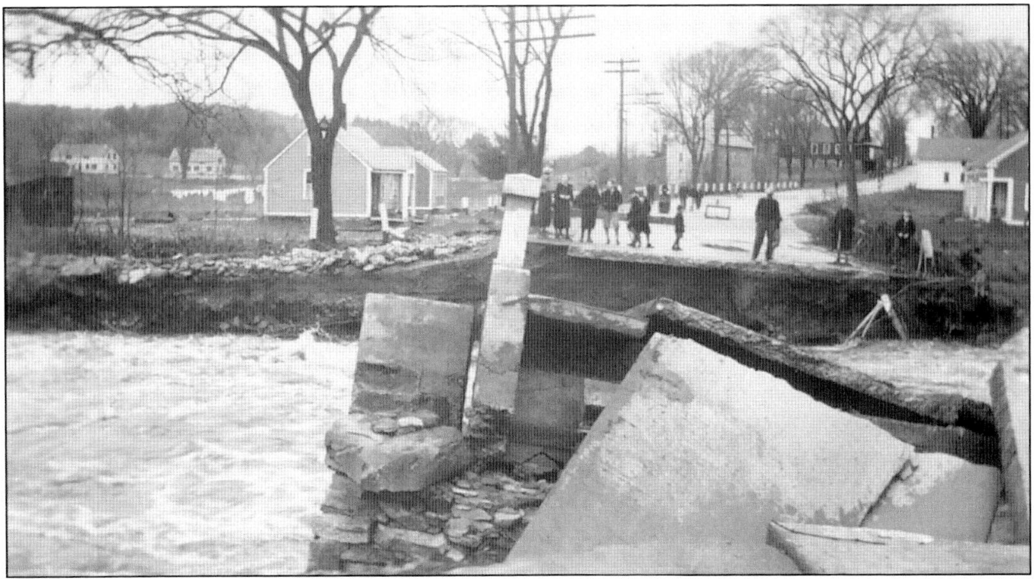

ATTAWAUGAN BRIDGE, ROUTE 12, THE FLOOD OF MARCH 1936. The rampaging Five Mile River caused widespread destruction. These photographs show the concrete bridge in Attawaugan on the road to Putnam, Route 12, that gave way before the violent floodwaters. The bridge was replaced in 1938.

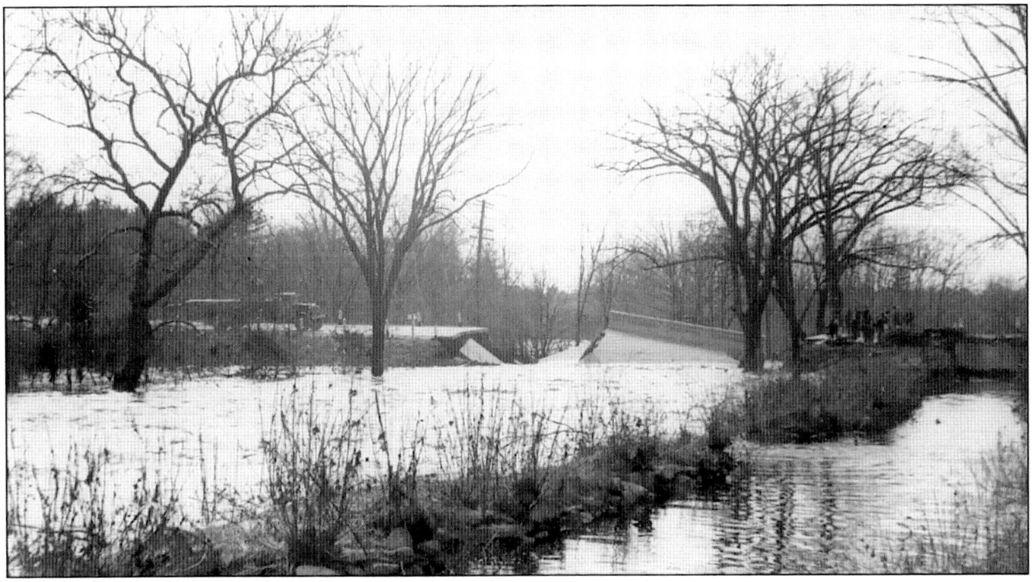

Three

BALLOUVILLE:

PINEVILLE, WARSAW, AND YOSEMITE VALLEY

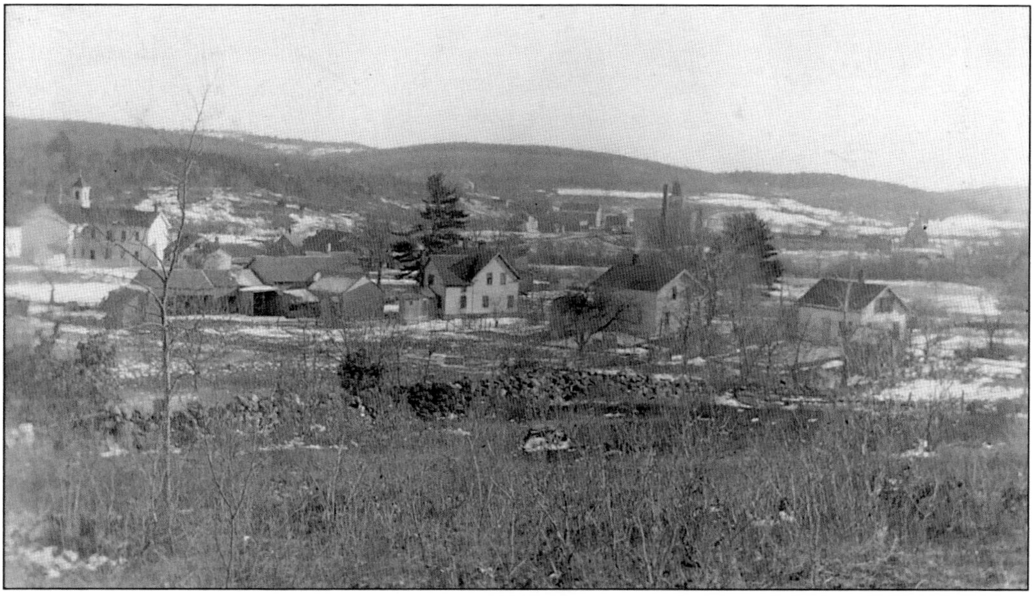

AN OVERVIEW OF BALLOUVILLE, C. EARLY 1900S. This view shows the Church of Five Wounds on the Ballouville Road in the upper right. To the left is the Ballouville Mill. On the far left, the back of the Ballouville School is visible. Ware Road houses are in the foreground. Breakneck Hill is the white area in the distance, left of center.

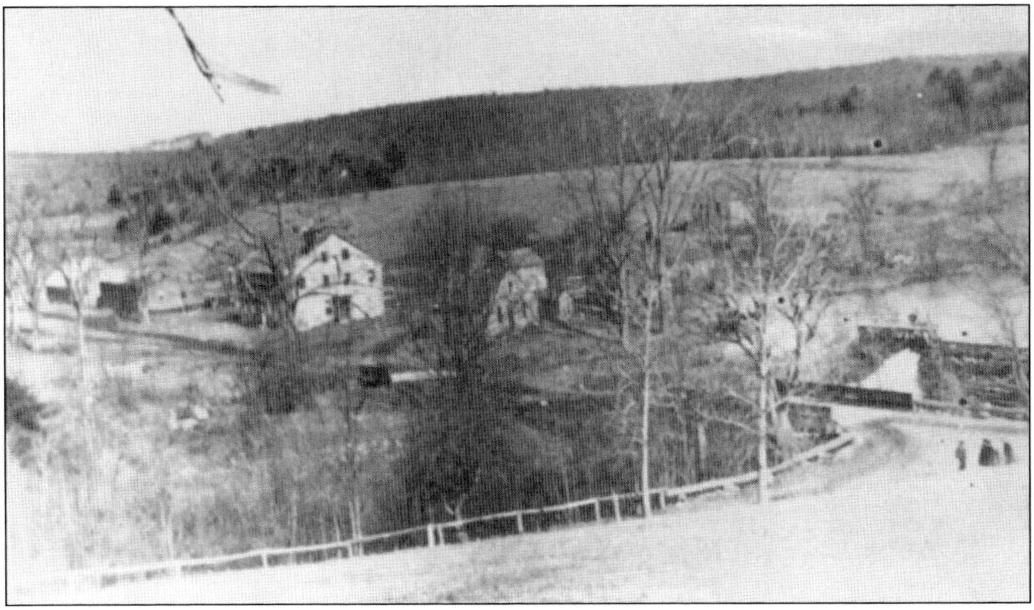

AN OVERVIEW OF DANIELS VILLAGE AND THE DANIELS FACTORY RUINS, 1888. Listed in the National Register of Historic Places, Daniels Village is the site of one of the first textile mills in Connecticut. Today, only the dam and stone mansion remain intact, although foundations of other buildings and tenements are visible. The site is located on the north side of the Five Mile River, near Stone Road in Pineville. The area was first settled in the early 1700s. By 1800, it was known as Talbot's Mills. In 1814, the well-established mill site was purchased by the Killingly Manufacturing Company, a cotton mill. Local residents joined with Rhode Island entrepreneurs and erected the cotton factory. Operated by the Howe family, the plant was called Howe's Factory. The Daniels family bought the property in 1845, and it then became known as Daniels Village.

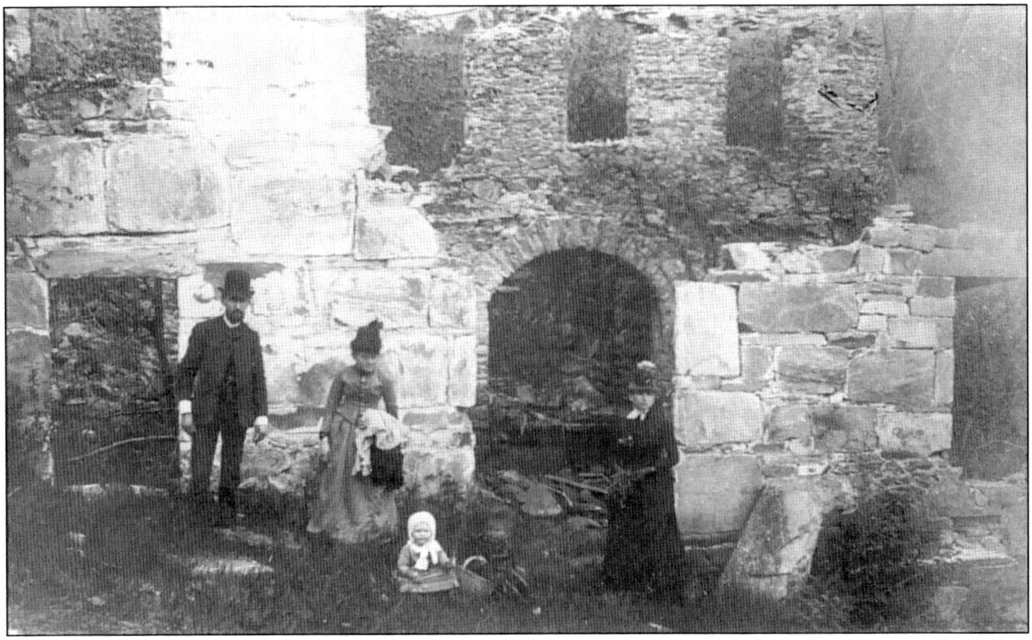

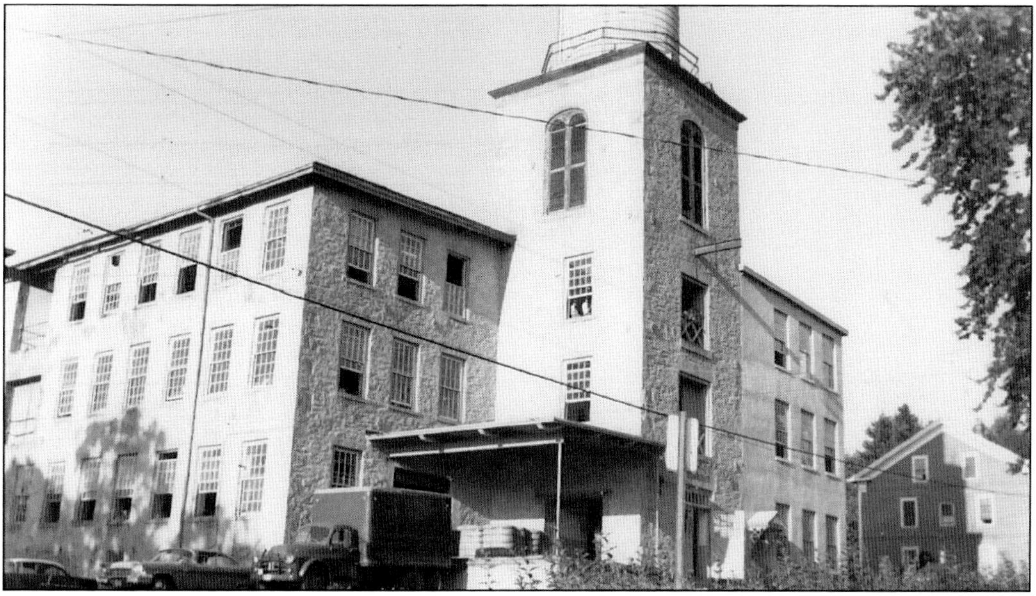

THE MILL OF BALLOUVILLE. Ballouville developed around the mill constructed by Leonard Ballou and his father-in-law, Jabez Amsbury. In 1825, the two men bought Asa Alexander's corn mill and water privilege on the Five Mile River and converted it to a cotton mill. Attawaugan Manufacturing bought the mill in 1860. Powdrell & Alexander purchased it in 1927 and operated it until the 1950s. Later, the mill was used by Hale Manufacturing for making specialty yarns.

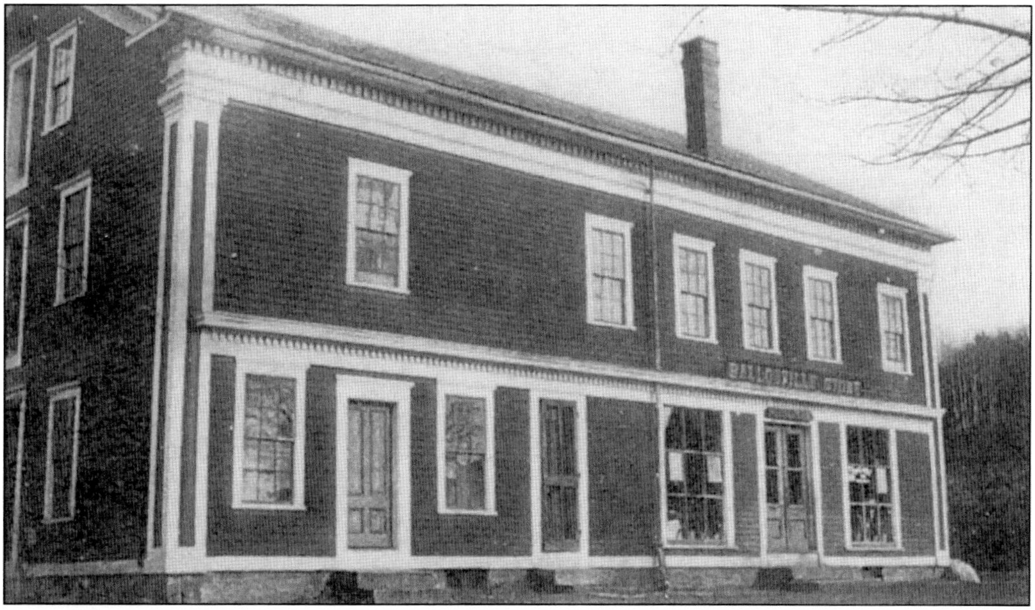

THE BALLOUVILLE STORE AND POST OFFICE, C. 1854. This store is among the most significant of the early mill-owned buildings in Killingly. Located on Ballouville Road east of the mill, it was built in 1854 by Jabez Amsbury and Leonard Ballou. Their successors, Powdrell & Alexander, sold the building to Peter Dumas in the mid-1930s. The store has housed the post office since 1882.

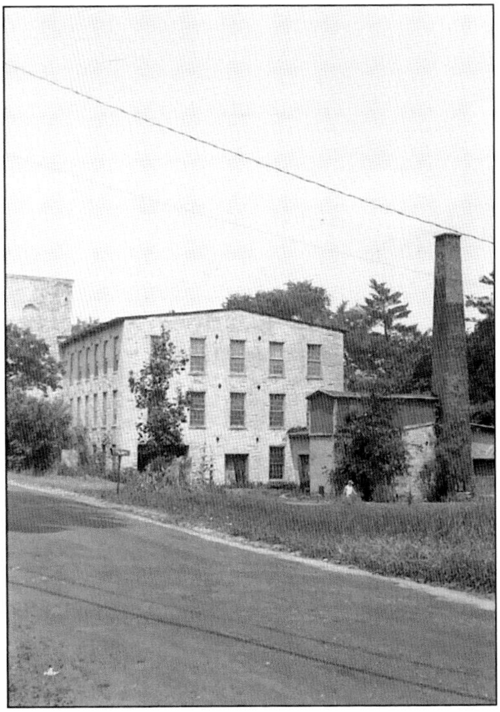

The Mill of Pineville. Jabez Amsbury took over operation of the Pineville Mill. Pineville's first mill burned in 1853. The mill was rebuilt in 1865. Powdrell and Alexander owned and operated the mill from 1927 to the early 1950s. In recent years, the building was used as a chicken house and then for light manufacturing.

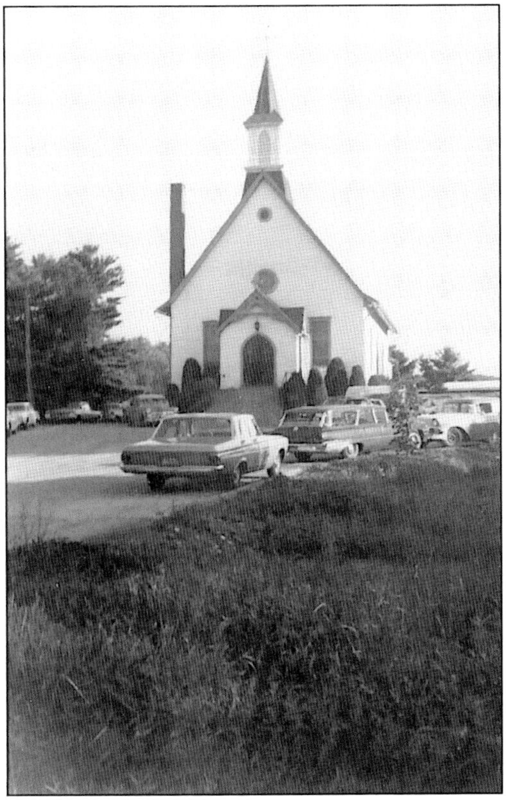

The Church of Five Wounds (St. Anne's), c. 1881. The spiritual needs of some of the Attawaugan and Ballouville workers were met by the establishment of the Attawaugan Methodist Church. However, as Catholic immigrants arrived in large numbers in the late 1800s, the Attawaugan Company acknowledged the change and donated land for the construction of a Catholic church in Ballouville. The church operated as a mission of St. Joseph's in Dayville.

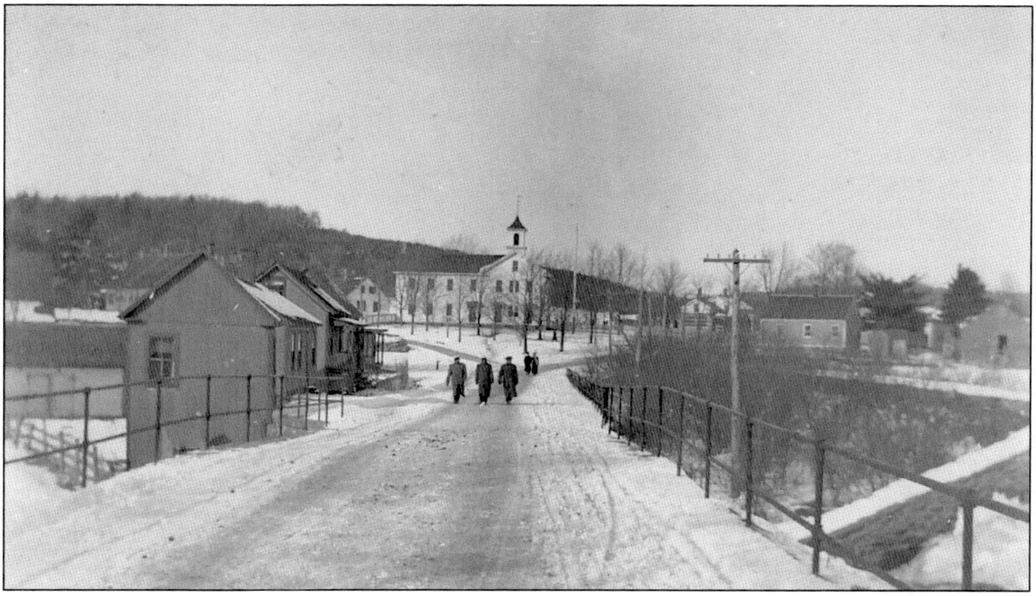

THE BALLOUVILLE SCHOOL, 1878. The district school for both Ballouville and Pineville was located at the junction of Ware and Pineville Roads on a lot donated by Mowry Amsbury, son of Jabez Amsbury. The school housed grades one through eight and was run by two teachers. It ceased being used as a school in the early 1950s. The LaBelle-Lemieux American Legion Post #183 has owned it since 1963.

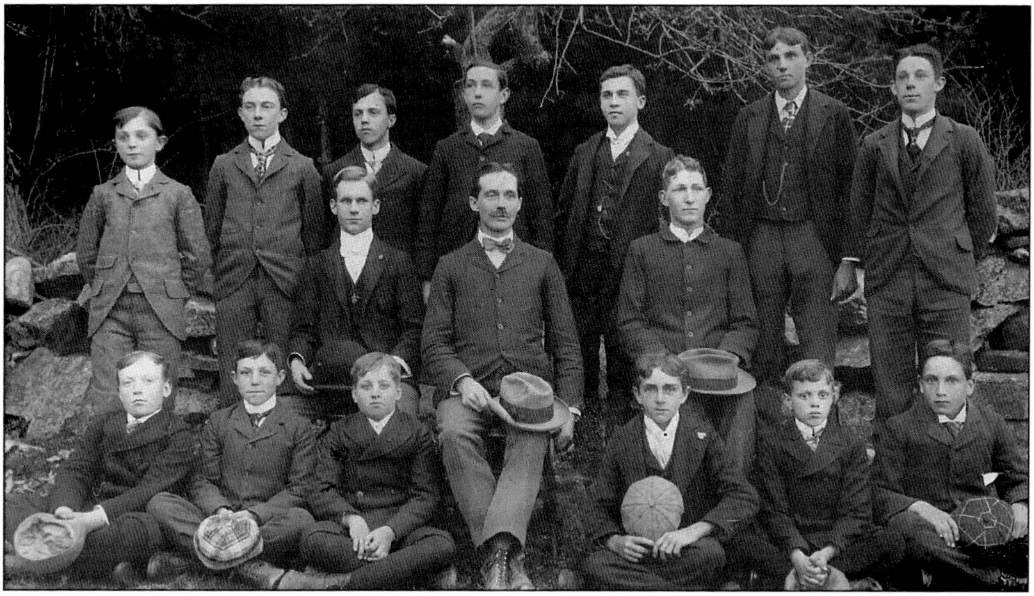

BALLOUVILLE SCHOOL STUDENTS, C. 1898. The teacher in the center was A.D. Tripp, who was also the principal of the school. Directly behind Tripp was James Elmer Keene. In the group were some children of the LaBelle family.

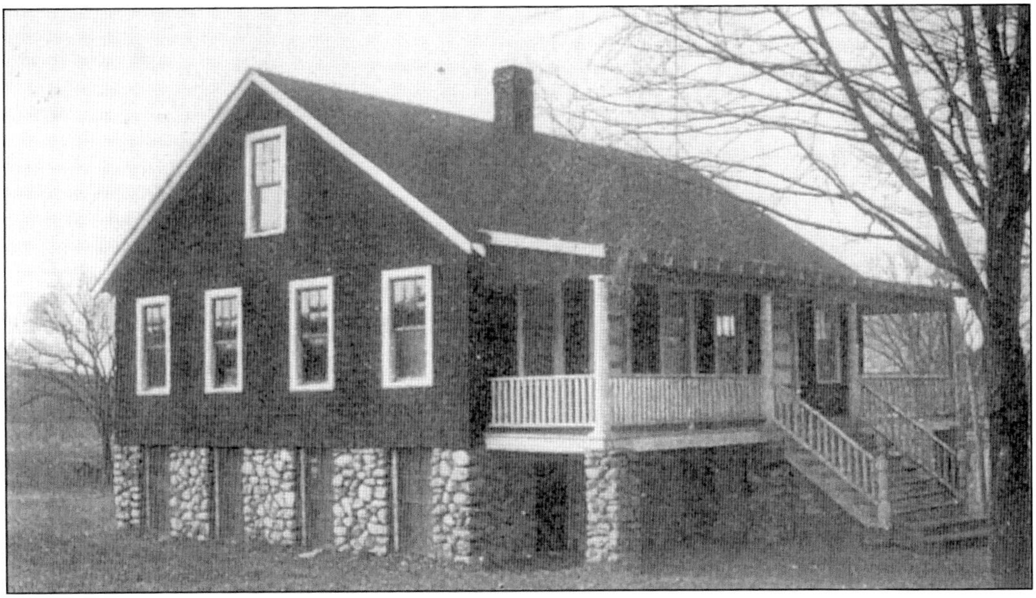

The Ballouville Mill Clubhouse, c. 1920. The Attawaugan Manufacturing Company constructed this bungalow on Ballouville Road as a clubhouse for its workers. The workers came to the clubhouse on their lunch breaks and played marbles and peggie, a stick game. Dances were held here on Saturday nights, with Miriam Keene playing the piano. In 1940, the clubhouse was converted into office space by Hale Manufacturing. Today, it is a private residence.

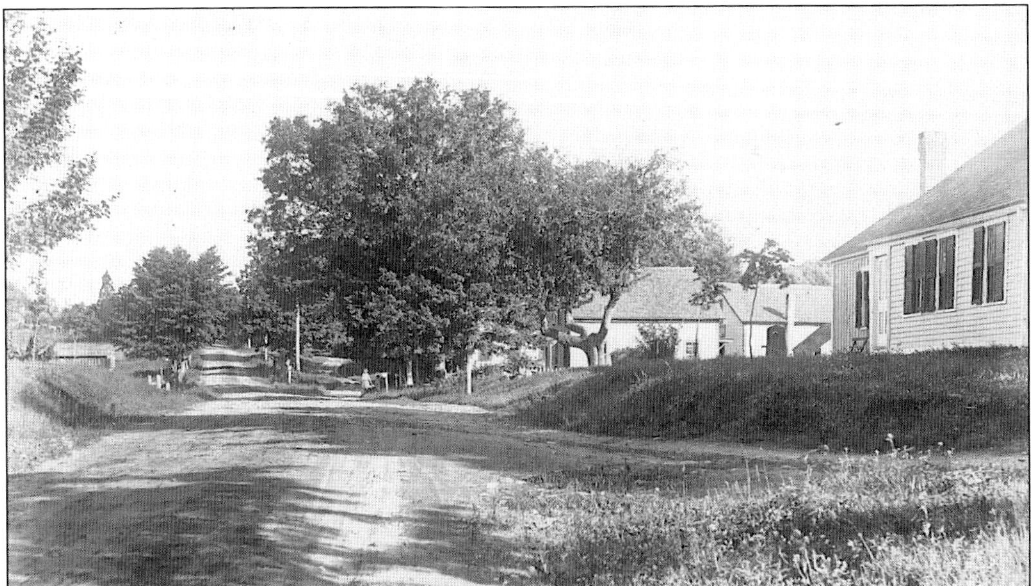

A Junction in Ballouville. This bucolic scene is at the junction of Ware Road (here called Putnam Road) and Pineville Road, looking toward Route 21. The road on the right leads to the Ballouville School. The Roscoe Chase House is on the extreme right.

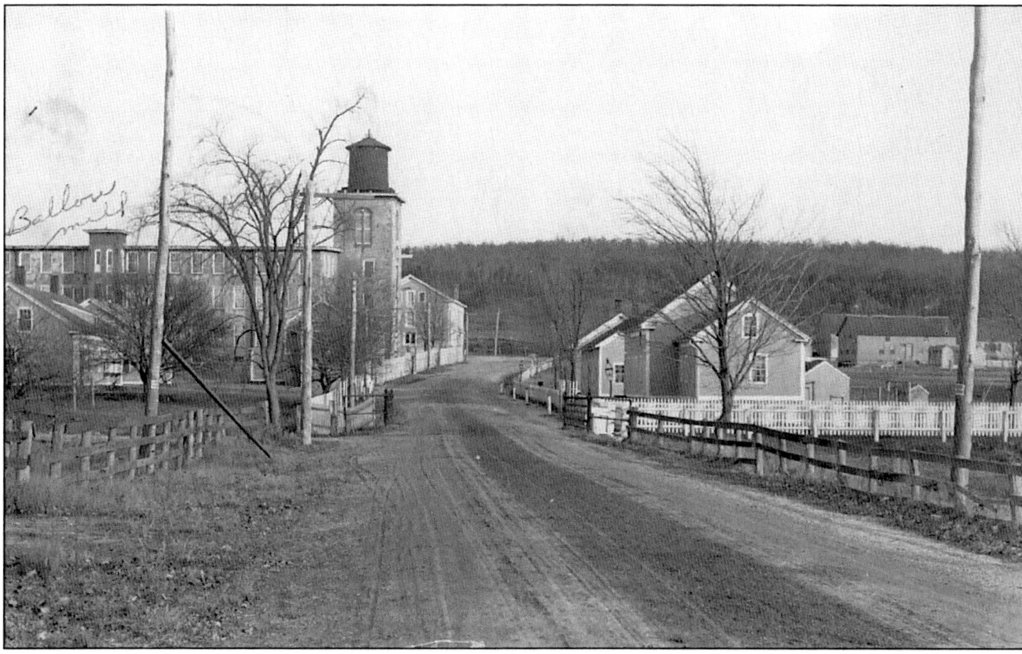

BALLOU'S MILL, C. EARLY 1900S. This tranquil scene is on the Ballouville Road. Ballou's Mill, owned by the Attawaugan Company, is on the upper left, and some of the mill houses are on the right.

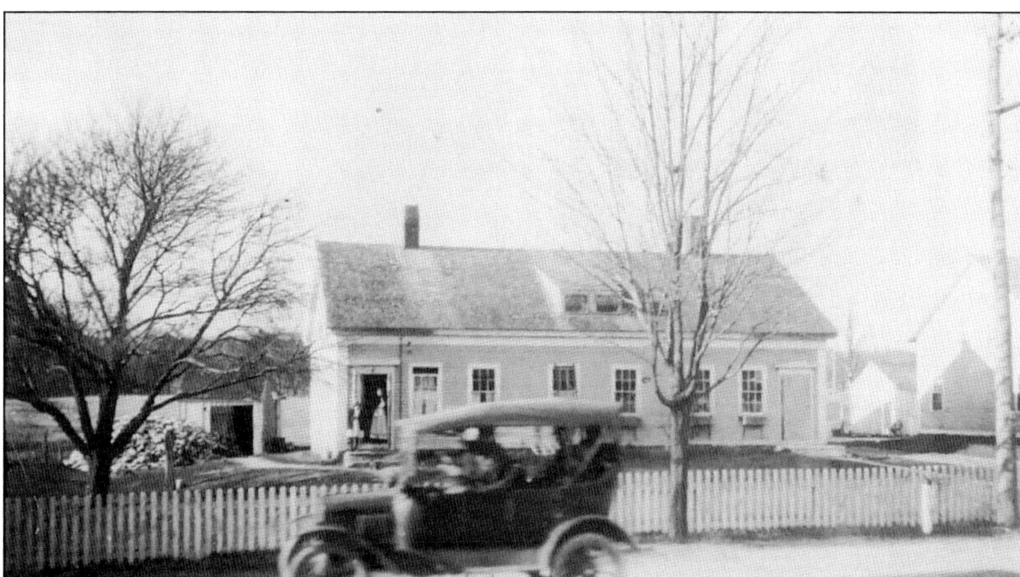

THE BALLOUVILLE MILL HOUSE. Mabele Pray's house on the Attawaugan-Ballouville Road is one of the neatly kept homes built by the mill owners for their workers. James Keene's Model T Ford is parked in front of the house.

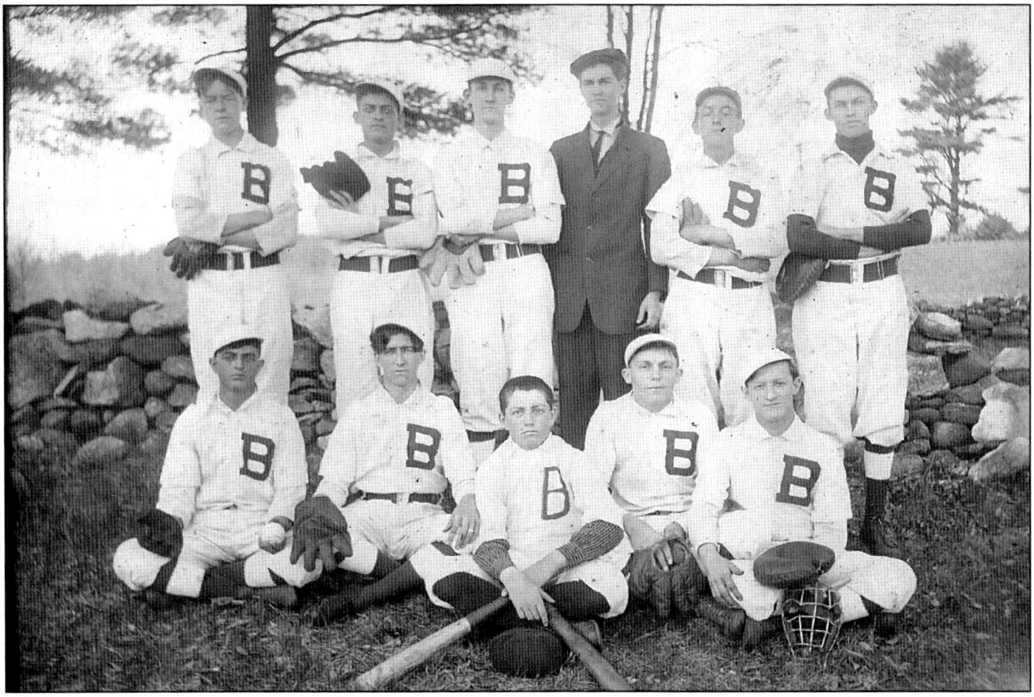

The Village Baseball Team, c. 1900. Every village had a baseball team, and Ballouville was no exception. Each village had a competitive spirit that made the games exciting for the players as well as the spectators.

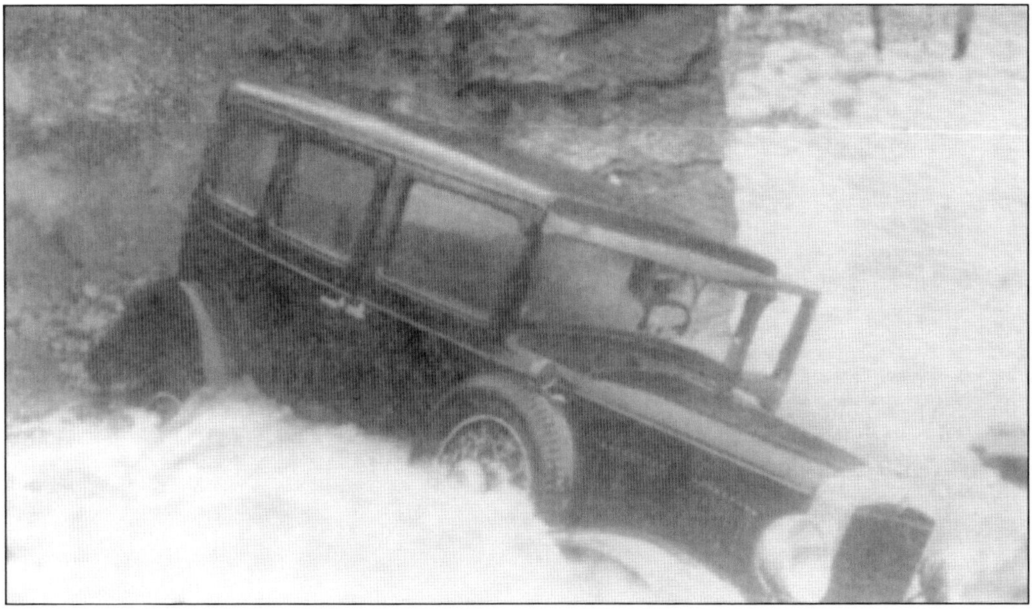

The Flood of March, 1936. The high waters of the Five Mile River caused the Ballouville-Pineville Road to cave in, sending the car of Patrick Durocher crashing 18 feet down into the raging torrent. Only a timely break in the eastern end of the dike at Pineville saved the dam. This photograph originally appeared in a booklet of pictures of the 1936 flood, published by the Bulletin Company in Norwich.

Four

DAYVILLE:

KILLINGLY CENTER AND ELMVILLE

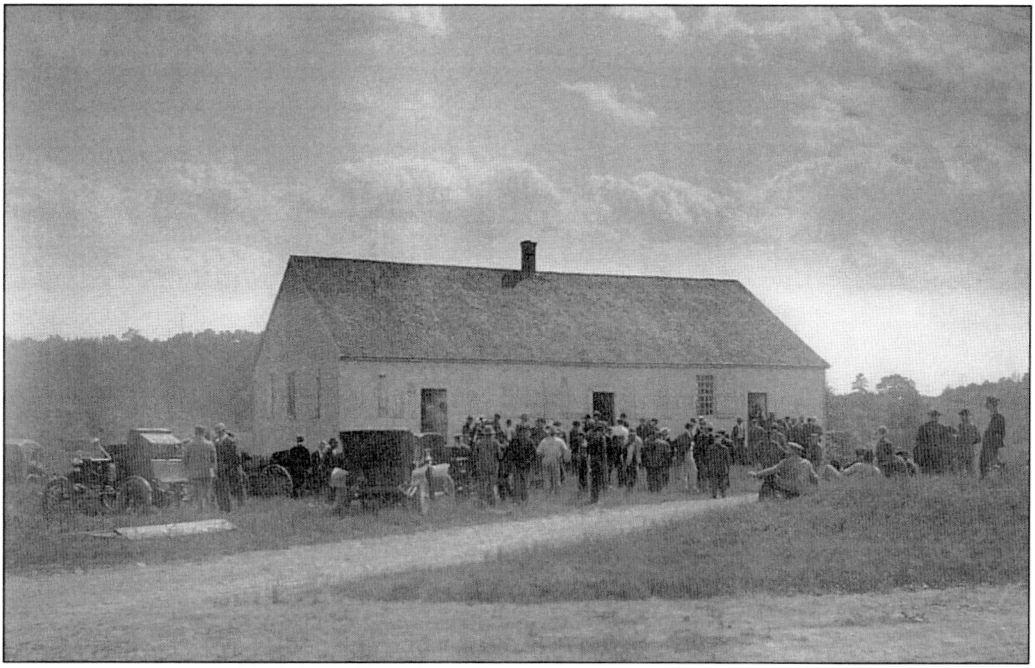

THE KILLINGLY CENTER TOWN MEETING HALL, c. 1785. The Breakneck Hill Congregational Church was moved to the intersection of Cook Hill Road and Route 101. The first town meeting was held there on December 12, 1785. The hall continued to be used for town meetings until 1906, when the town purchased the Music Hall in Danielson. The old building was sold by the town in 1922 and was demolished in 1933.

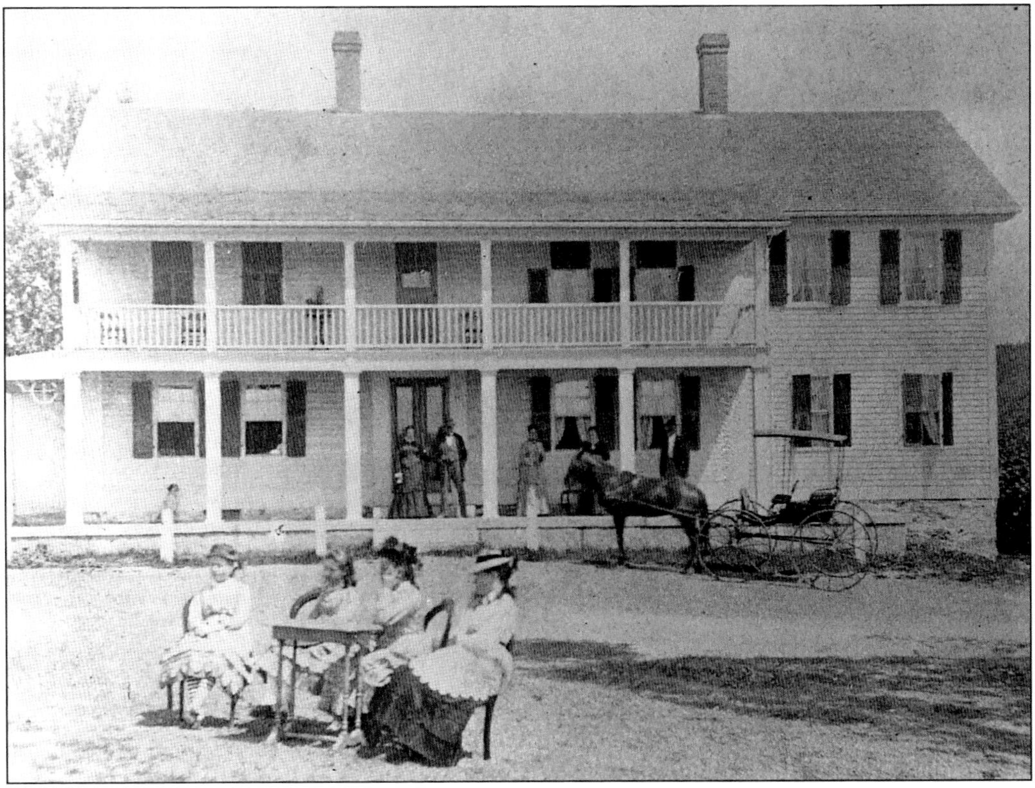

KINGSBURY'S HOTEL, C. 1790. The oldest extant structure on Route 101 in Killingly Center was known in its early years as the Jeremiah Field Tavern, a stagecoach inn. George Kingsbury operated it in 1839. A 19th-century double-tiered porch survived into the 1930s. The building is now divided into apartments.

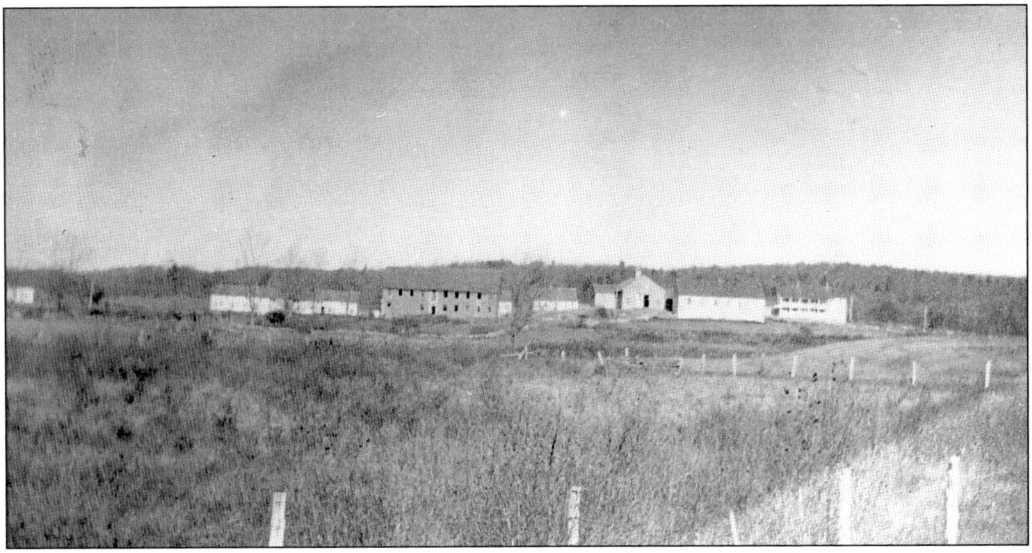

THE KILLINGLY CENTER MILL. The mill adjacent to the old town meeting house was constructed in 1824 and was sold to Joseph and Samuel Hutchins. The mill disappeared prior to 1932. The Kingsbury Inn is visible on the right.

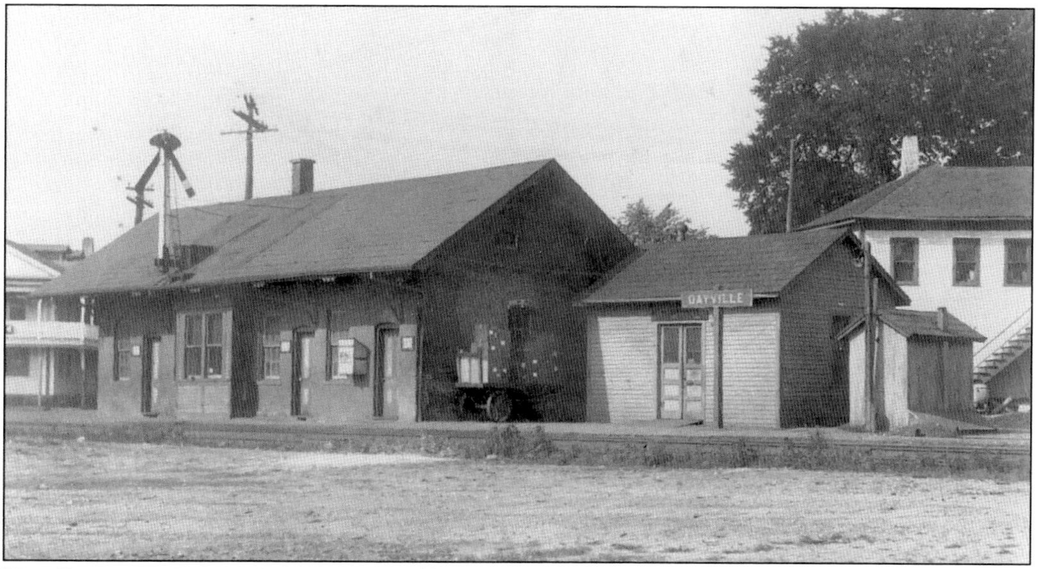

The Dayville Depot Square. Dayville was originally called Daysville after Capt. John Day, who owned and developed the water privilege along the Assawaga (Five Mile) River. With the construction of the Norwich & Worcester Railroad in the 1830s, the depot became the freight hub for other manufacturing sites along the river and Whetstone Brook. The mills picked up the cotton at the Dayville depot, hauled the bales to their factories, and shipped the finished goods the same way.

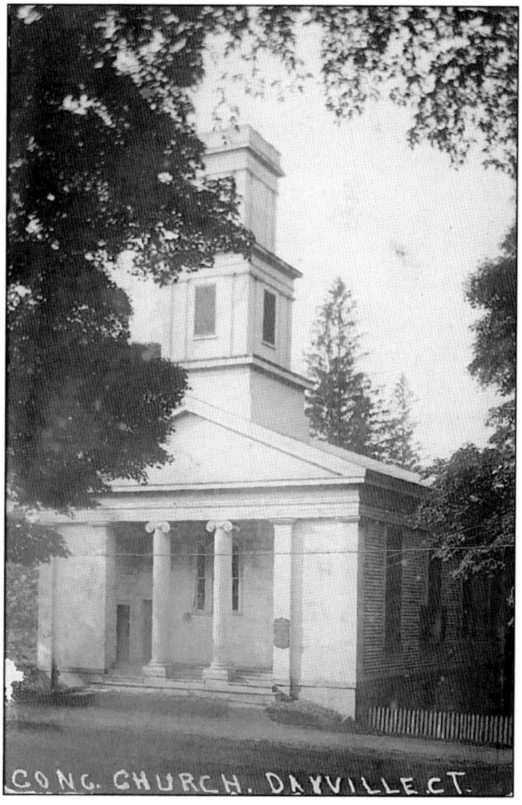

The Dayville Congregational Church, 1849. By 1849, the village of Dayville had grown to such a size that a separate Dayville Congregational Church was organized. It was built by carpenter Alexander Blanchard in the Greek Revival style of architecture. The Rev. Roswell Whitmore, former pastor of the Westfield Congregational Church in Danielsonville, served as pastor until 1857.

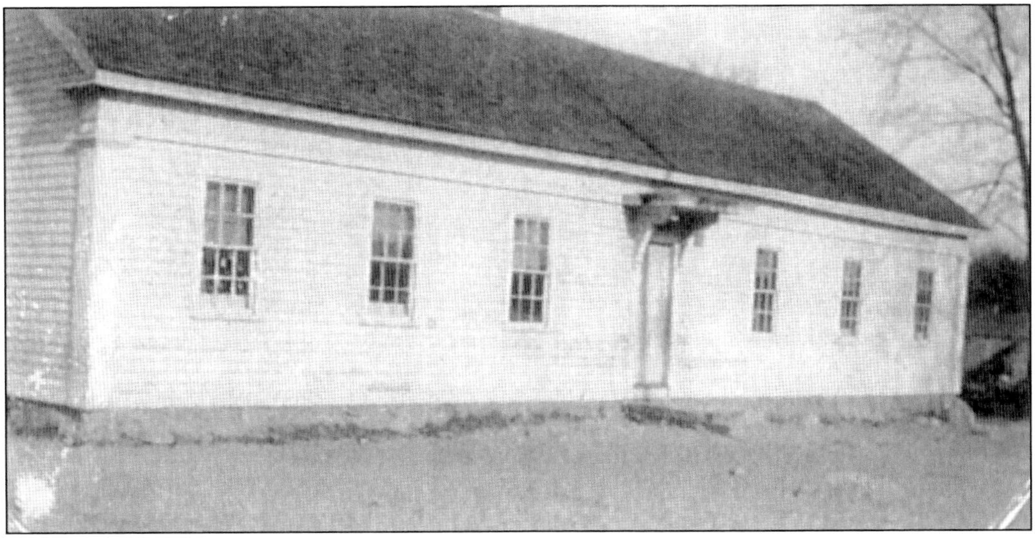

THE KILLINGLY CENTER SCHOOL, 1848. A one-story building at the intersection of Route 101 and Dog Hill Road served as a one-room schoolhouse for the town's fourth district. One teacher instructed some 30 students. According to historical accounts, the building was constructed by resident Julius Thomas and was sold to the Killingly School District in 1877. By that time, the population had doubled and an addition was built on the school.

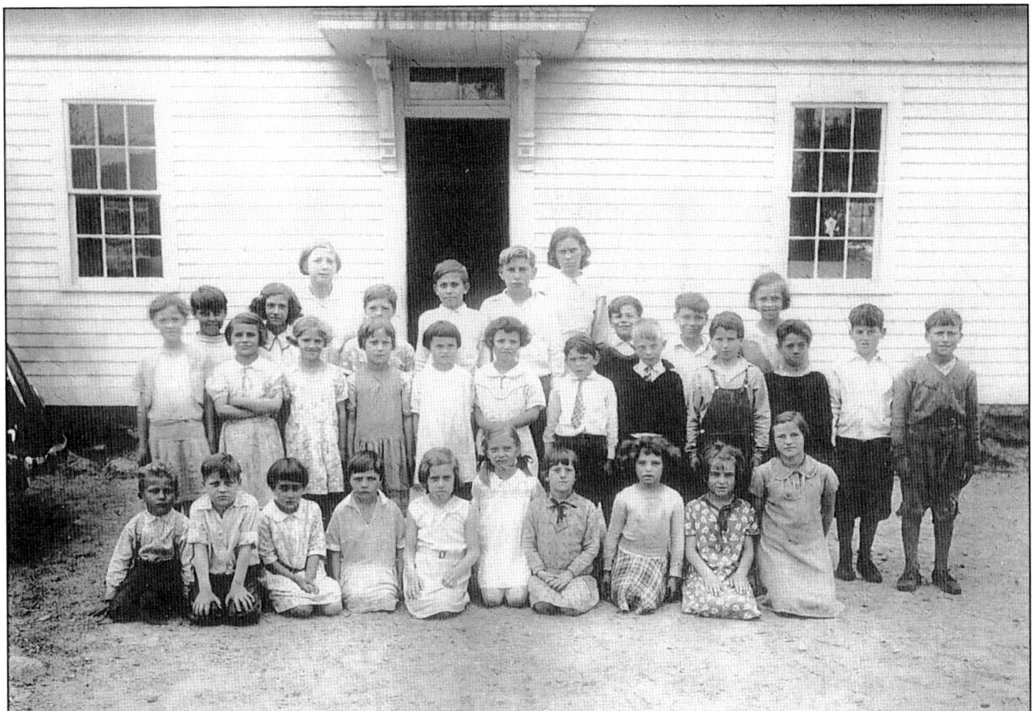

A KILLINGLY CENTER SCHOOL CLASS. The children pictured in front of the Killingly Center School were in grades one through four in 1932–33. The teacher was Flora (Keach) Eyers. The school is now the Killingly Grange Hall.

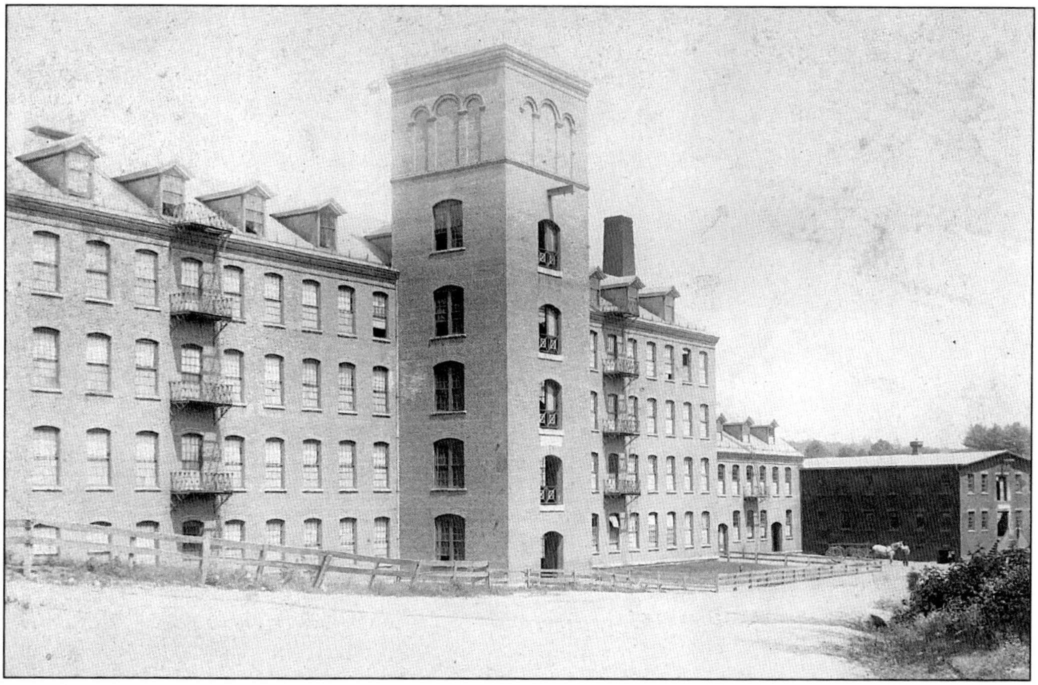

THE SAYLES MILL, c. 1846. John Day, a well-to-do farmer with interests in real estate, built this mill and leased it to the manufacturing firm of Asher Starkweather. A series of lessees operated at the site for some 25 years. Then, in 1858, Harris and Sabin Sayles bought the property. Since the original building had been destroyed, they put up a new structure, which was enlarged several times to accommodate increased business.

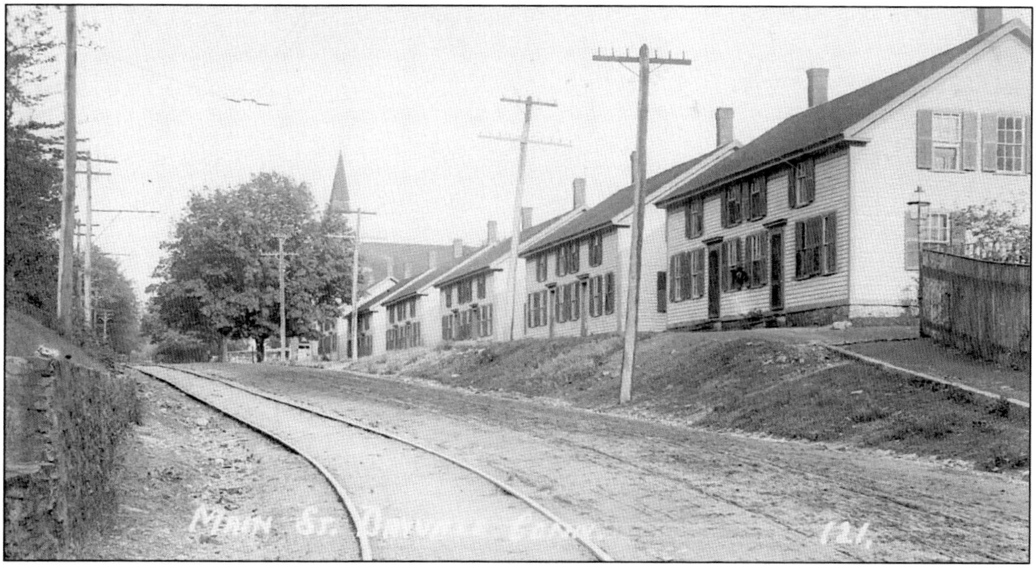

SAYLES COMPANY MILL HOUSES. After building a new brick mill in 1882, Sabin and Harris Sayles built numerous mill houses for the use of their larger work force. These houses were typical of those provided by mill owners during the Industrial Revolution. They enabled the workers to be within walking distance of the factory. In the center of Dayville, the mill owners built a company store and a meeting hall in the large brick block, *c.* 1873.

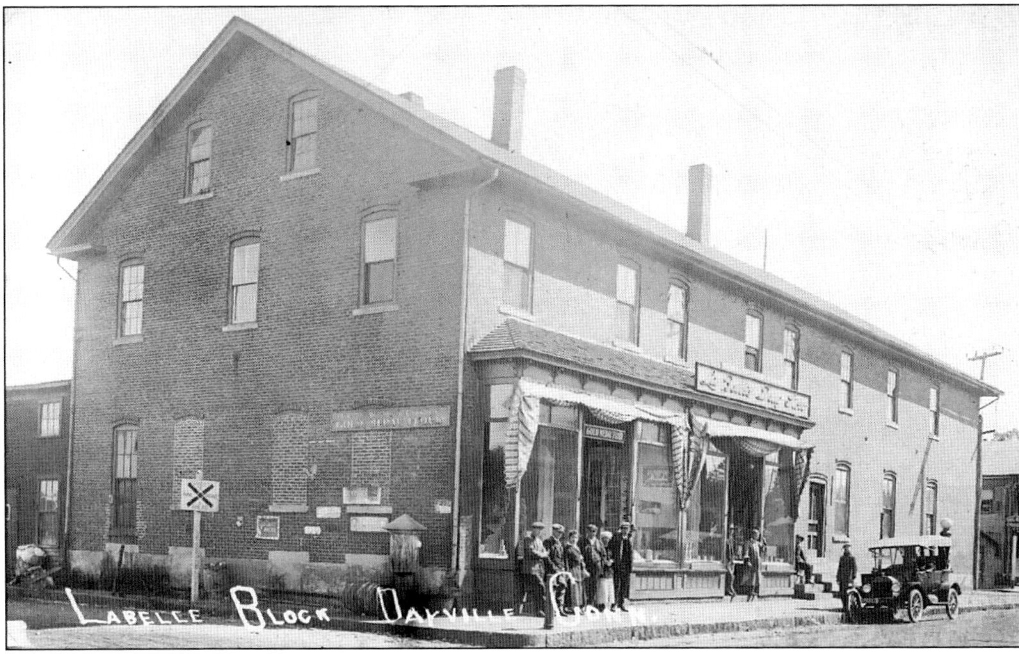

THE SAYLES-LA BELLE BLOCK (THE COMPANY STORE), 1873. Sabin L. Sayles, the village's 19th-century industrialist, built the block on Main Street that is probably the oldest extant commercial structure in Dayville. It accommodated three stores and a meeting hall upstairs. In 1900, it was sold to William LaBelle, who had opened a drugstore there in 1895. LaBelle originally worked as a master mechanic in the textile mills but turned to pharmacy when his health failed.

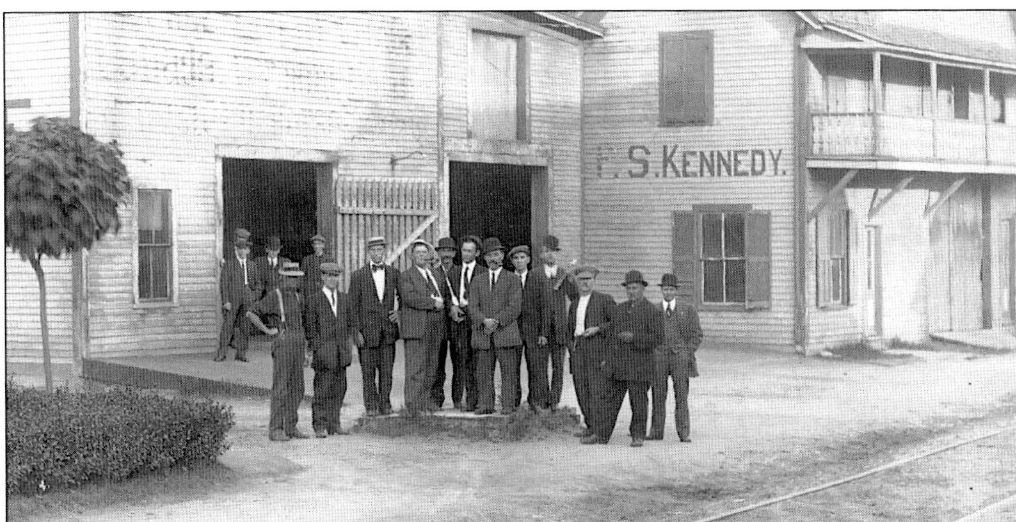

THE F.S. KENNEDY FUNERAL PARLOR AND CARRIAGE HOUSE. In 1888, Frank S. Kennedy bought the Kennedy Hotel from his father, Lorenzo Kennedy. Earlier, in 1880, he had purchased the undertaking establishment of Mowry Amsbury in Danielson. In addition he operated a sales stable, buying three to six carloads of horses a year in Canada and the West and selling them to local buyers.

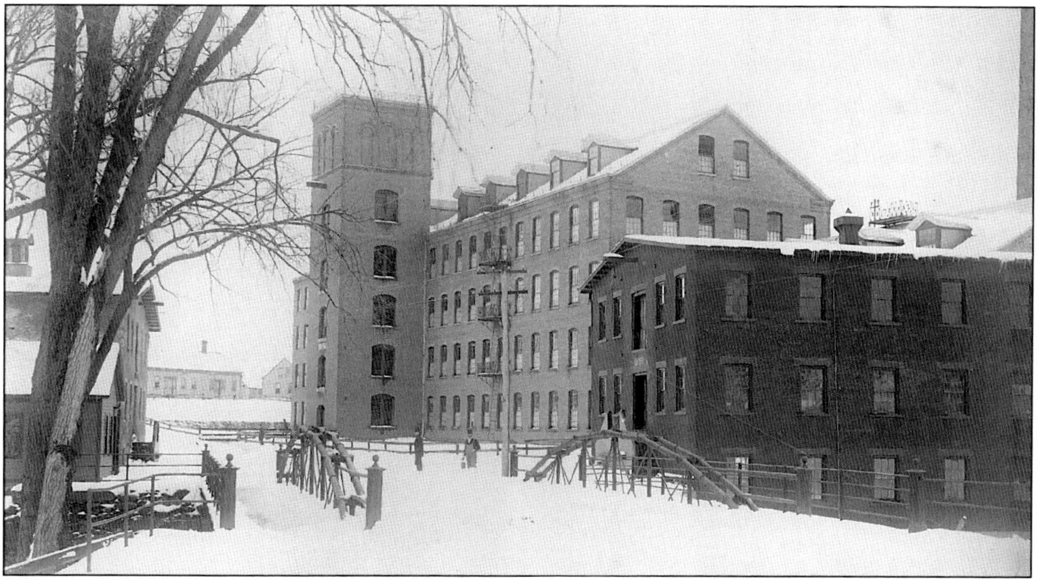

The Assawaga Woolen Mill, c. 1903. After the Sayles Company closed its operation, the mill ran for ten years as the Dayville Woolen Company. Dayville then sold out to the Assawaga Company, which prospered during the World War I period. A new weave room was added in 1918, and many new houses were built on Sayles Avenue. The mill is the largest and most centrally located building in the village, attesting to the importance of textile manufacturing to this region.

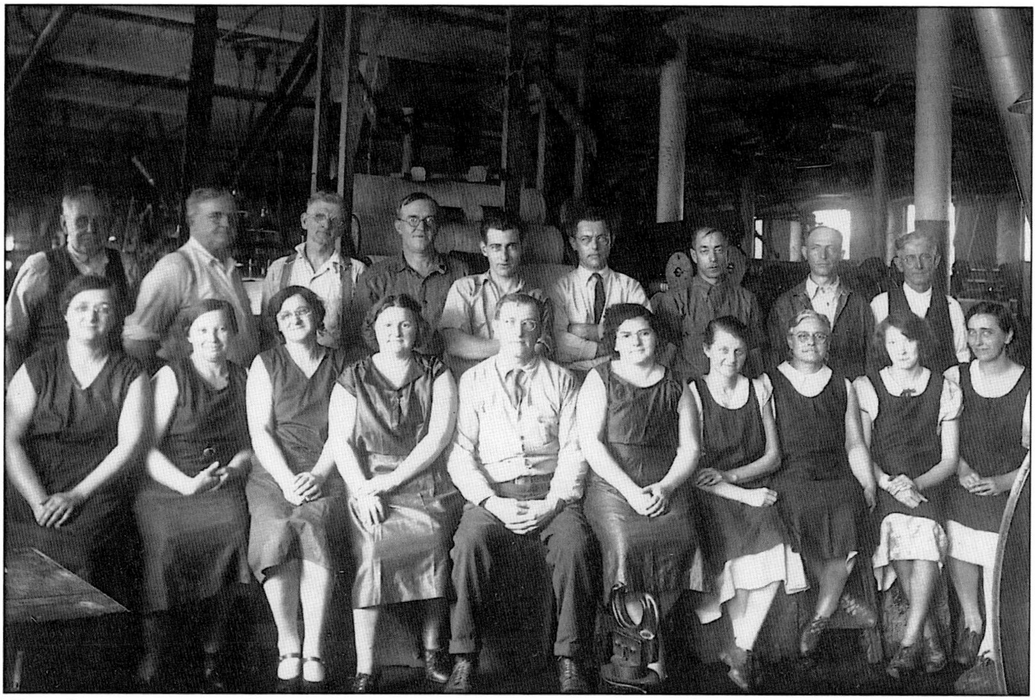

The Spooling and Finishing Department, mid-1930s. This group from the Assawaga Company includes A. Gingras, R. Foster, A. Barry, A. Pechie, W. Janes, S. Mathieu, H. Weaver, N. Janes, M. Morin, J. Roy, F. Janes, C. Harris, and C. Janes.

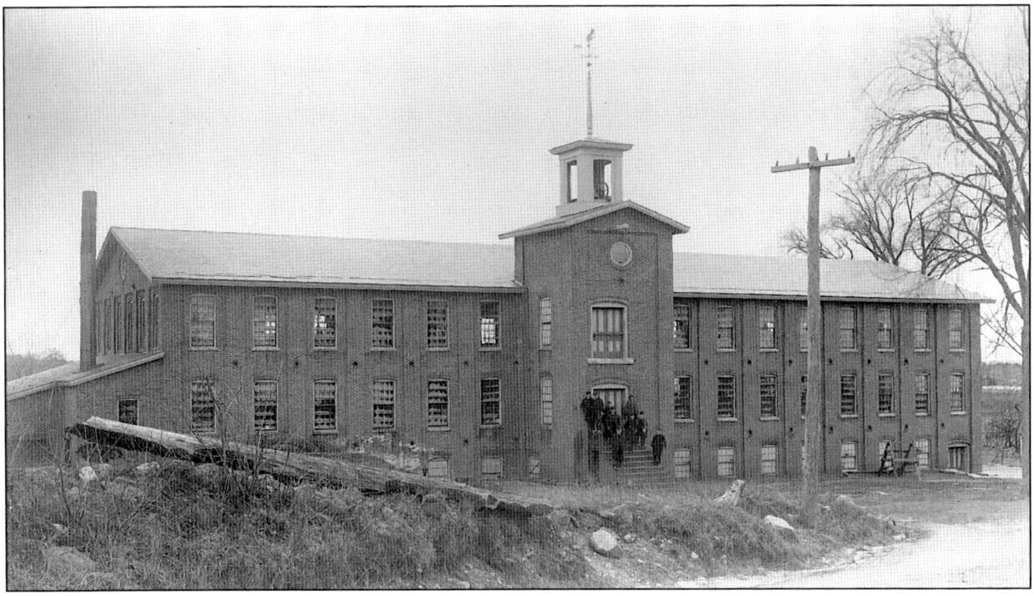

THE DEXTER WOOLEN MILL, C. 1875. This brick mill was built for Alfred Potter to replace a frame mill that had occupied the site since at least 1800. It was used by many companies to produce a variety of textiles until 1933, when Danielson Manufacturing Company, a mill supply manufacturer, moved in. Danco later diversified and become one of the major suppliers of injection-molded nylon products in the United States.

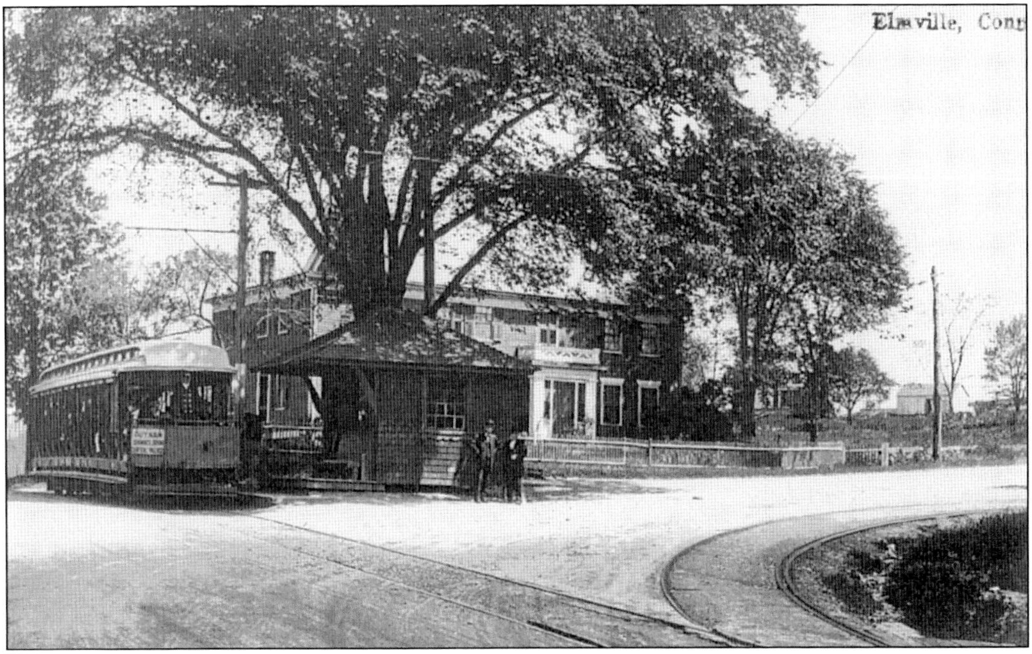

THE ELMVILLE TROLLEY WAITING STATION. The Elmville Stand was the connection of the Providence & Danielson electric railroad and the People's Tramway Company, which ran from Danielson to Putnam. The Providence & Danielson was a passenger and freight line. A freight and milk car made one trip a day from Danielson to Providence. After the line was abandoned in 1920–21, the old waiting station was used for years as an ice cream parlor and lunchroom.

The Old Dayville School. This school was constructed on the northeast corner of Route 101 and the Town Farm Road. In 1853, Thomas Evans was one of the teachers in the school. By 1878, Evans had become an entrepreneur and had built the large Evans block in Danielsonville.

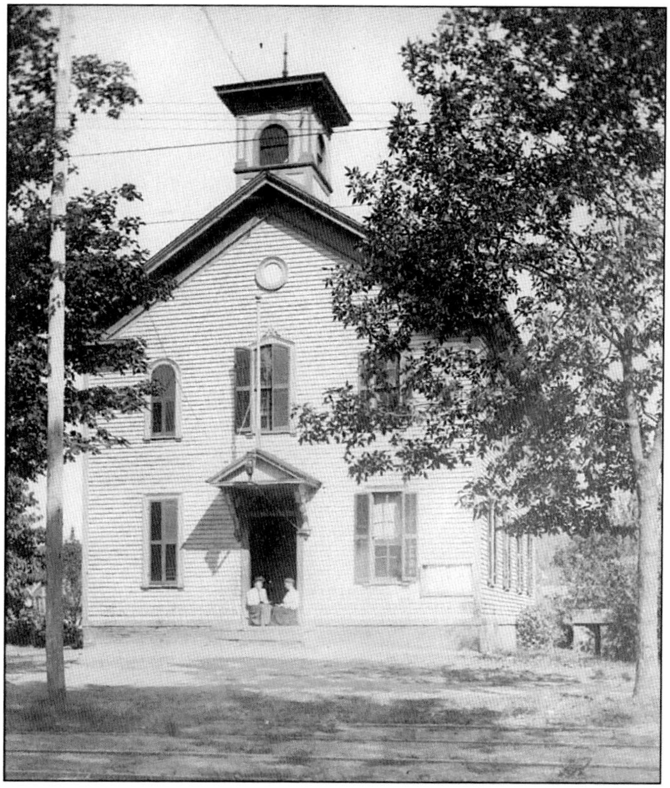

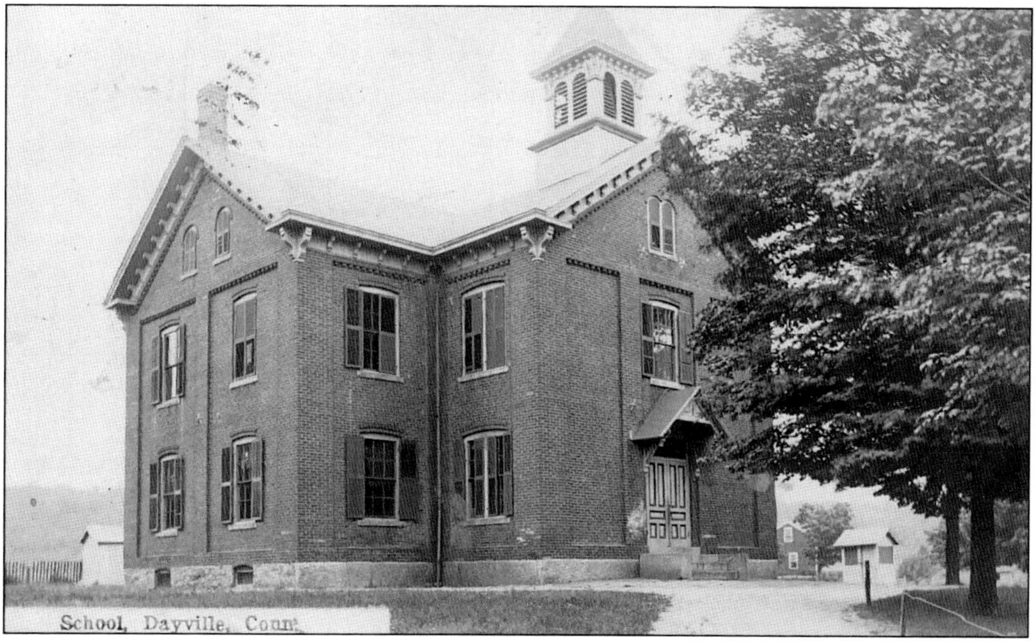

The Later Dayville School, 1875–80. This Dayville School was possibly the only brick grammar school in the town at that time. The school closed in 1948 and was torn down in the early 1960s. The bell was saved and was placed in the new Killingly Intermediate School on Upper Maple Street.

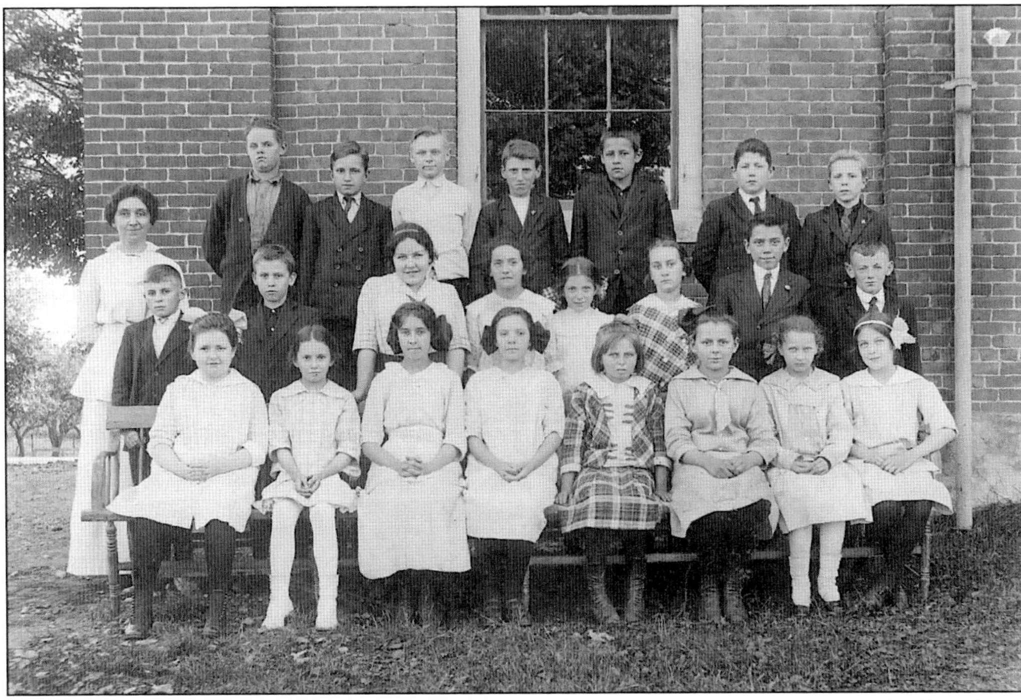

A Dayville School Class, c. 1916. The teacher of this class was Miss Duffey. Some of the schoolchildren include C. Lamothe, M. Mullen, W. Coffee, C. Harris, C. Lehrer, and A. Fortier.

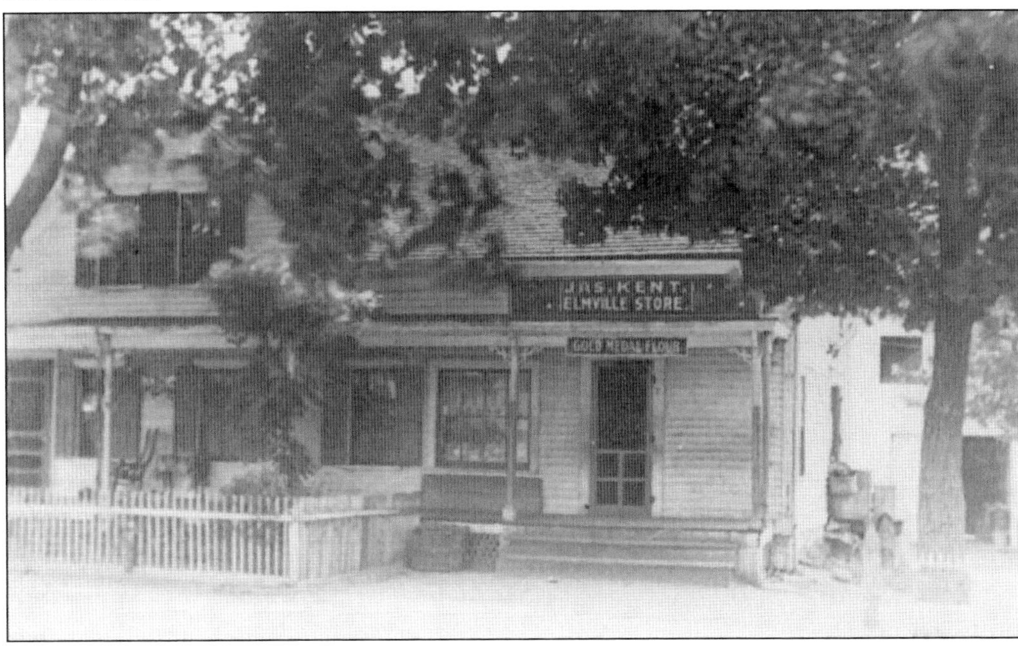

Kent's Store, c. 1884. William Kent built his house on the west side of the highway from Danielsonville and Dayville, just south of the Whetstone Brook and what was Potter's Mill. A wing that was added to the north side of the dwelling housed the Elmville store, which was operated by James Kent and successors from the early 1900s to the late 1950s.

St. Joseph's Roman Catholic Church, 1881. Mass was first celebrated in Dayville at Sayles Hall in 1869. Sabin L. Sayles donated the land for the church on Main Street. The wooden church built in the Gothic Revival style was at first a mission of the Danielsonville church. St. Joseph's Church is one of the earliest Catholic churches remaining in Windham County.

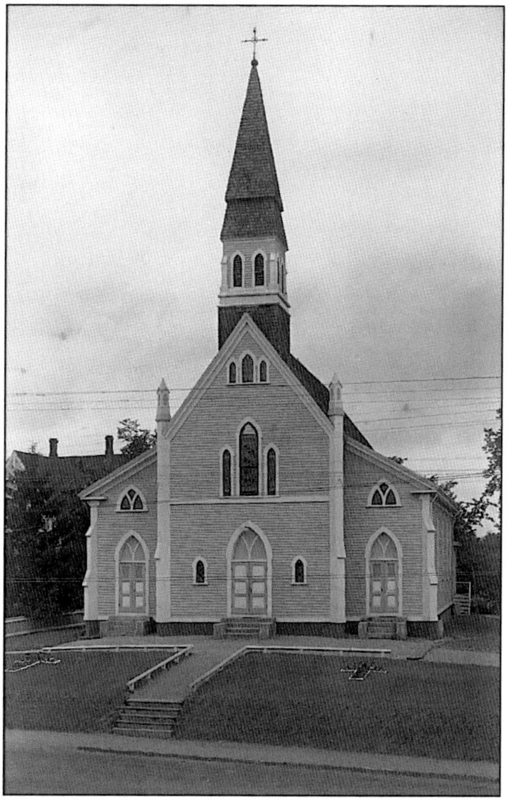

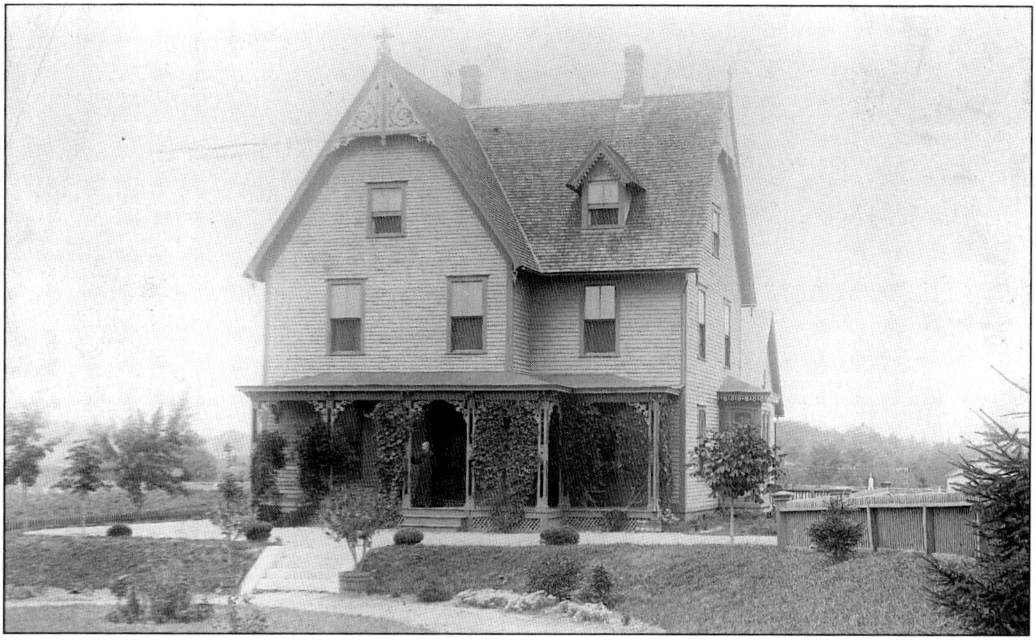

St. Joseph's Parsonage. The Rev. Thomas Ariens became the first resident pastor of St. Joseph's Church. He had the parochial residence built in 1882.

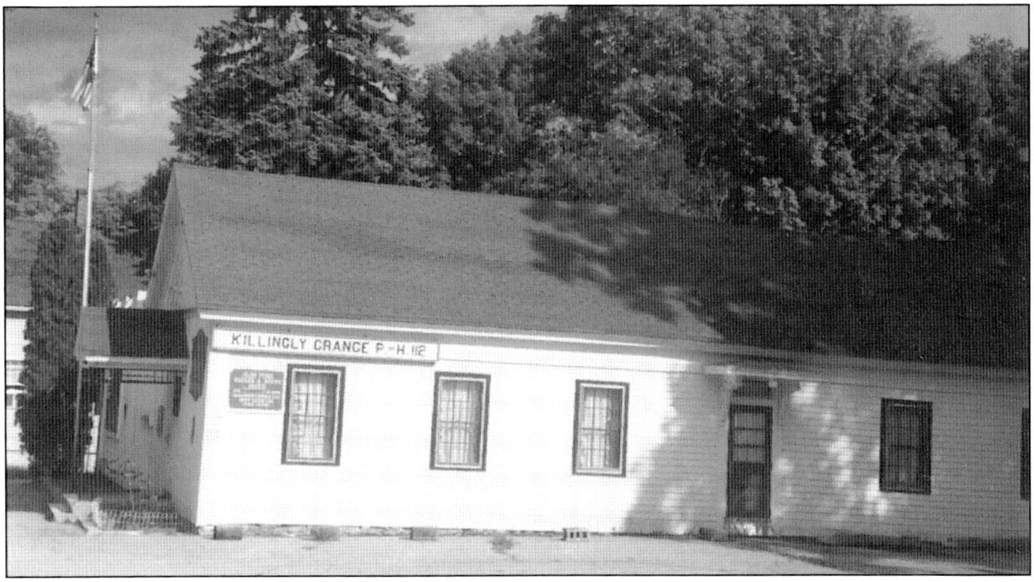

Killingly Grange #112, 1890. The Killingly Grange was organized with 13 charter members. The first meeting was held in the Grand Army Hall in Dayville. It was originally known as the First Grange of Killingly. The grange bought the Killingly Center School in 1948 and added another room in 1960. Through the grange, local farmers were offered a place to gather socially and later provided with a means of buying staples and grain in quantity.

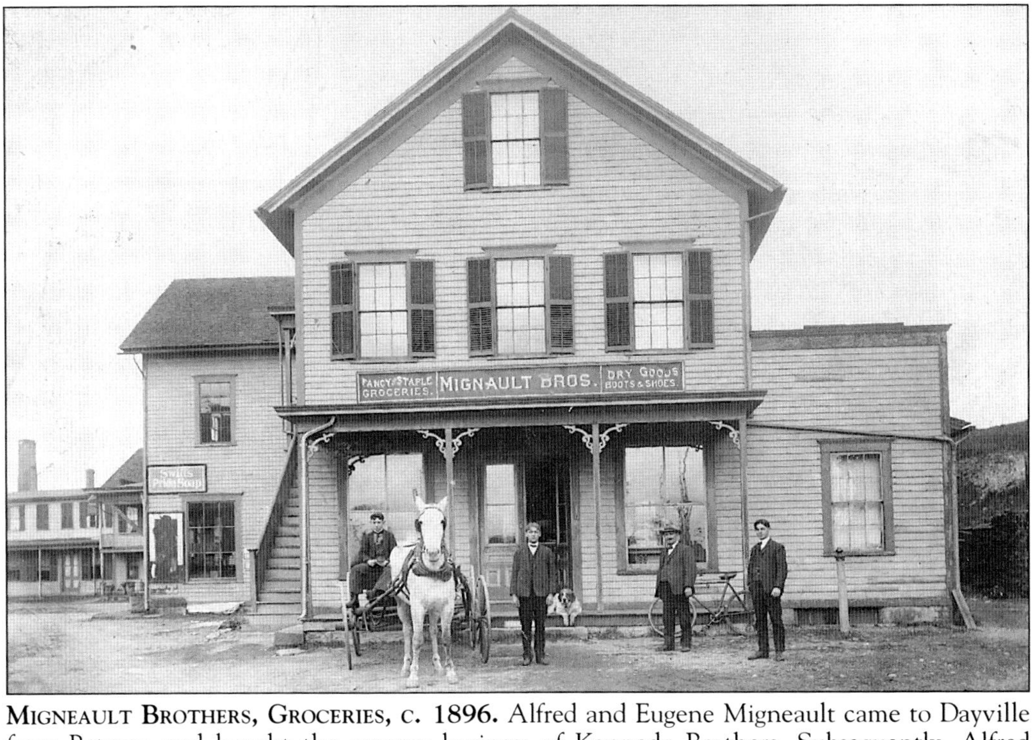

Migneault Brothers, Groceries, c. 1896. Alfred and Eugene Migneault came to Dayville from Putnam and bought the grocery business of Kennedy Brothers. Subsequently, Alfred acquired his brother's interest. He had a reputation for honest business dealings. Upon his death in 1912, his wife, Annie (Casey) Migneault, continued to operate the store.

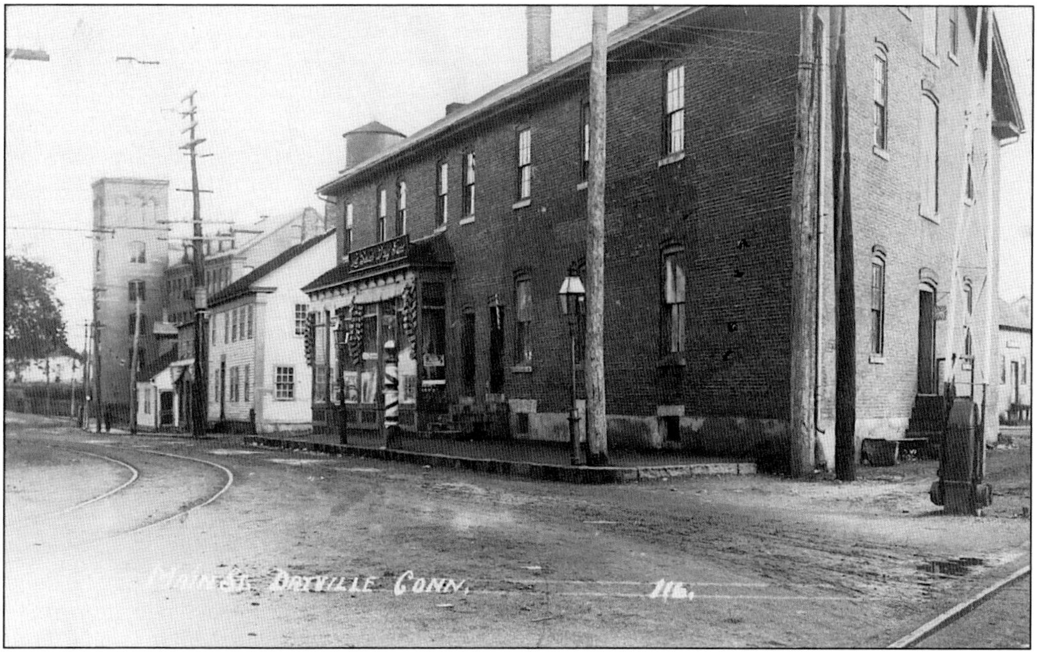

MAIN STREET SCENES. Dayville was more than simply a mill town. Houses here are associated with merchants, carriage makers, machinists, carpenters, doctors, lumber dealers, and others who made Dayville a commercial as well as an industrial center.

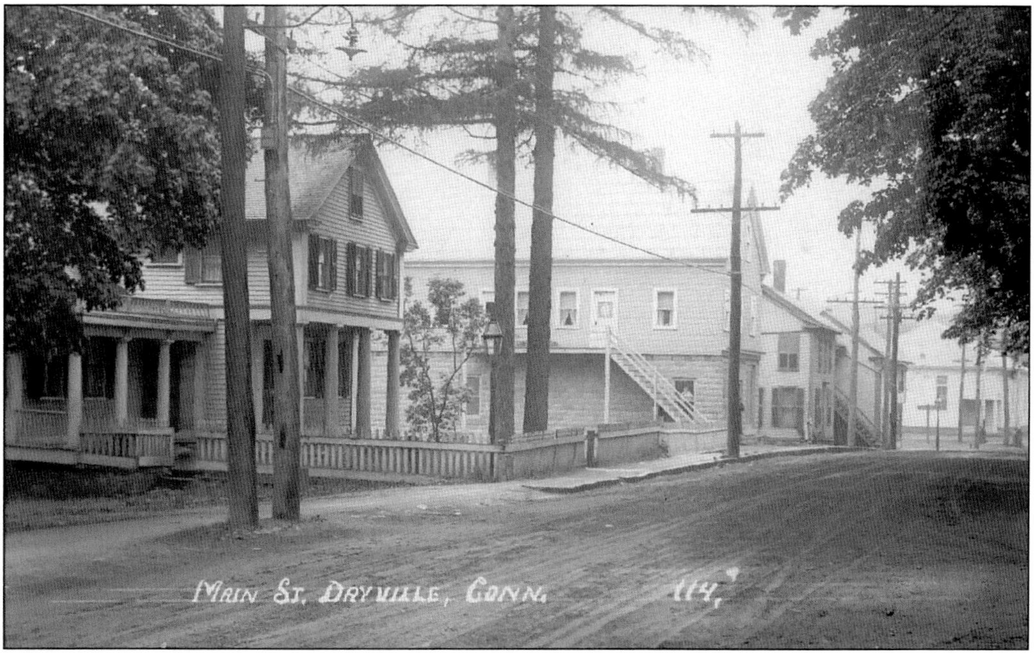

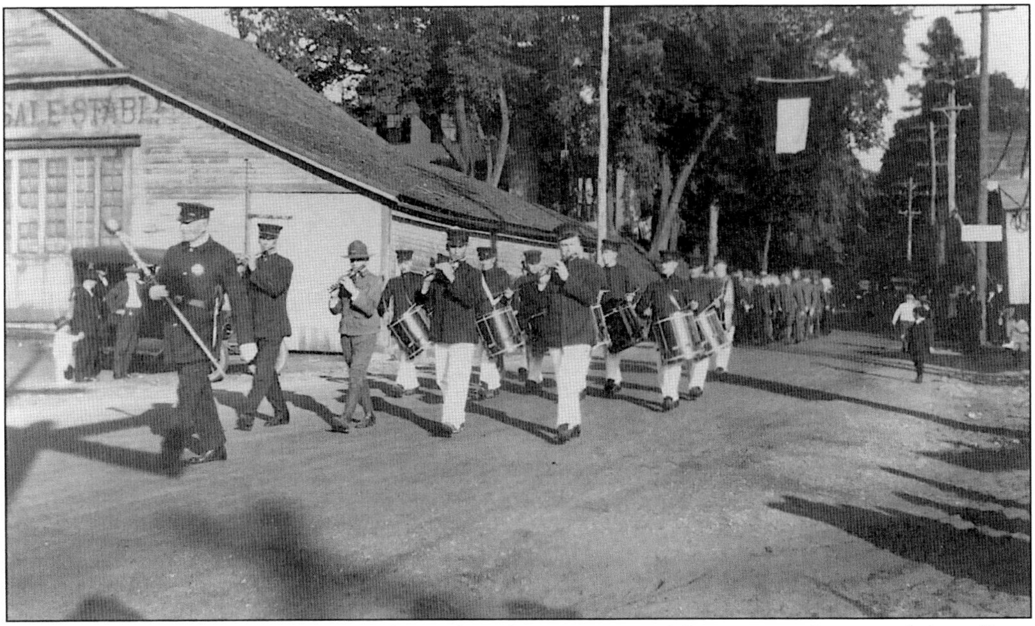

A Dayville Parade. People have always found a reason to celebrate something, and the village of Dayville is no exception. Parades took place on patriotic holidays and even at election time. This parade was held in the early 1900s.

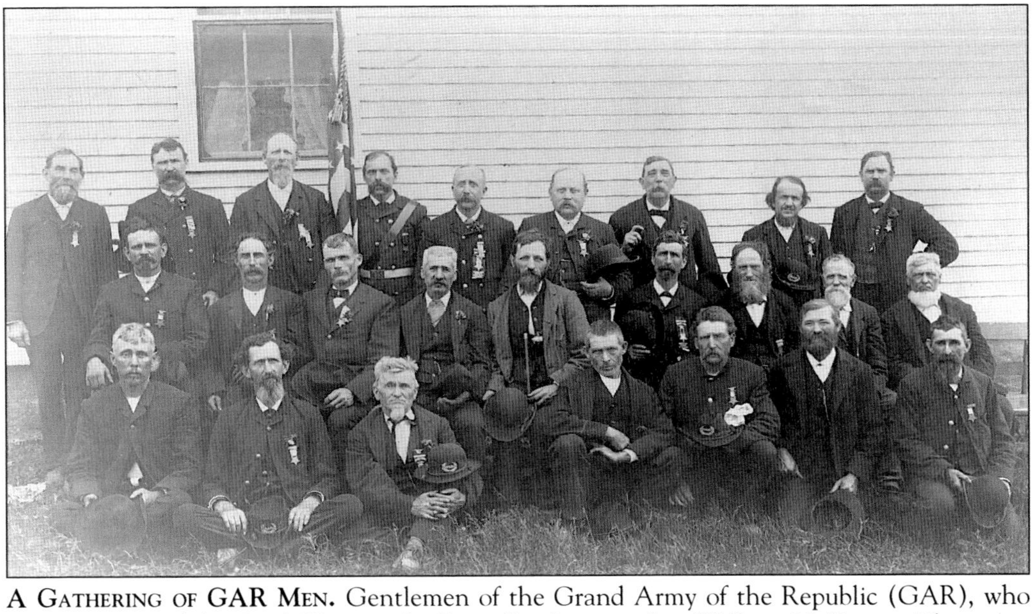

A Gathering of GAR Men. Gentlemen of the Grand Army of the Republic (GAR), who were veterans of the Civil War, sat for Dayville photographer William H. Brown. The group met in the Grand Army Hall in Dayville.

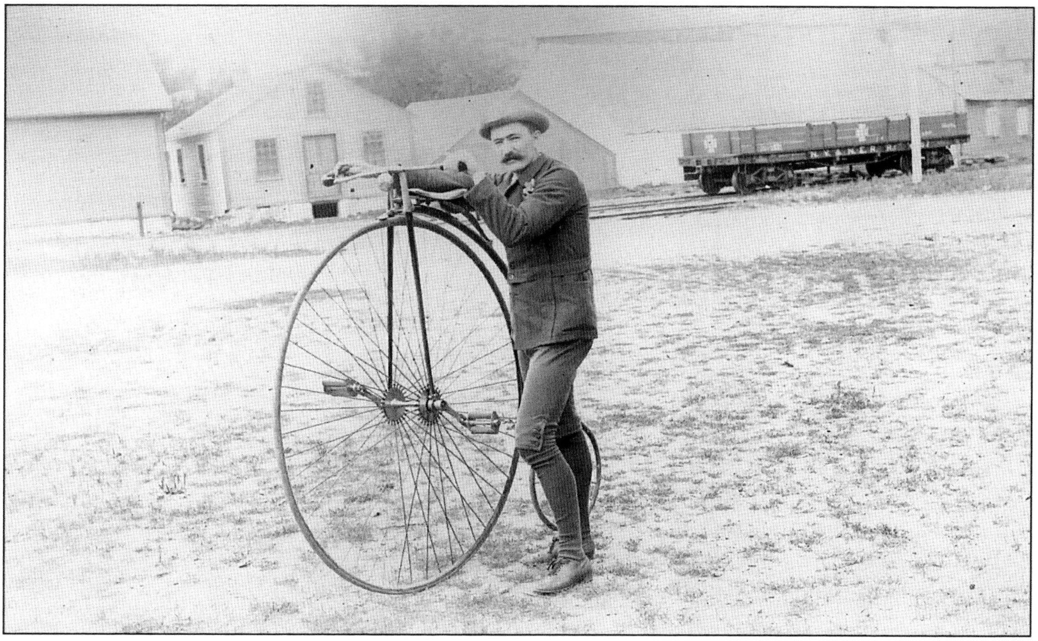

George Brown with a Cycle. George H. Brown of Dayville poses with his high cycle, called an ordinary. His brother, noted photographer W.H. Brown, took the photograph. James Stanley invented the ordinary in 1873 in England.

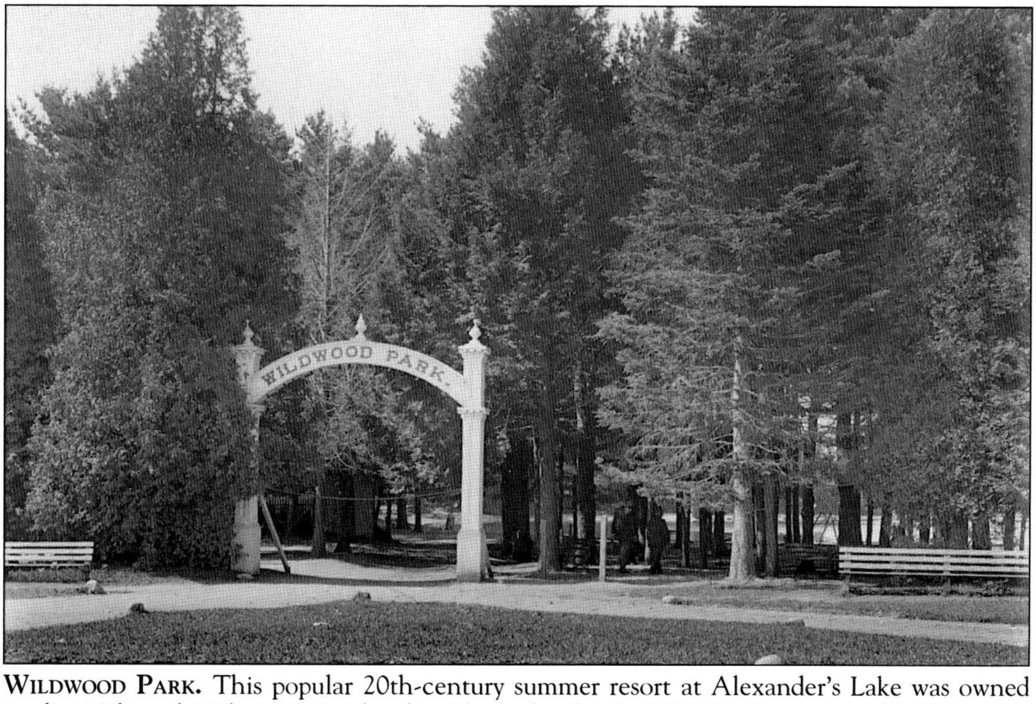

Wildwood Park. This popular 20th-century summer resort at Alexander's Lake was owned in the 18th and 19th centuries by the Alexander family. The family was involved in many of Killingly's textile mills, as well as in brick manufacturing. In 1890, the People's Tramway Company developed a resort on leased land on the east side of the lake. In 1919, the lake and acreage were sold to Patrick Sheridan, father of John Sheridan, the current owner.

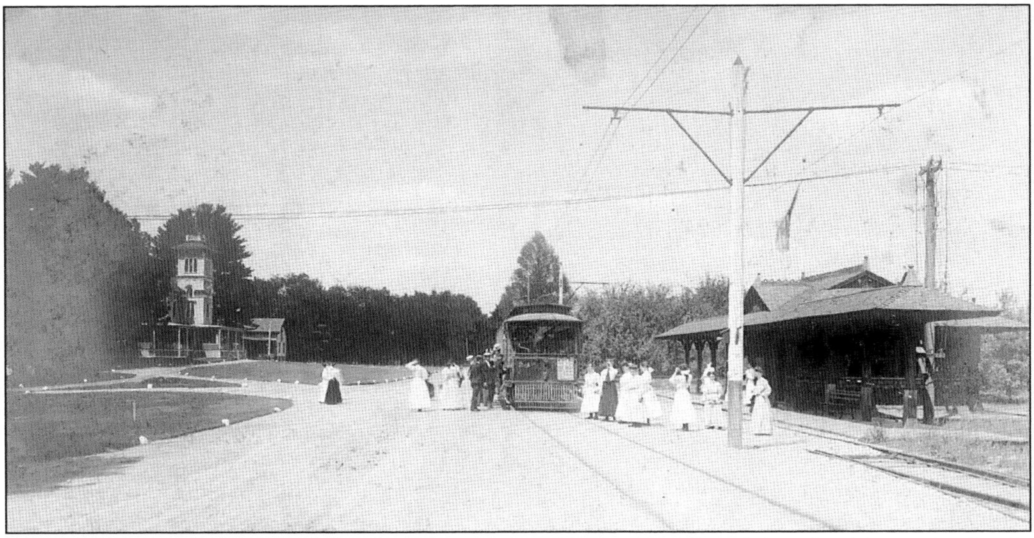

A Trolley Stand and the Alexander Family Mansion. At their lake, the Alexander family built this fabulous Italianate villa, *c.* 1865. The mansion was later converted to a 40-room hotel, and in 1935, it was demolished. Trolley service to Wildwood Park was provided by the People's Tramway Company and also the Providence & Danielson line, which terminated in Elmville. A transfer station was built across the street from the lake so that passengers could change to the north-south line.

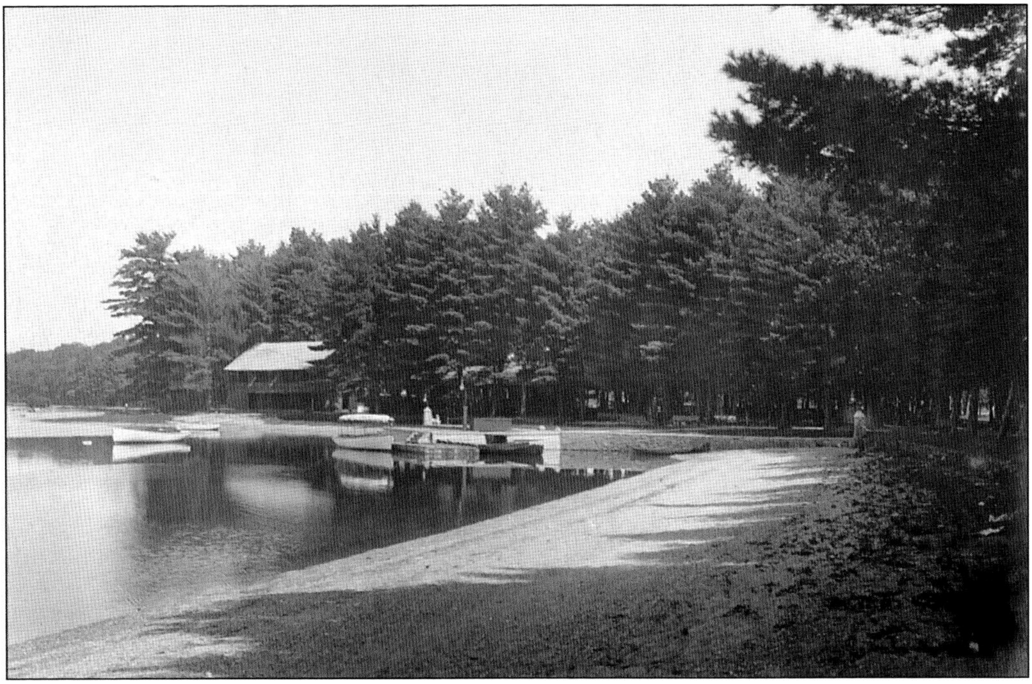

Wildwood Park, or the Lake. The People's Tramway Company was a subsidiary of the People's Light & Power Company. It was common for electric companies to expand into electric street railways or traction companies, as they were sometimes called. Wildwood Park became a popular spot for day trips. Swimming in the lake was not permitted until 1939 because, prior to that, it was a dedicated reservoir.

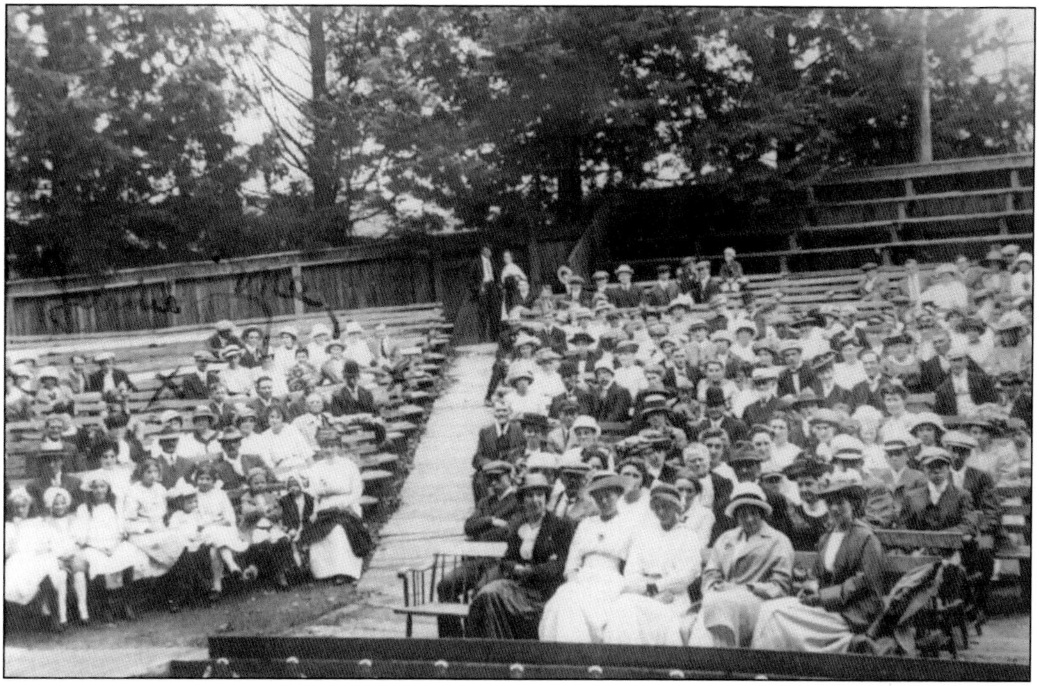

The Amphitheater at Wildwood Park, c. 1901. An amphitheater was located between the Sheridan home and the park on the lake side of the street. It was billed as an elegant summer theater, with strictly high-class vaudeville entertainment. Dancing was the attraction on Wednesday and Saturday evenings. A newspaper in 1901 announced the Labor Day program: two concerts on the stage of the theater, a tub race, a greased-pig chase, and a fireworks display.

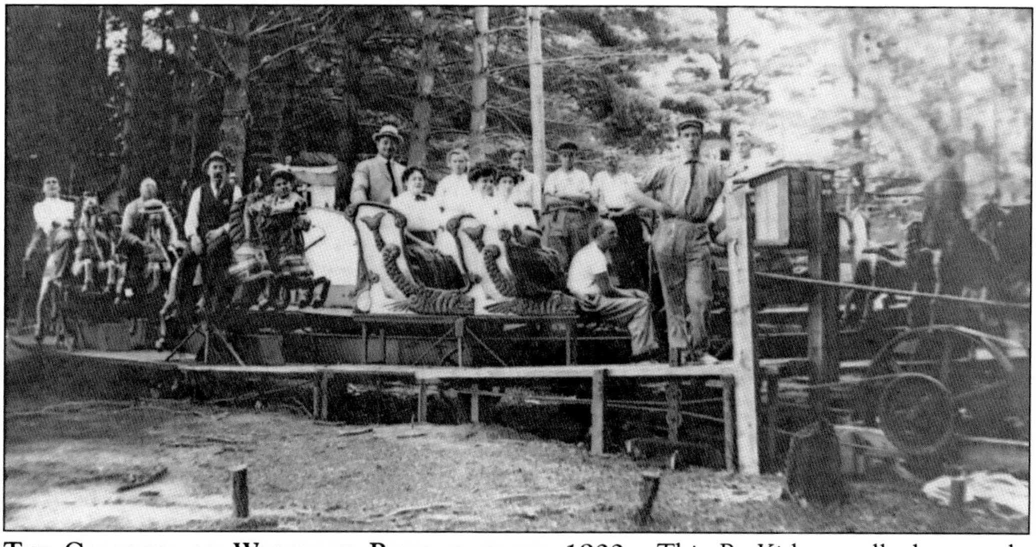

The Carousel at Wildwood Park, c. early 1900s. This R. Kirkconnell photograph, provided by Avery Tillinghast, shows one of the attractions for park visitors. The carousel, located just north of the trolley station on the east side of the street, was popular with people of all ages. Another attraction was the swinging chairs. Throughout the summer, trolleys made their first stop at 5:24 a.m. and then every half hour all day.

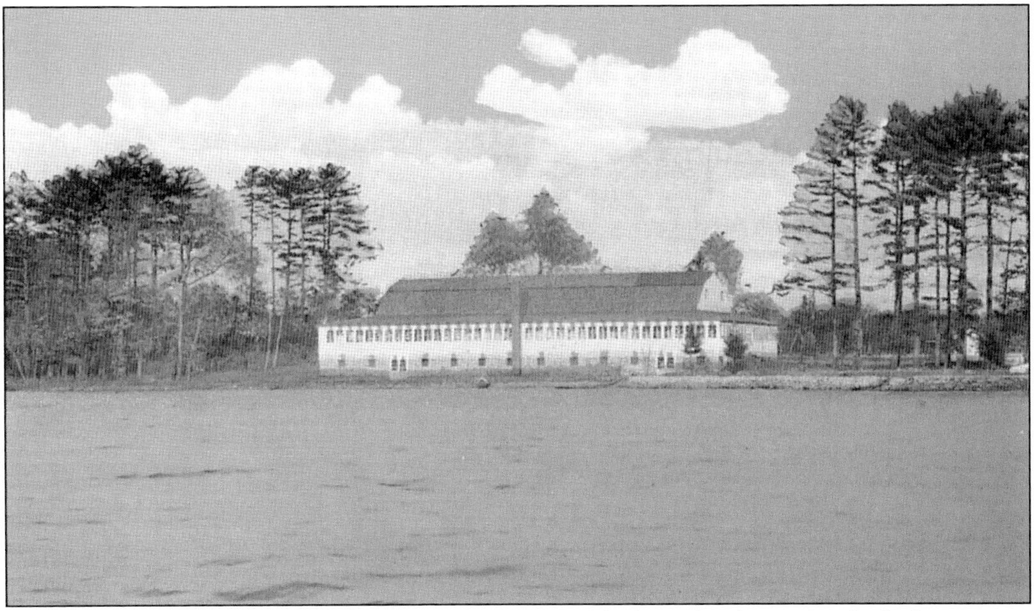

The Dance Pavilion, 1923. In addition to leasing lakefront land to individuals for summer cottages, Patrick Sheridan erected a dance pavilion. It was the fourth to stand in the park. Sheridan held ballroom dances through the 1940s. The hall was also used for square dances and roller-skating. The dances ceased in the 1950s and the skating stopped in the early 1980s. The building is now closed.

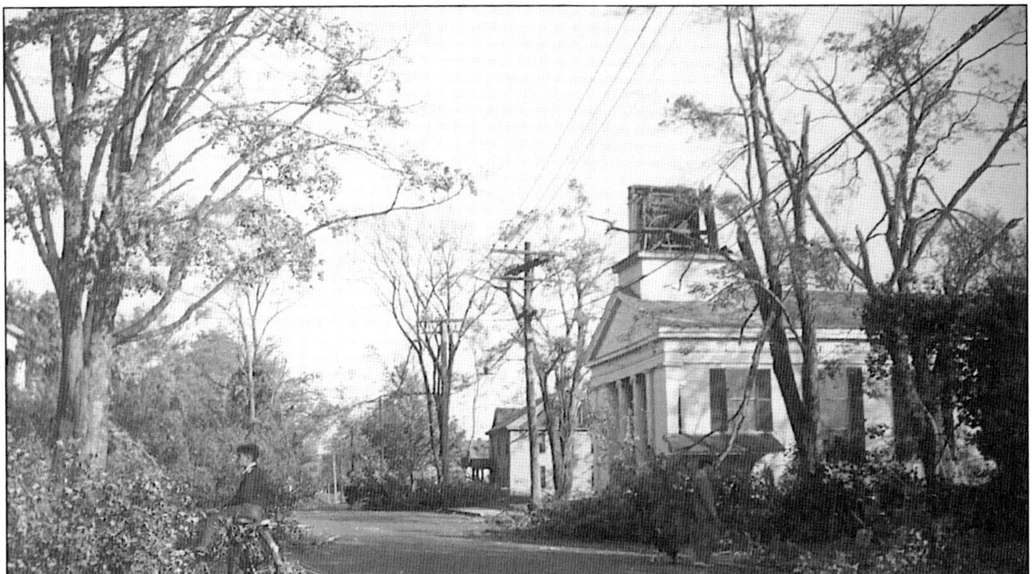

The Hurricane of 1938. The Dayville Congregational Church was one of the casualties of the devastating Hurricane of 1938. Extensive damage was done to the Assawaga Woolen Mill. The village lost many of the beautiful trees that lined the streets.

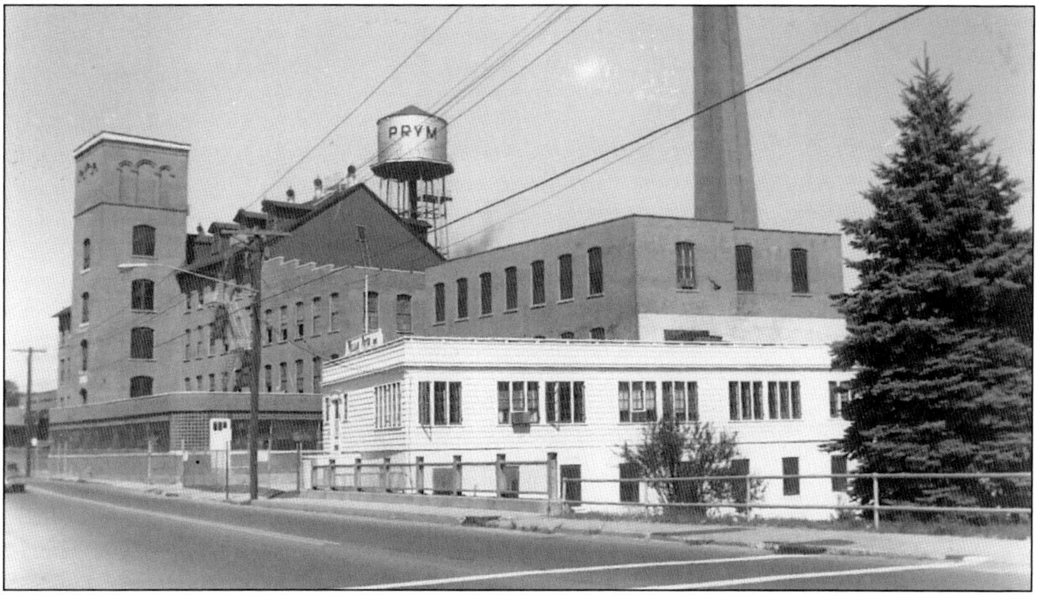

William Prym's. Textile production came to an end in the Depression, but wire manufacturer William Prym bought the Assawaga Woolen Mill in 1939. Prym's company manufactured items such as small metal notions, common pins, snap fasteners, hooks and eyes, and Cover-Your-Own buttons and buckles. The company's main sales office was in the Empire State Building in New York City.

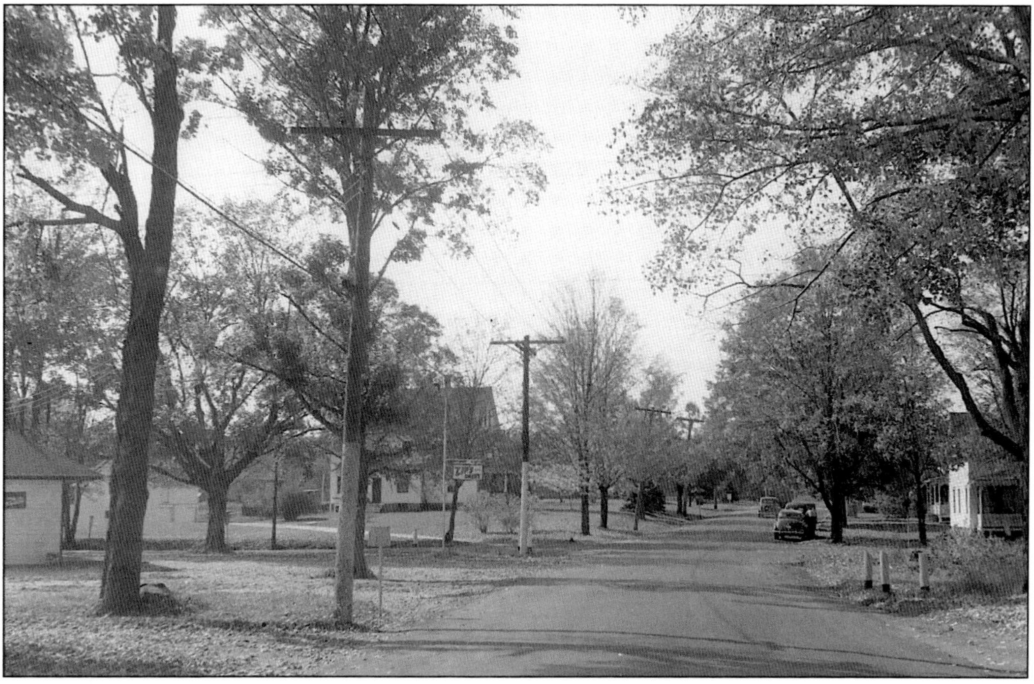

Zip's Dairy, c. 1940. This photograph from John MacDonald shows the popular ice cream stand on the corner of Maple and Main Streets. There was an added attraction on Saturday nights—outdoor movies. People sat in their cars or on blankets on the hill and watched films shown on a screen set atop the dairy stand.

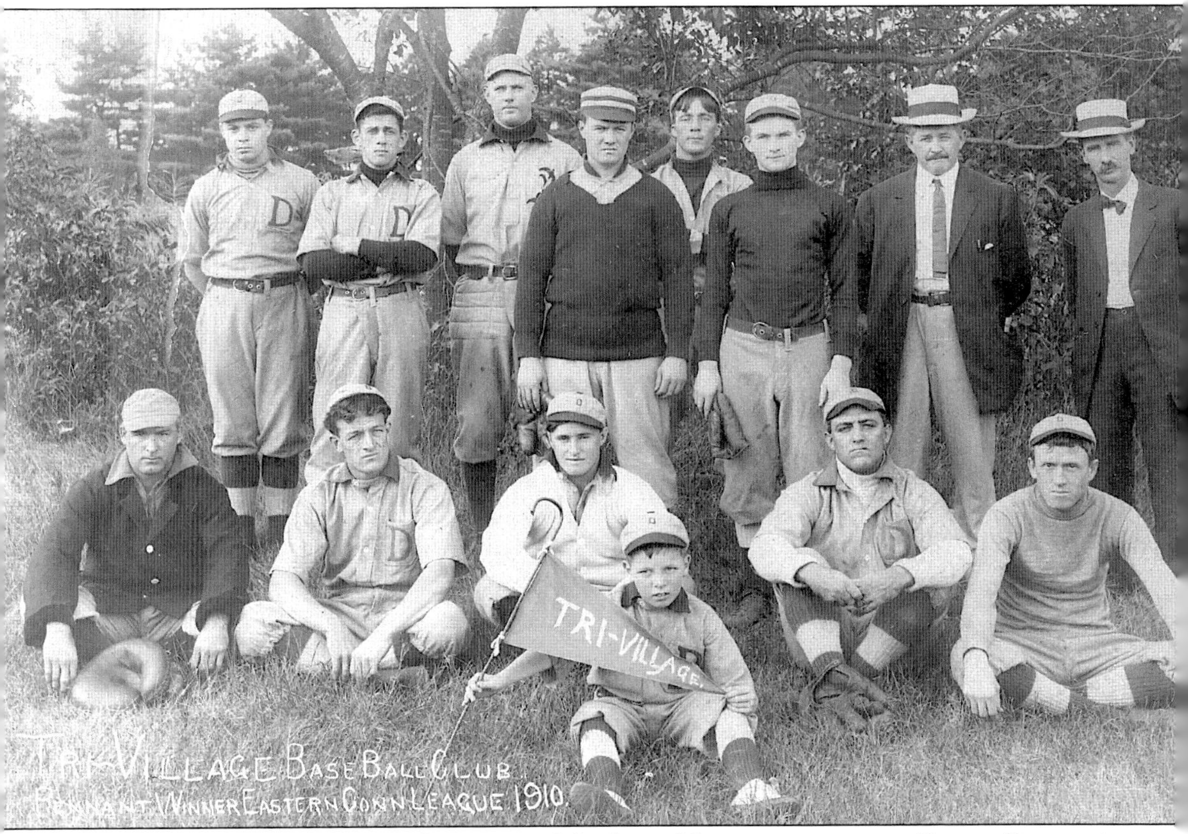

THE TRI-VILLAGE BASEBALL CLUB, 1910. Members of the pennant-winning Eastern Connecticut League were D. Page, W. Mellor, Howard, McManus, A. Brooks, W. Clark, J. Walker, P. Daly, J. LaBelle, Bulkley, Bergstrom, and bat boy Wayland Elliott.

Five

East Killingly:

Chestnut Hill, The Valley, Tucker District, and Kentuck Woods

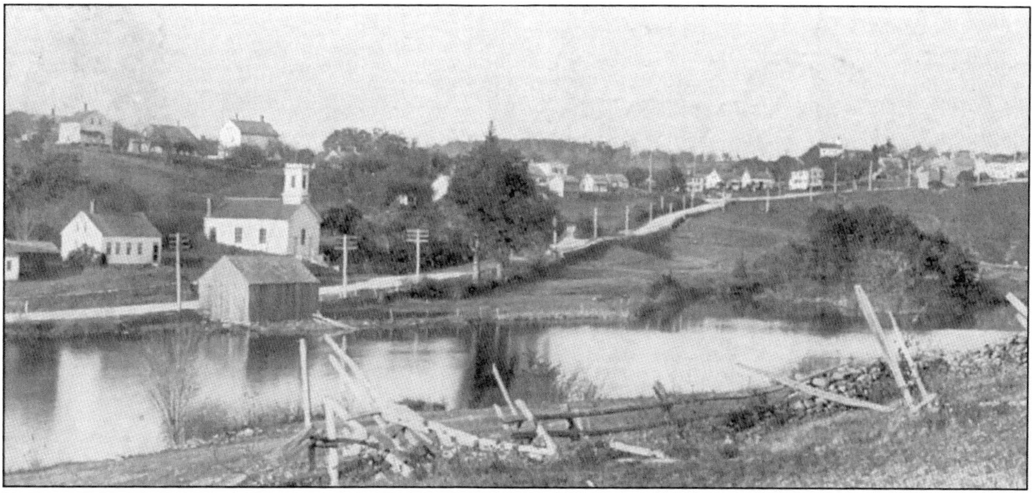

Pleasant Valley, c. early 1900s. This is the picture-book scene looking up Valley Road toward the top of the hill in East Killingly. The church on the left is the Free Will Baptist Church.

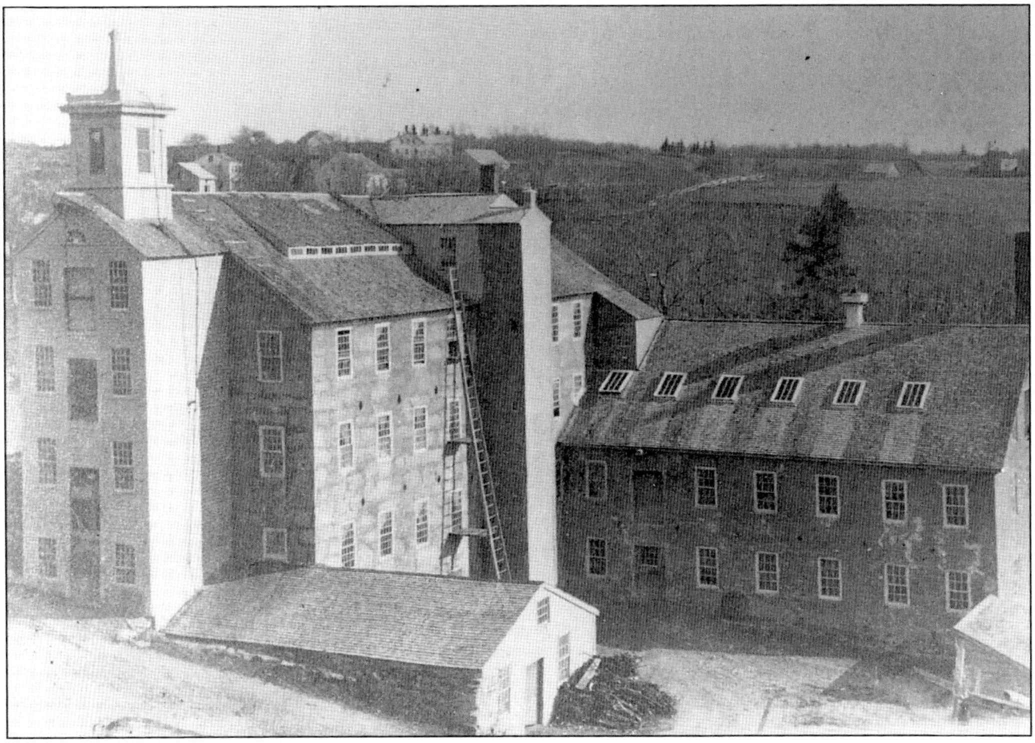

THE JUDGE YOUNG MILL, C. 1815. This mill was built of stone from a nearby quarry. Various wings were added until its final capacity was 6,000 spindles and 100 looms. The business prospered until the decline of small cotton industries in New England. The mill was destroyed by fire on December 16, 1902. The image of this old mill appears on the logo of the Killingly Historical Society.

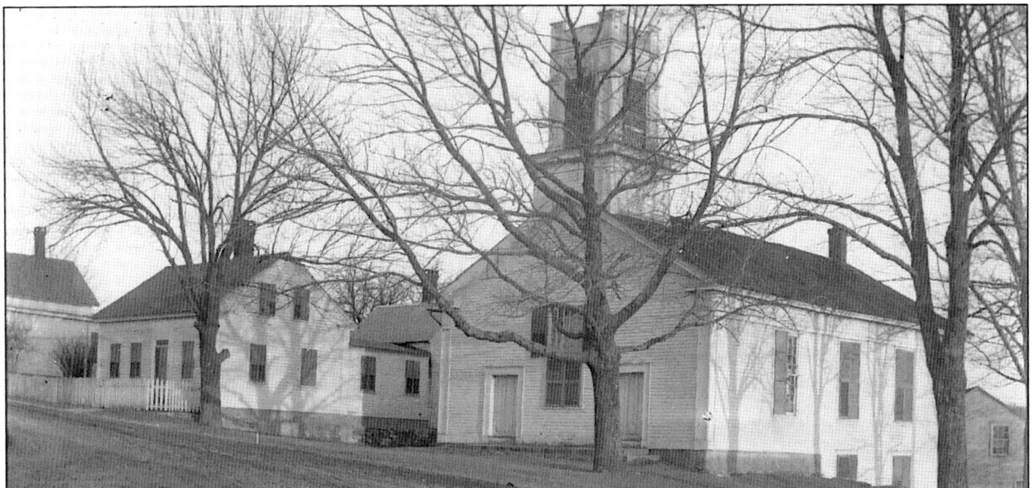

THE UNION BAPTIST CHURCH, 1836. The Baptist church was organized in the East Killingly area in 1776. A meetinghouse was erected in 1807, one mile north of where a new church was built in 1836. After the move, the name changed from Killingly Baptist to East Killingly Baptist. In 1912, the Free Will Baptists in the Valley gave up their church and joined the East Killingly congregation. This time, the name, changed to the Union Baptist Church.

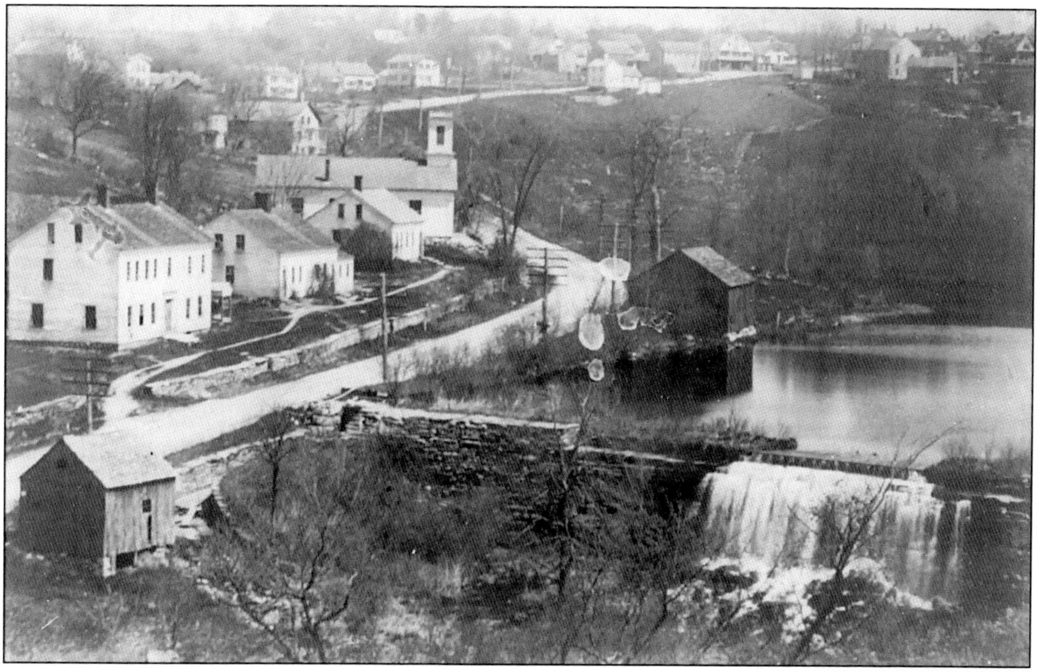

The Free Will Baptist Church, c. 1840. This church was organized in East Killingly prior to 1840. After the congregation joined with the East Killingly Baptist Church in 1912, the building was used as a dance hall and for other entertainment, known as the Jolly Social Club.

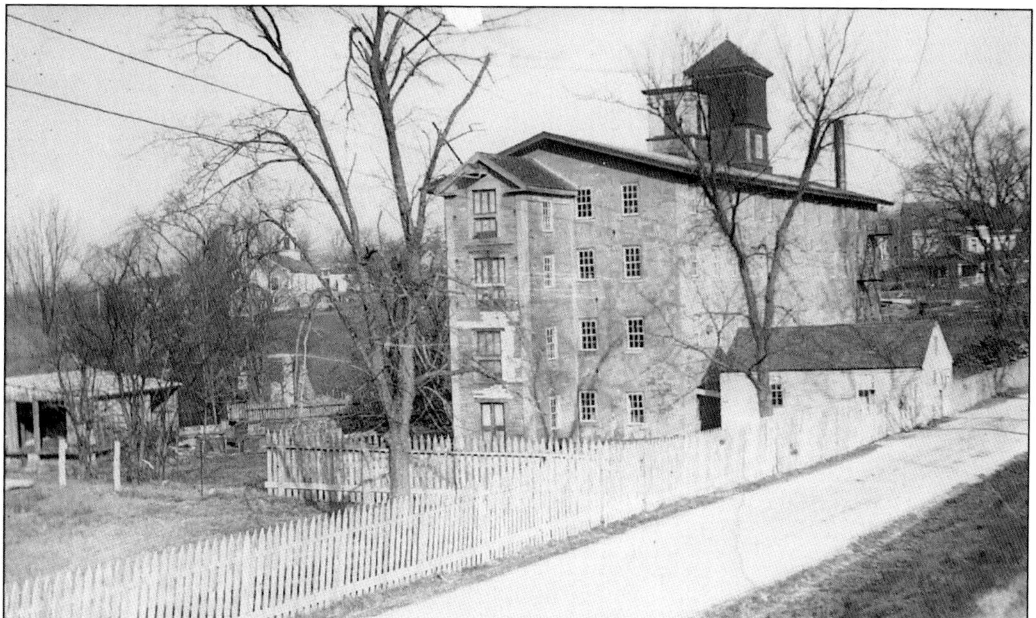

Acme Cotton Products, 1846. When the stone mill was originally built on the west side of Bailey Hill Road, it was called the Chestnut Hill Mill. Later, it was known as the Ross Mill. In 1874, it turned out 25,000 yards of cotton sheeting a week. In 1925, after several other owners, the mill became Acme Cotton Products Company and produced medical supplies there until moving to new facilities in the mid-1970s.

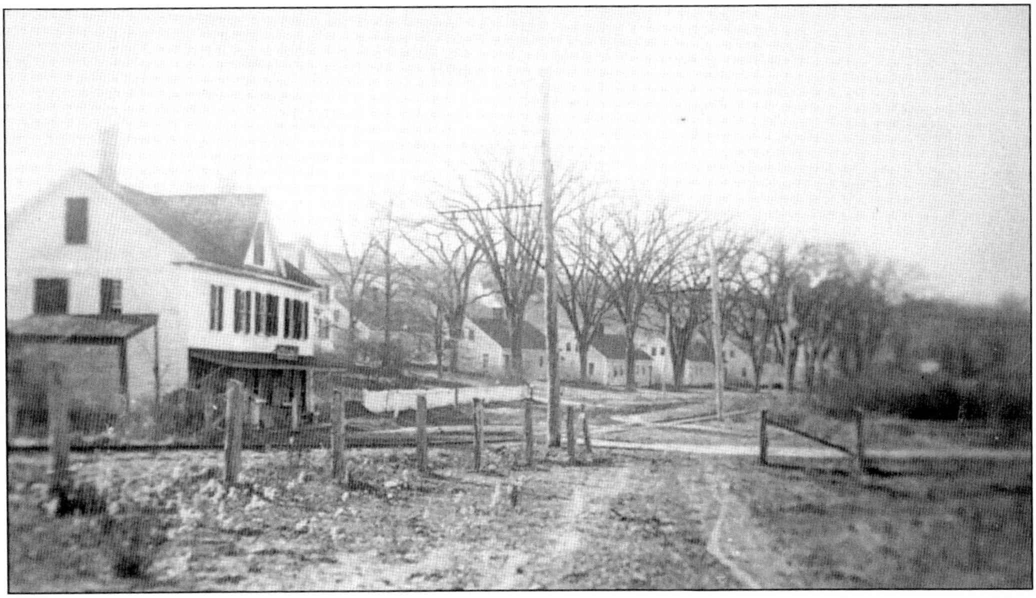

The Newton-Wells Store, c. 1848. This store, located on Valley Road near the trolley tracks in the lower village, was an example of a small, general merchandise emporium. William A. Newton, who operated a shop on the first floor, purchased the store in 1861 from Isaac Fuller. The family of Arthur Wells, who also had a factory job, ran the store for 50 years, from 1924 to 1974. A gas pump stood out front.

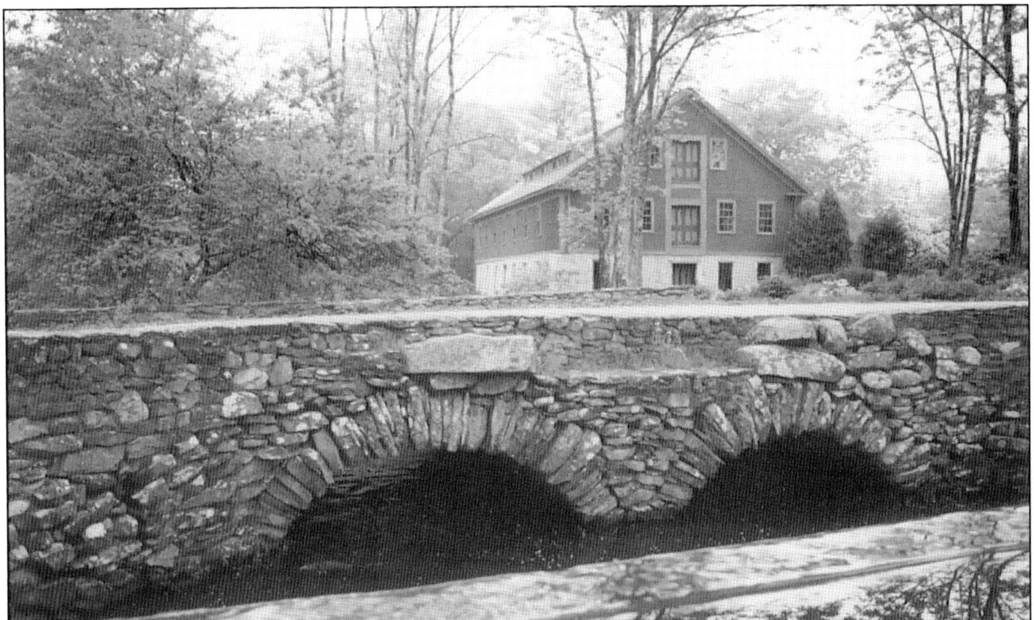

The Peeptoad Mill and Bridge, c. 1850. Located on Peeptoad Road in Killingly Center, this mill is listed in the National Register of Historic Places along with the stone double-arch bridge. The site has housed an ax and hoe shop, saw and grain mill, and machine and blacksmith shop. In later years it was a yarn mill and then a hide-processing and warehousing facility for Danielson Manufacturing Company. It is now a residence.

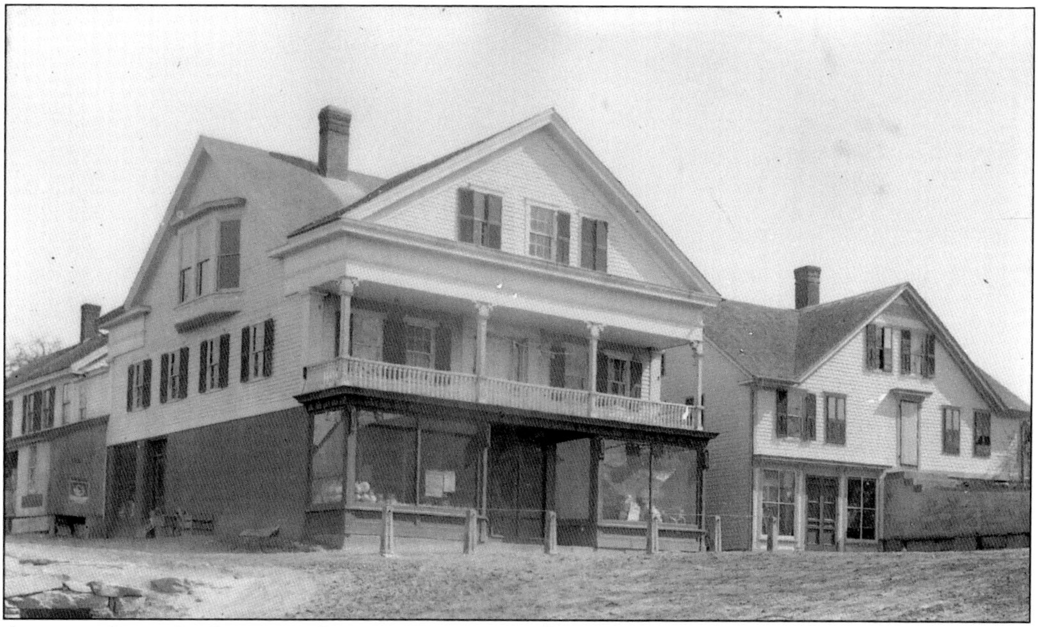

ALMOND PAINE'S GENERAL STORE, C. 1852. Allie Paine's Store, as it was known to local residents, was located on the corner of North Road and Route 101 in East Killingly. The store carried everything from shoes to dried fruit, wallpaper, and all kinds of food. It served the surrounding farms, as well as the mill village, for over 100 years.

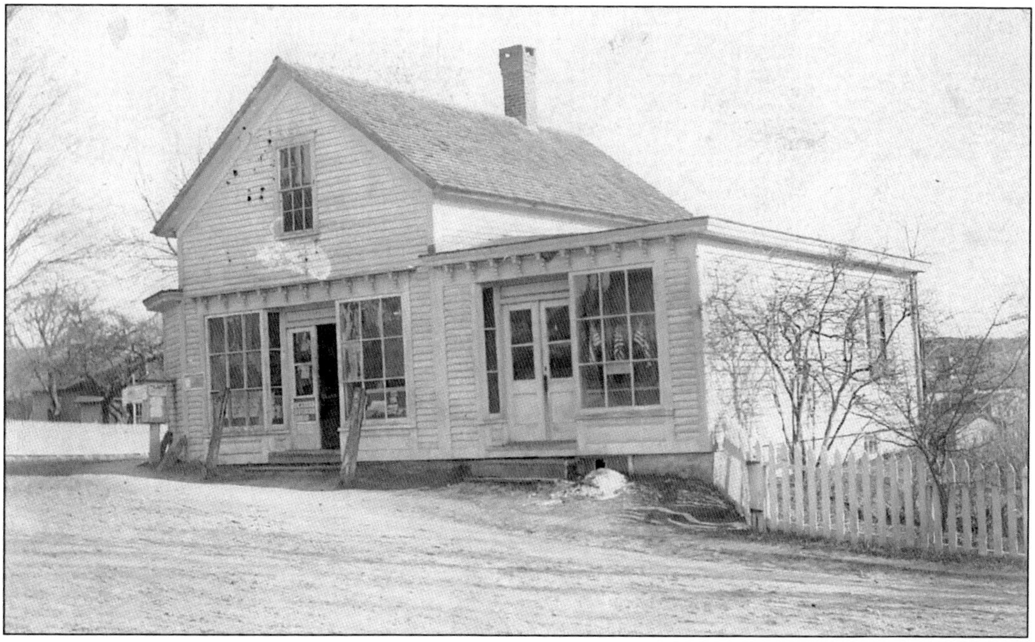

THE WELLS-SMITH STORE, C. 1860. For well over 100 years, various owners have operated a store in the building on the southwest corner of Route 101 and Bailey Hill Road in the center of the village. Richard and Stephanie Wells ran the Wells Store from 1949 to 1975. When James Smith owned the store, his brother, Robert Smith, ran the post office in the western portion of the building.

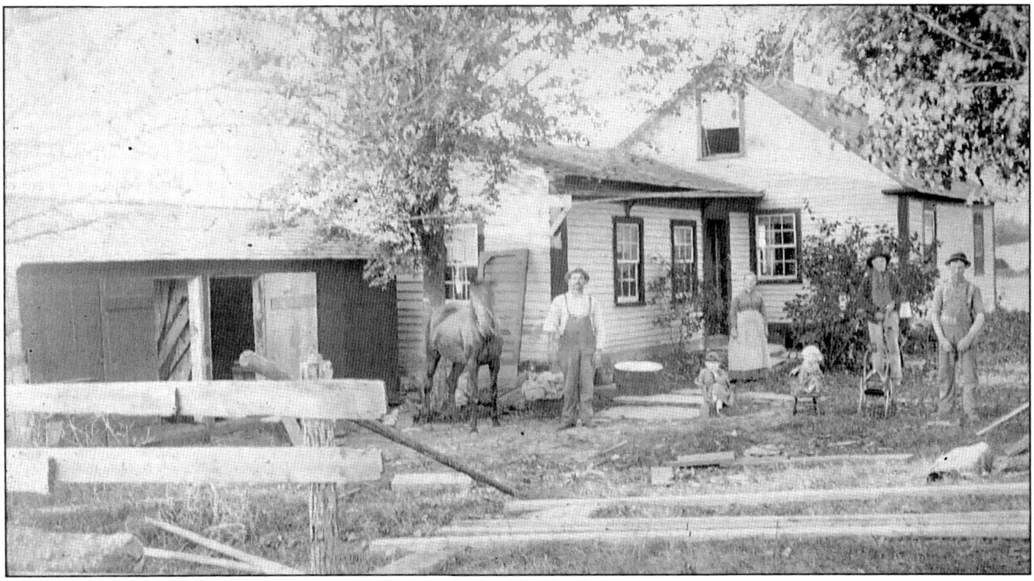

The Hiram Wells House, c. 1860. This small house was built for Jonathan and William Aldrich on Bailey Hill Road land that had been in the family for many years. The house was sold to Hiram Wells, who occupied it until his death in 1897. Jonathan Smith owned it from 1897 to 1920. Pictured here are Hiram Wells, Jonathan Smith and his wife, and two of their children, Ray and Elizabeth.

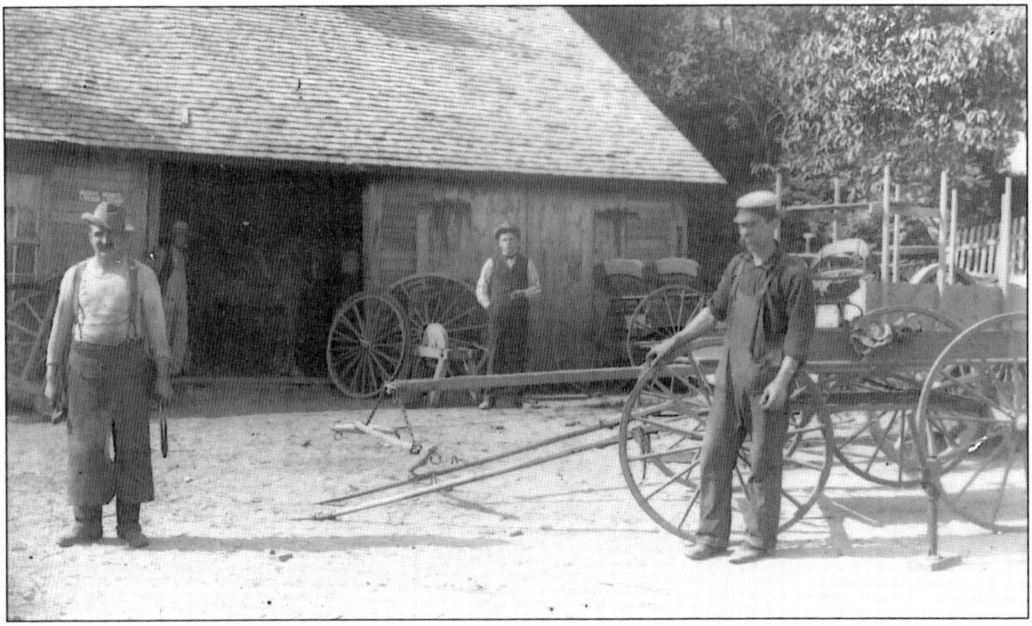

Cyrus Smith's Blacksmith Shop, c. 1869. Cyrus Smith built this blacksmith shop prior to 1869. Cyril B. Shippee operated it during the early 1900s. It was one of the last blacksmith shops in the area. It collapsed c. 1950, during a severe wind and rainstorm.

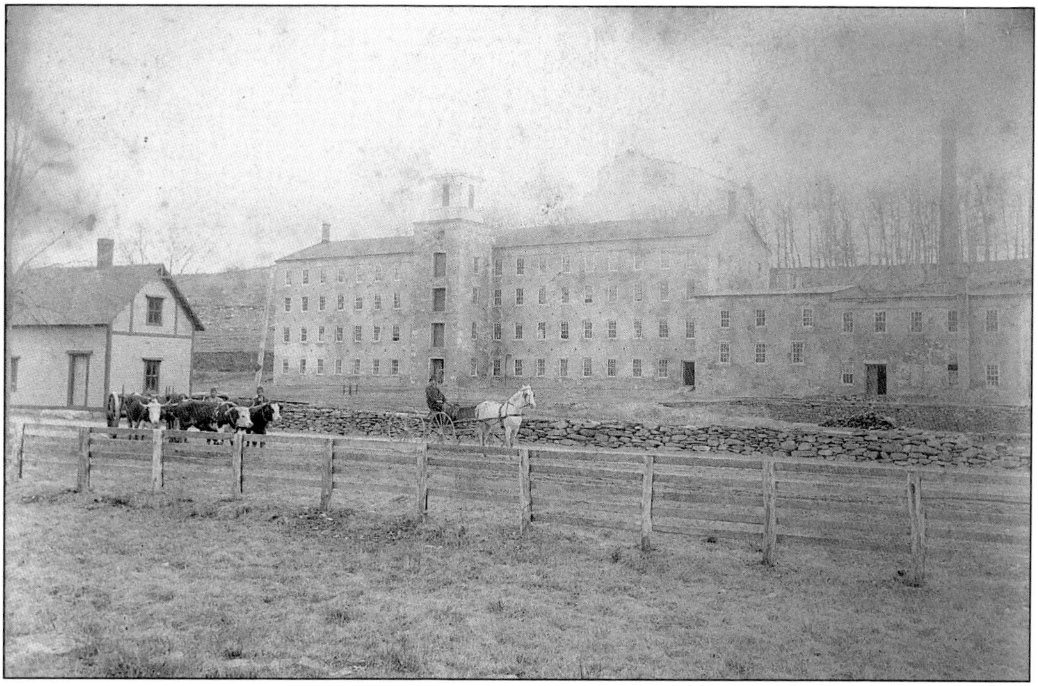

The Whitestone Mill and Employees before 1890. The Whitestone Mill was built in 1858 on Valley Road. Associated with this cotton mill were two large stone tenements, a boardinghouse, and several smaller dwellings. The tenements housed 12 families each. The mill was used by later owners or lessees for producing bed comforters and carpet linings, book cloth, and as a bleachery and dyeing works. It burned to the ground on December 3, 1922.

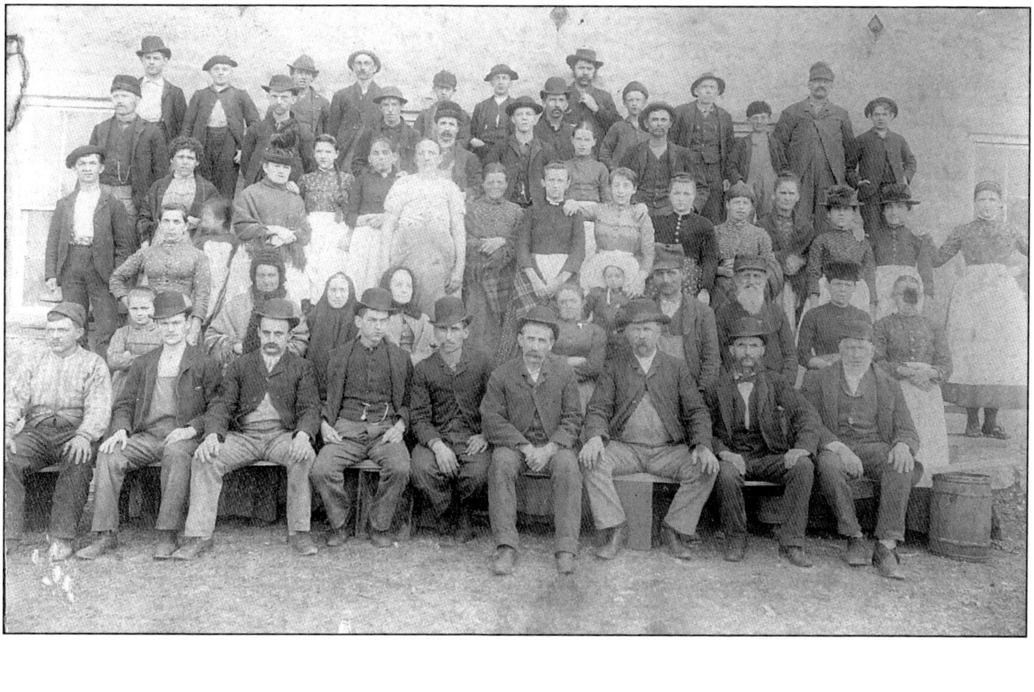

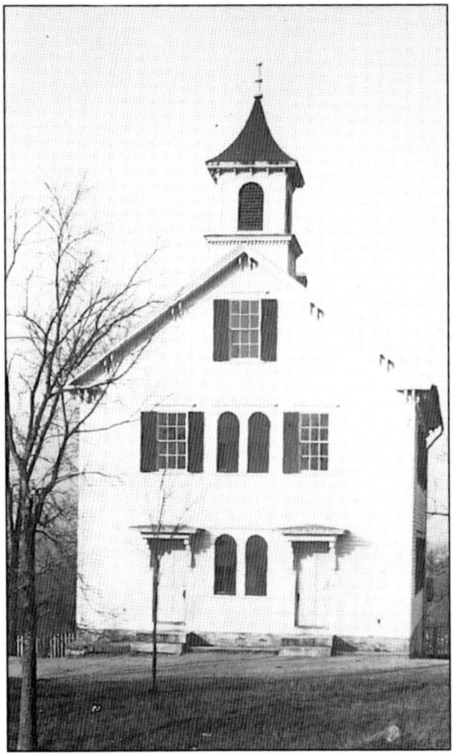

The East Killingly School, c. 1875. The East Killingly School was built on a North Road lot conveyed to School District No. 12 in 1874 by Hassel [sic] Peckham. Running water was installed in 1928. The school closed in 1952, after all students were assigned to the new Killingly Memorial School. The Byron A. Carroll Post of the Veterans of Foreign Wars purchased the old school from the town in 1957.

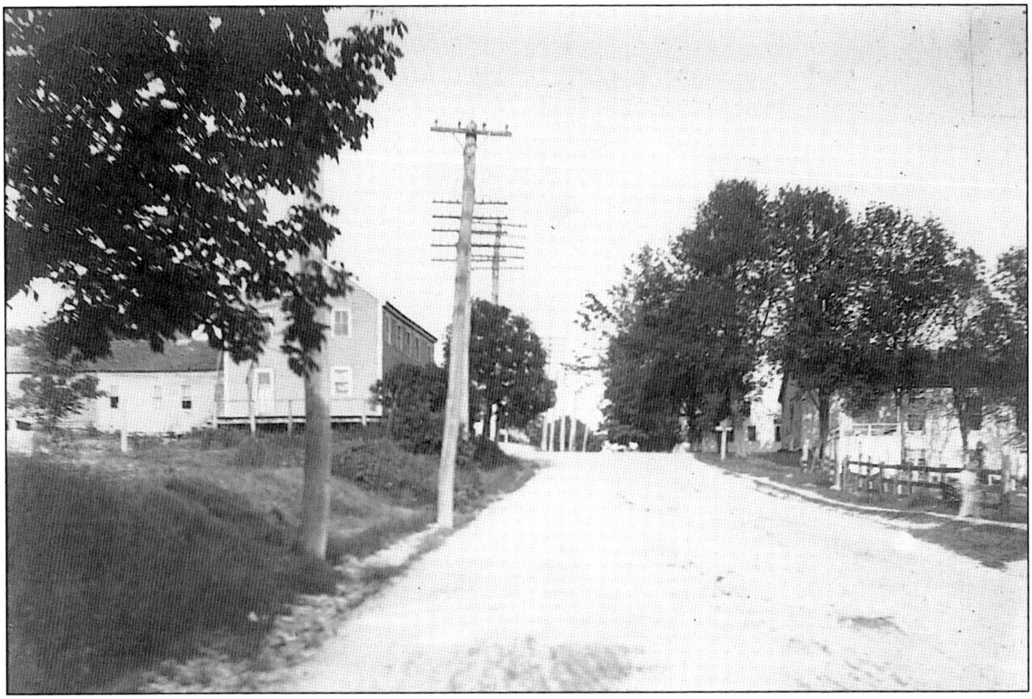

The Sayles Store, c. 1900s. Albert Sayles's store was on the west corner of North Road and Route 101. By the 1930s, it had become famous as Shippee's Dance Hall. The building was torn down in the 1960s.

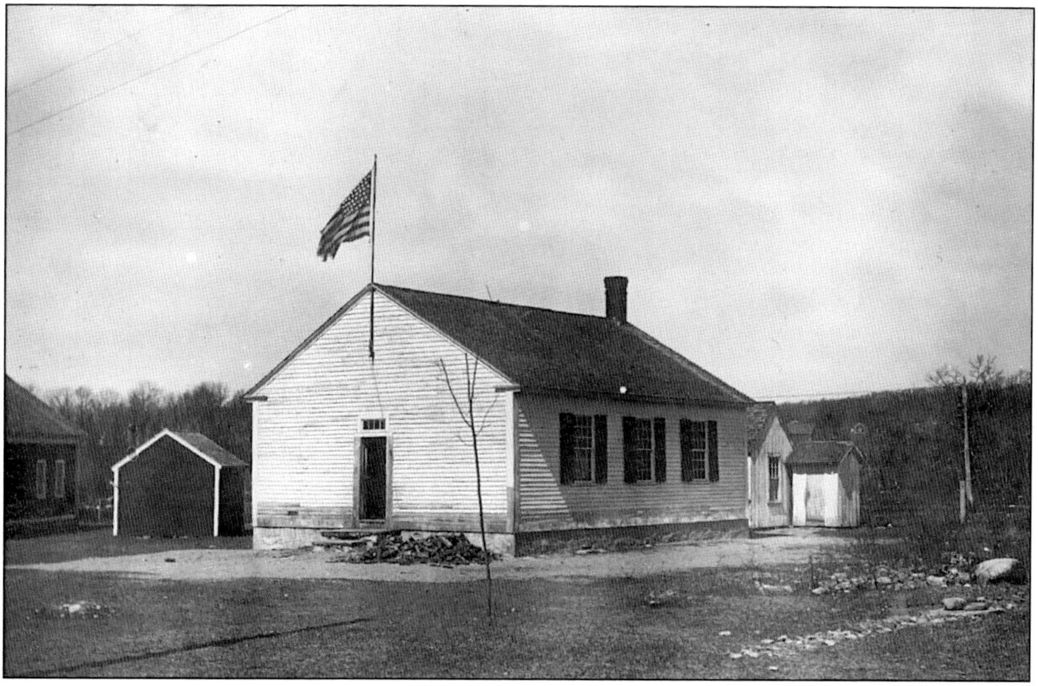

The Valley School, c. 1902. This school was located on the corner of Valley and Peeptoad Roads in the Valley section of East Killingly. It was built to replace one that burned on the same property, which was donated to the town by Timothy E. Hopkins. The school remained in use until 1952, when it was sold to Postmaster Phil Lewis, who converted it into a private residence.

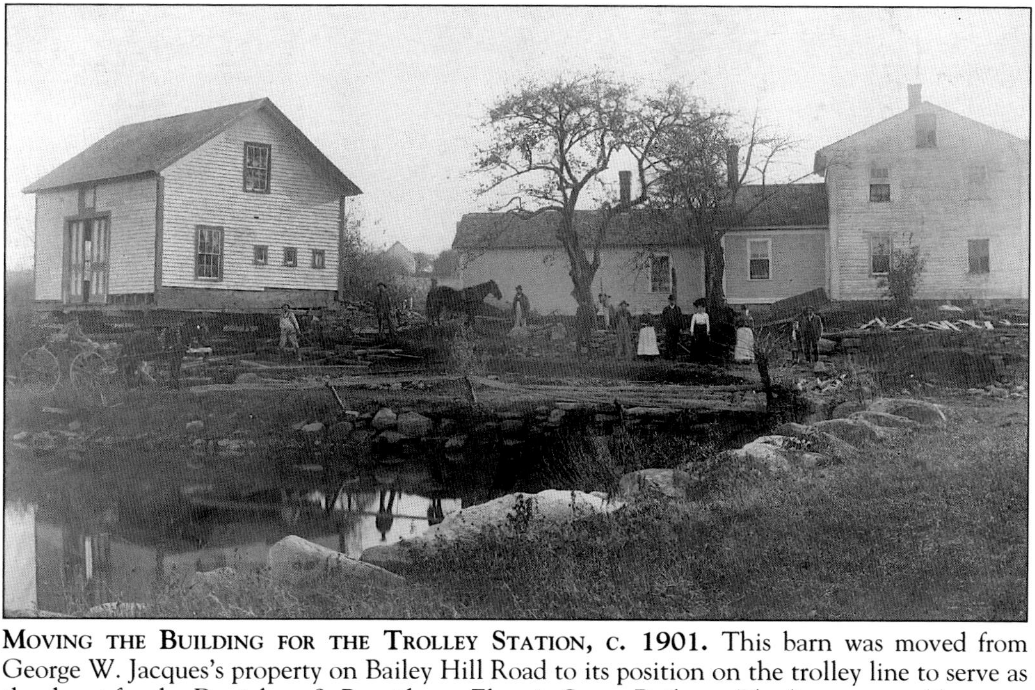

Moving the Building for the Trolley Station, c. 1901. This barn was moved from George W. Jacques's property on Bailey Hill Road to its position on the trolley line to serve as the depot for the Danielson & Providence Electric Street Railway. The line operated between 1902 and 1920.

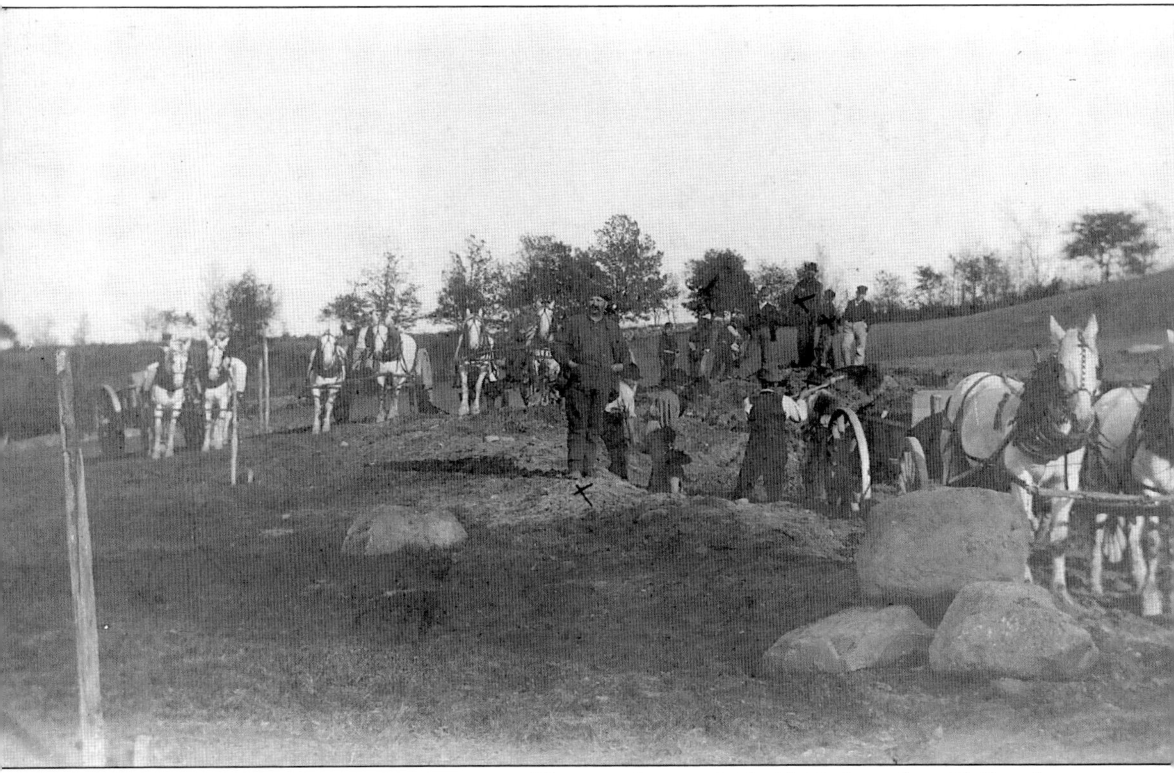

BUILDING THE PROVIDENCE-DANIELSON TROLLEY LINE, 1902–1903. Jonathan H. Smith, center, was in charge of all the teamsters who worked on the trolley line. Others in the photograph with their teams are identified as William Harold, Frank Wood, Percy Greene, Daniel Meehan, and Ray E. Smith. Some of the team drivers were young boys who worked as hard as the men.

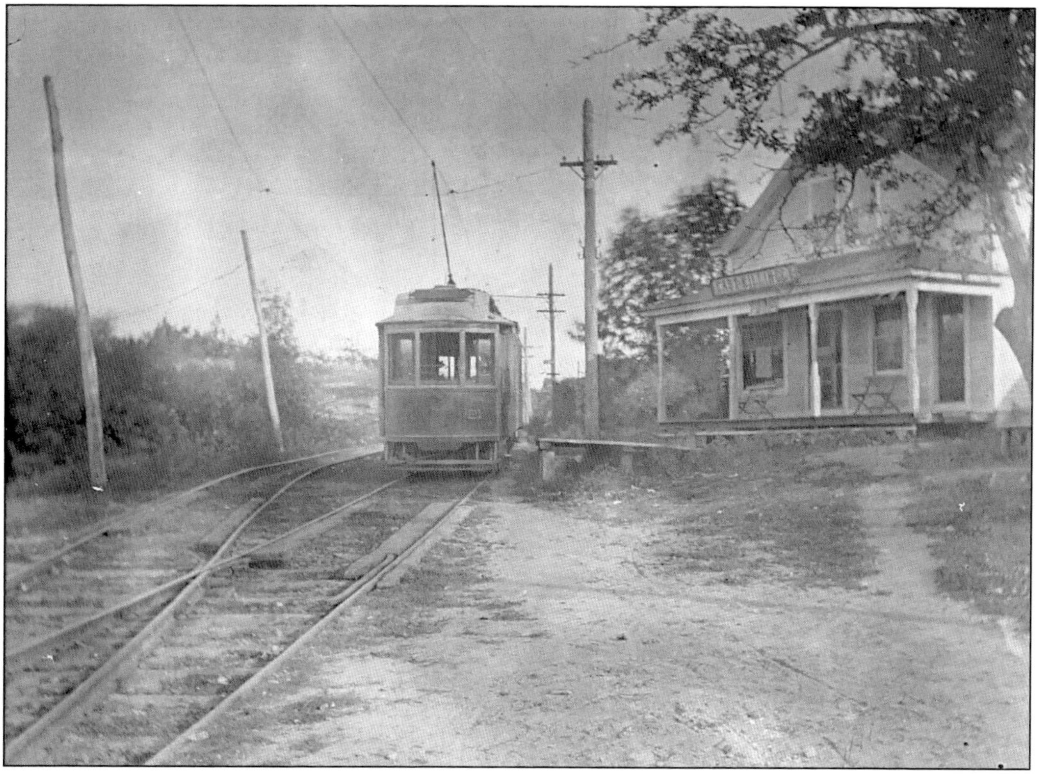

The East Killingly Depot. Although the railroad bypassed East Killingly, the electric street railway provided both passenger and freight service to Providence from 1902 until 1920. The right-of-way was south of Whetstone Brook, which it paralleled all the way to its terminus in Elmville.There, it connected with the Shore Line route to Alexander's Lake, and to Webster and Worcester, Massachusetts. A substation in Rhode Island powered the line.

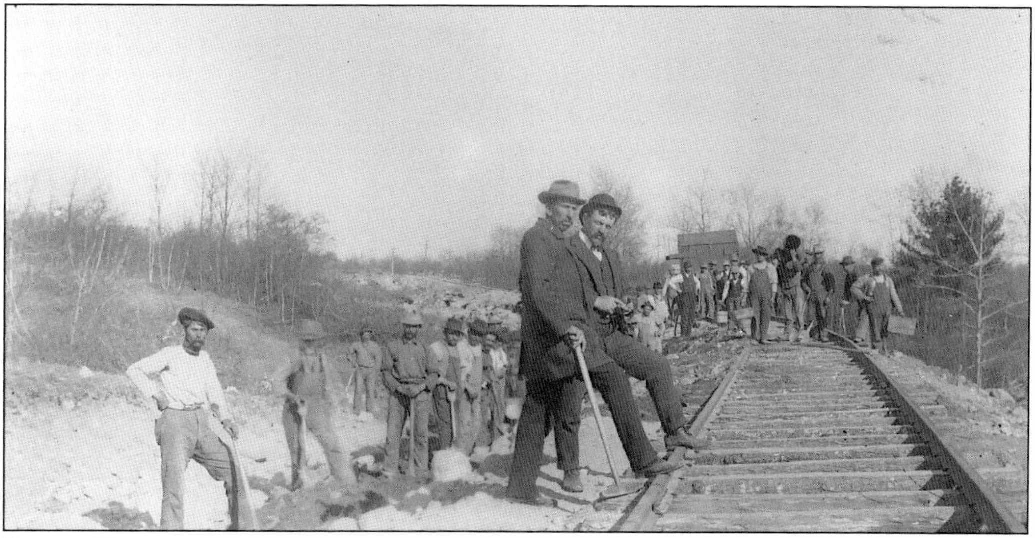

Spiking Rails in Position, 1902–1903. Building the electric railway lines required a work force of about 100 men and very little in the way of machinery. The crew pictured here was working on the trolley line from Danielson to Providence.

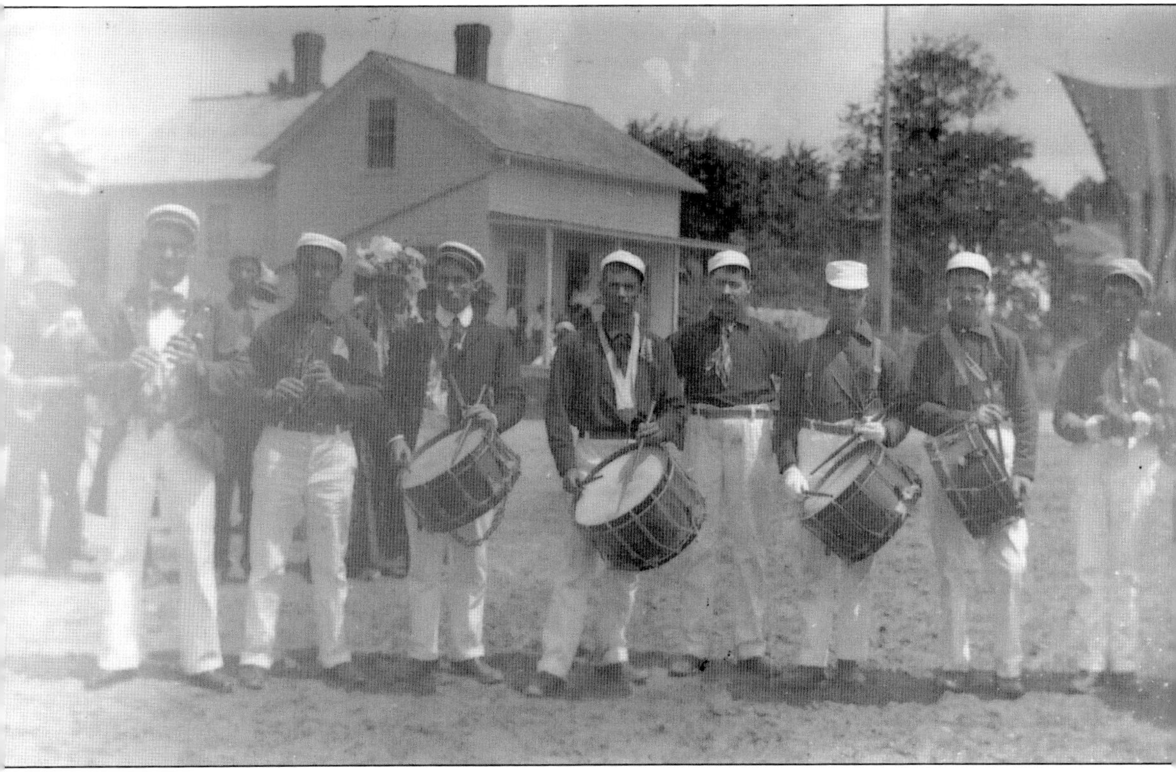

THE EAST KILLINGLY FIFE AND DRUM CORPS. East Killingly residents celebrated holidays and Old Home Days with lively music. The Fife and Drum Corps was one of the groups that provided that music.

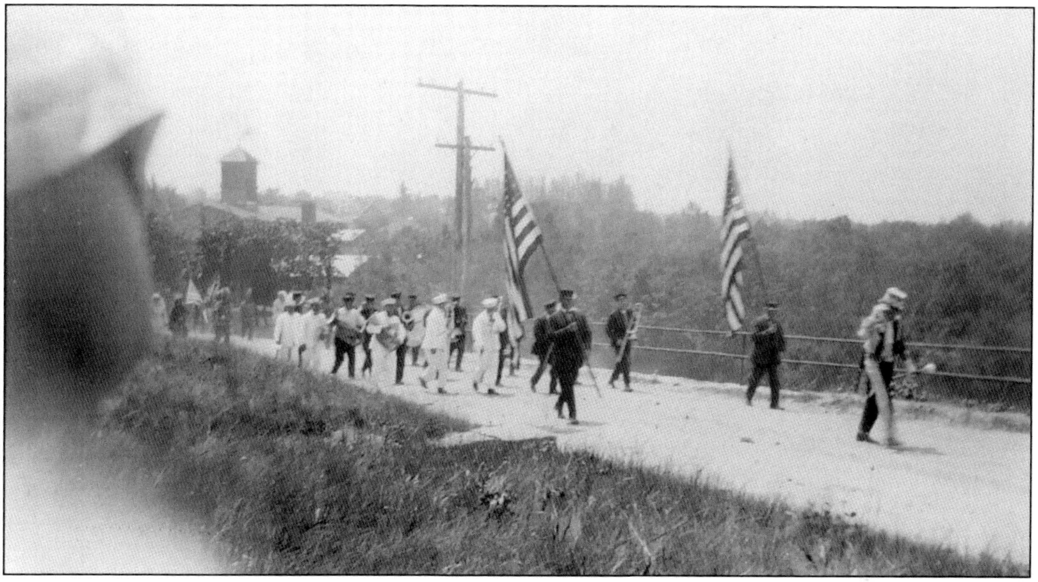

A Fourth of July Celebration, 1924. Uncle Sam leads the parade during East Killingly's holiday festivities. "Grandpa" Williams is identified as the speaker of the day, as he stands on the platform side of the cannon, now part of the Killingly Historical Society's collection.

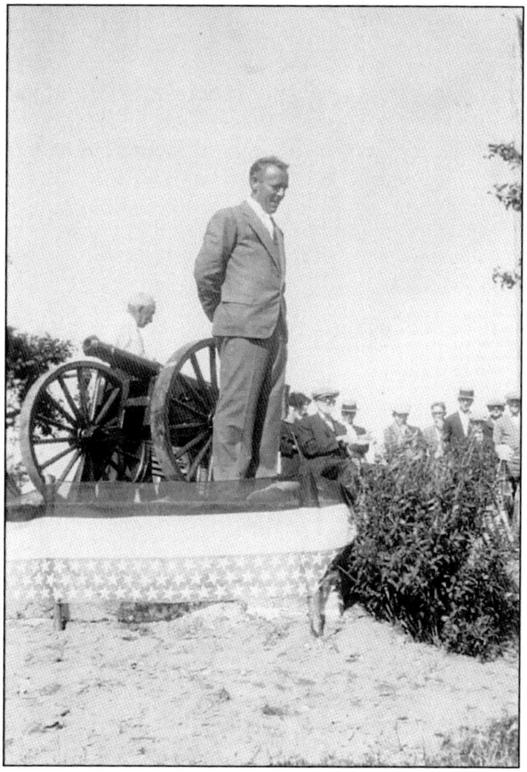

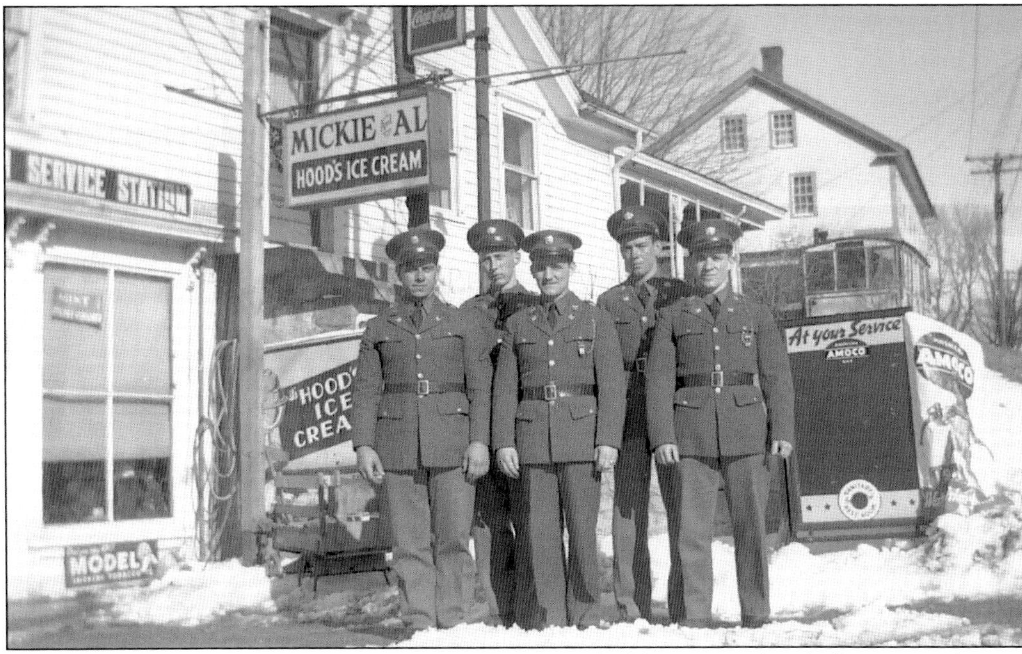

HOME ON LEAVE, 1941. North Ridge Gang boys who had been on a baseball team paid a visit to their former coach Nina McGinty. They are, from left to right, Charles Ladd, Howard Smith, Al Spicer, Lewis Woodward, and Russell (Gus) Beaudry. Their coach and Al Moffitt ran this luncheonette on Route 101, next to Allie Paine's Store.

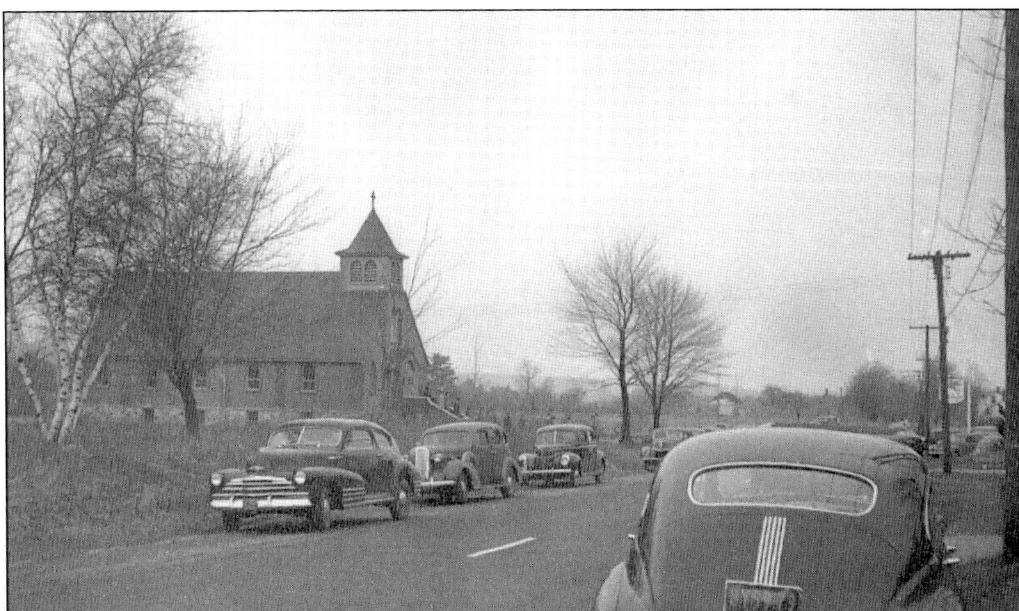

OUR LADY OF PEACE CATHOLIC CHURCH, 1944. This lovely church was established as a mission of St. James Church in Danielson. The sanctuary was built in 1944–46 on a lot purchased from Fred Smith. Fr. Anthelme Mollard was instrumental in having the church established in the East Killingly section of town. Many parishioners also remember the faithful service of Fr. Francis X. Baldwin.

Six

Rogers:

Williamsville and Goodyear

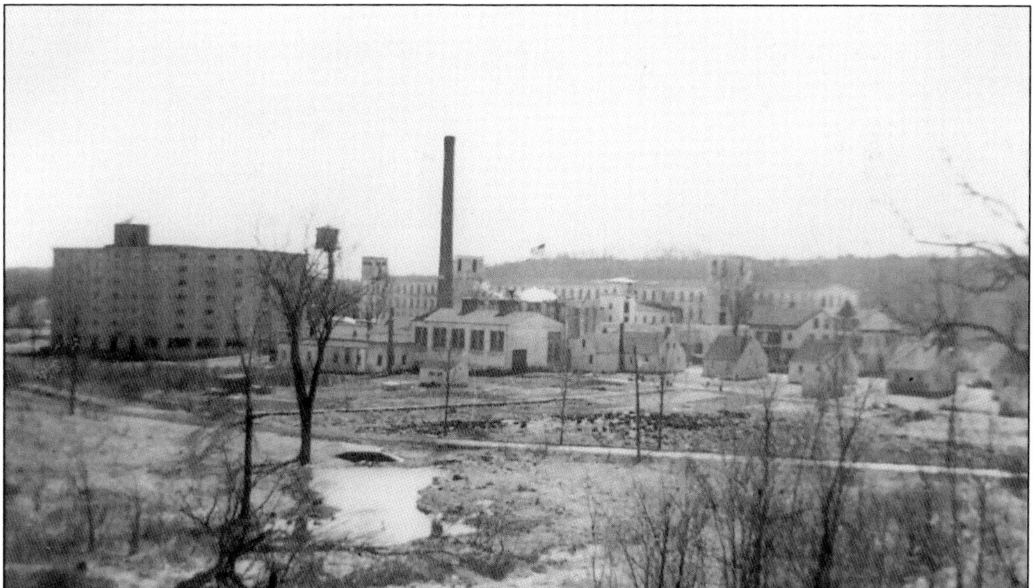

The Goodyear Company, 1912. A partnership of local men, headed by Robert Boys, succeeded in interesting the Goodyear Tire & Rubber Company of Akron, Ohio, in using the Williamsville mill to produce the cotton duck needed as reinforcement material in rubber tires. Goodyear bought the village in 1913 and became the first tire company to produce its own cloth-laminating material. The village name was changed to Goodyear in 1916.

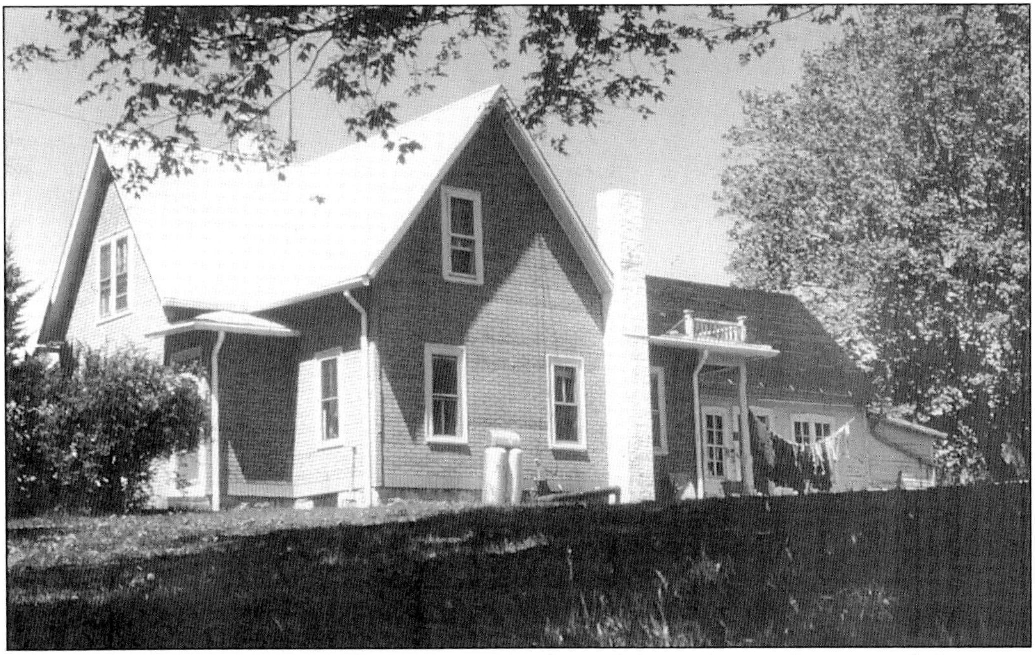

THE POTTER-ARNOLD BOBBIN SHOP, C. 1849. One of the earliest utilizations of the water privilege in Williamsville was by Robert N. Potter at his bobbin- and spool-making shop on Litchfield and Boys Avenues. Potter became partners with Alonzo and Orrin S. Arnold, who continued to run the shop after Potter's death in 1879. The shop burned *c.* 1900, but the site still has the remains of the former business. This photograph shows Potter's home.

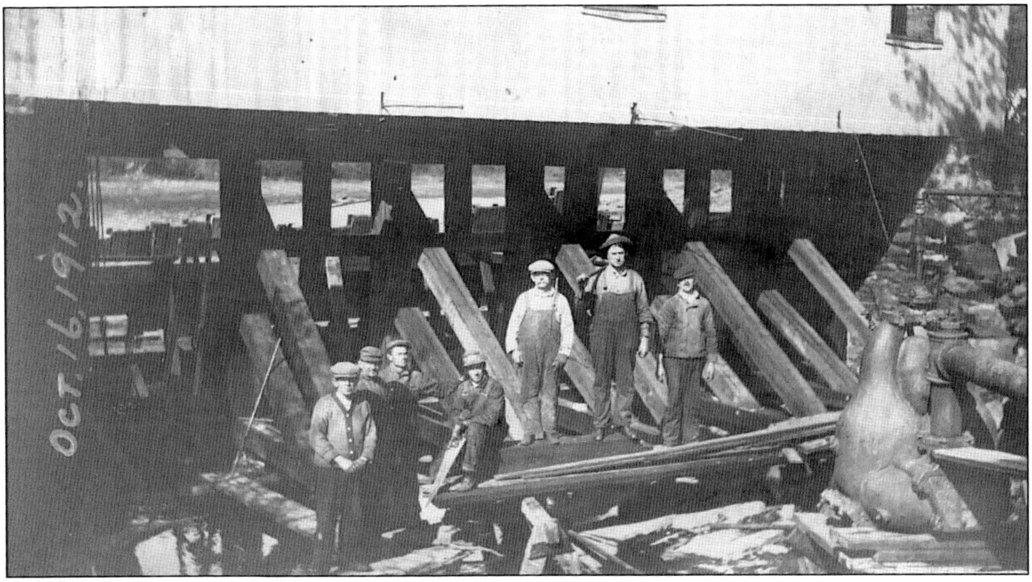

WILLIAMSVILLE, C. 1900. In 1826, Caleb Williams of Providence bought 27 acres, along with the privilege to use waterpower from the Quinebaug River, from Asa and William Alexander and John Day. Williams built a factory village, which he named Williamsville. This is a scene of some of the men building the dam. In the late 1820s, Williamsville consisted of little more than the tenant houses and the mill, which was equipped to make cloth from bales of cotton.

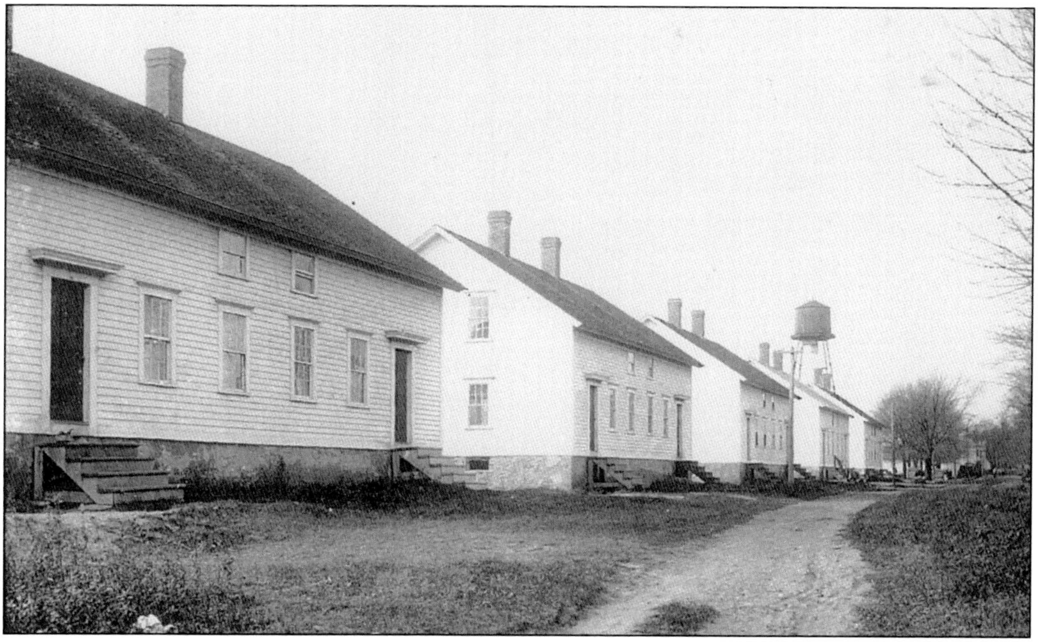

The Williamsville Mill Houses. In 1886, the Williamsville Company owned 105 tenements. In later years, the houses pictured here were destroyed by floods.

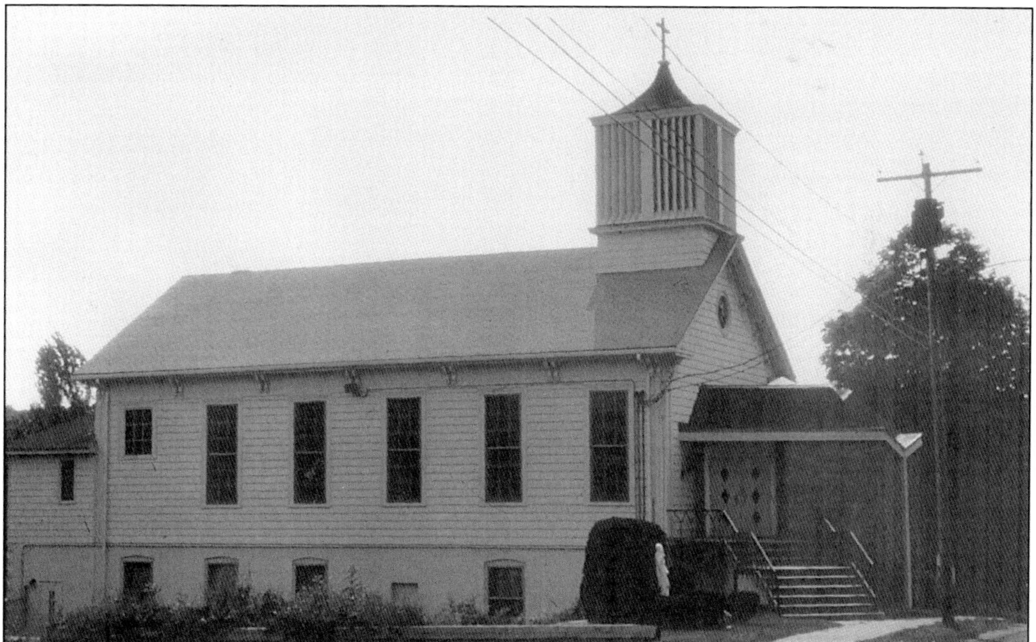

The Williamsville Church (St. Ignatius Church), 1868. The Williamsville Company erected this building as a school and church for its workers. School was held in the basement, and church services were held in the upper room. In 1883, a Congregational Church was organized with about 30 members. In later years, when the church was slated to be torn down, Dayville pastor the Rev. Ignatius Kost sought and received the bishop's approval to buy the church and land, which then became St. Ignatius Church.

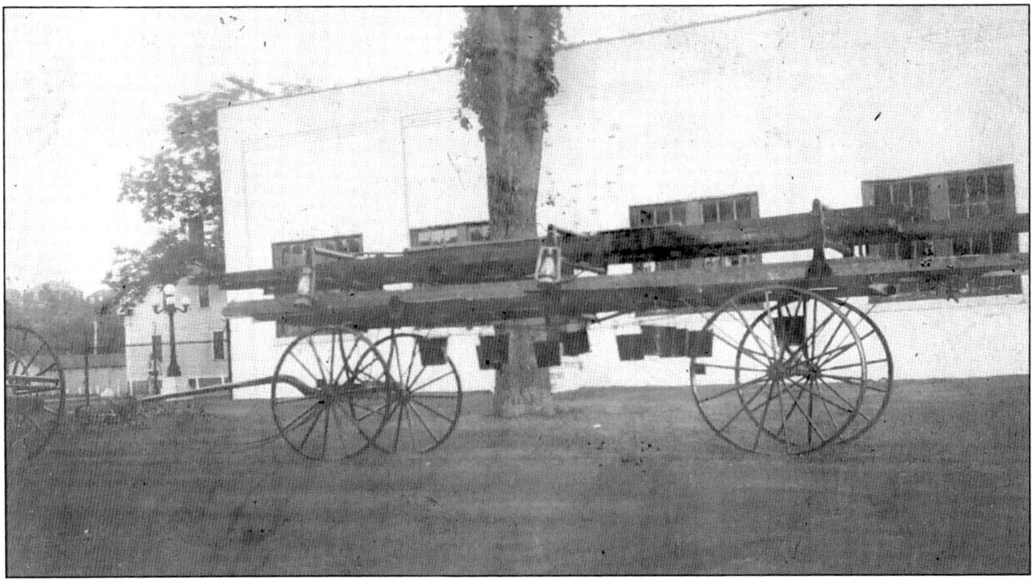

THE WILLIAMSVILLE FIRE COMPANY, 1833. The Williamsville Fire Company was organized to look out for the welfare of the fast-growing community of Williamsville. When the first members of the company responded to a fire call, they traveled on foot, pulling a hose reel behind them. The company claims to be the oldest volunteer fire department in Connecticut. The members described their territory as "the area they could cover in 10 minutes, pulling the apparatus." A replica of the Williamsville Company's first pumper is displayed at the Henry Ford Museum in Dearborn, Michigan.

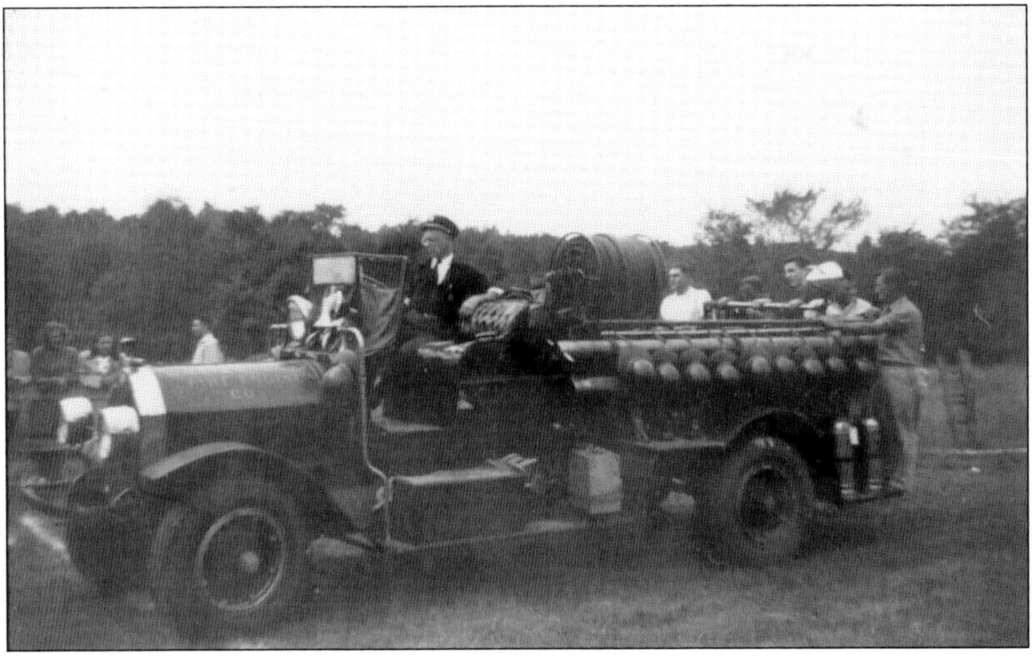

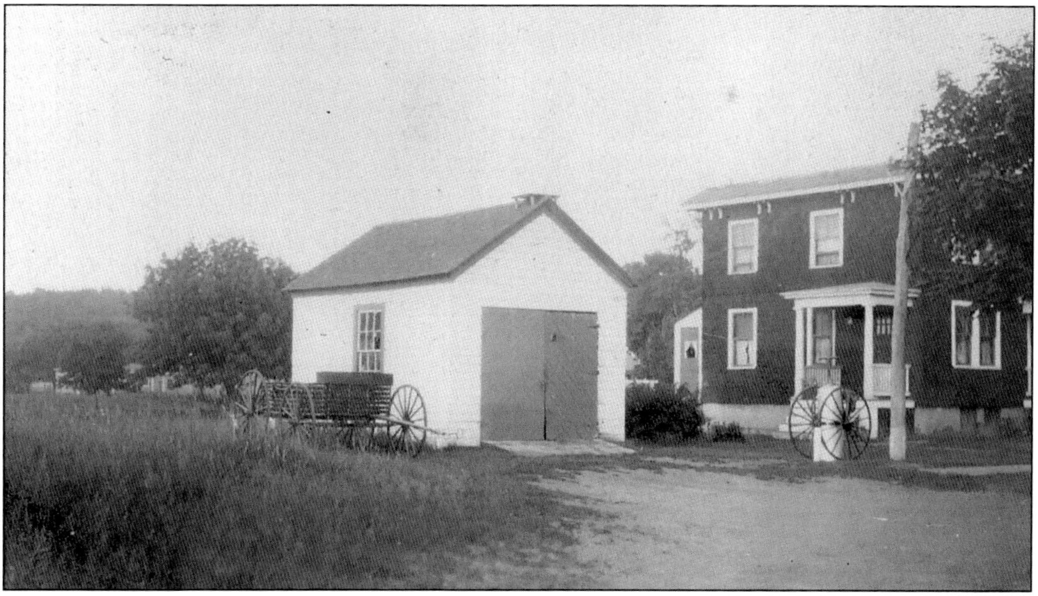

Boys Avenue Hose House #3. This hose house was part of the fire protection system provided for Goodyear Heights. At one time, the fire apparatus in the lower village was kept in the storehouse at the mill.

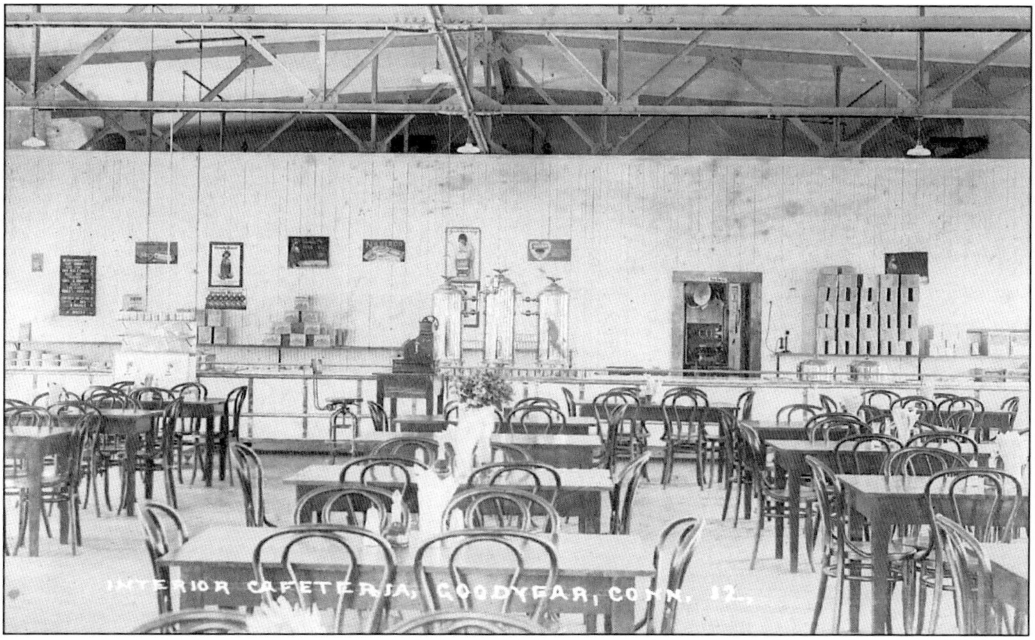

The Cafeteria of the Goodyear Mill. A four-room school was built in Williamsville in 1915. In 1922, a teacher's contract called for a salary of $950, paid in 10 monthly payments. The school burned in May 1945. For a number of years, school was held in this cafeteria. That space is now the main office of the Rogers Corporation. After the end of World War II, the town embarked on a series of school construction projects. The Goodyear School was the first to be replaced. Upon its completion in 1948, the first modern school in the town was opened.

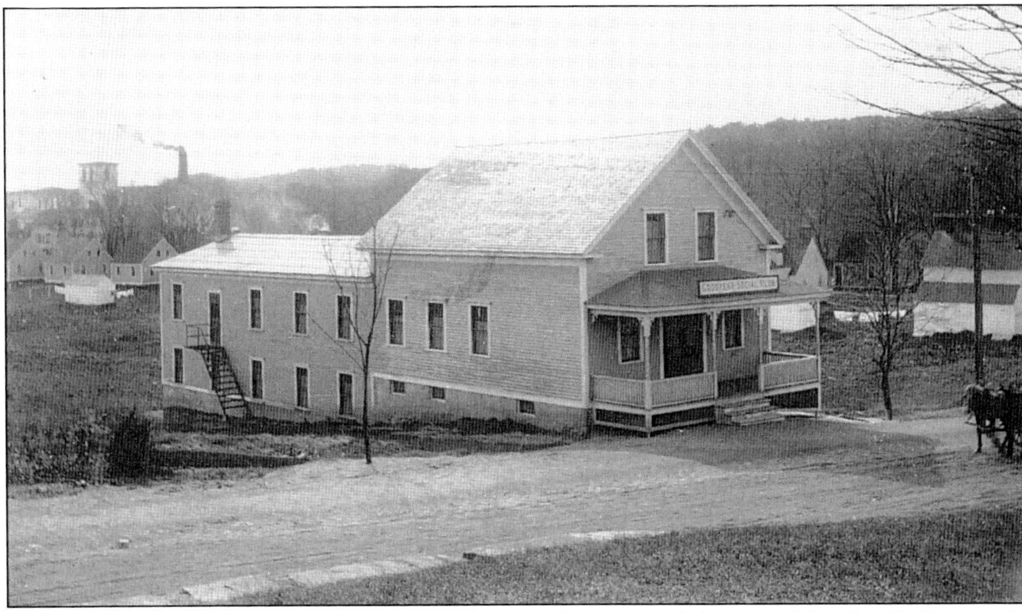

THE GOODYEAR SOCIAL CLUB, C. 1915. This was the social club erected by the Williamsville Company. The Goodyear Cotton Company continued using it for social occasions. The club was sponsored and subsidized by the Goodyear Company, which encouraged its use for sports and social events. Since 1939, the Rogers Community Club has owned the building.

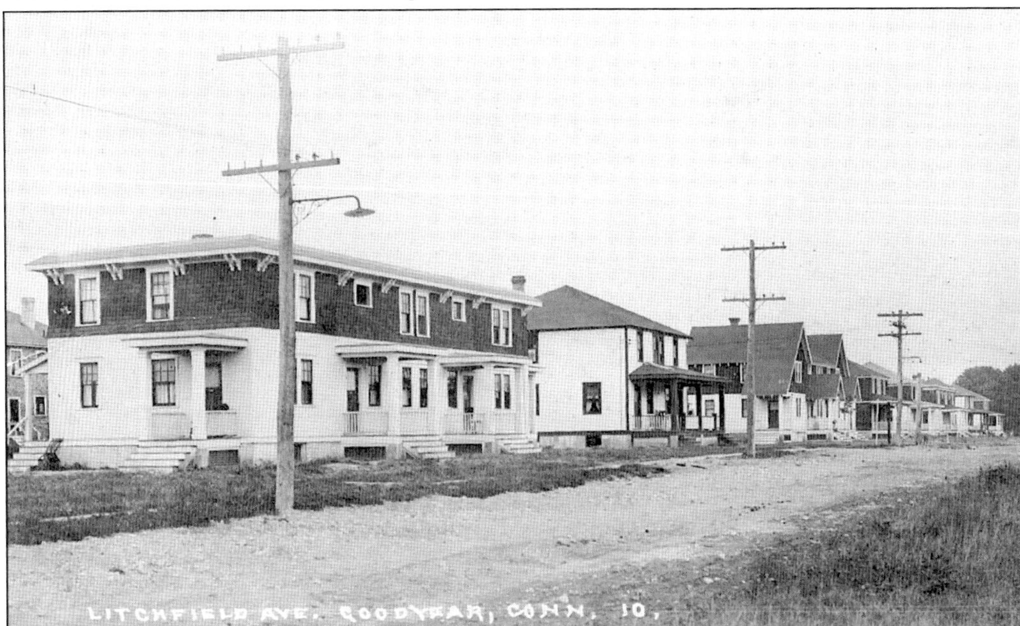

LITCHFIELD AVENUE. The Goodyear tire business increased in the years after World War I. The Goodyear Company expanded its facilities to handle this increase. Under the direction of General Manager Robert Boys, the company designed and built a whole new village. Goodyear Heights was built on a knoll overlooking the old village. Its streets were well laid out, splendidly lighted, and fully supplied with modern sanitary facilities. Goodyear Heights contained 84 modern homes.

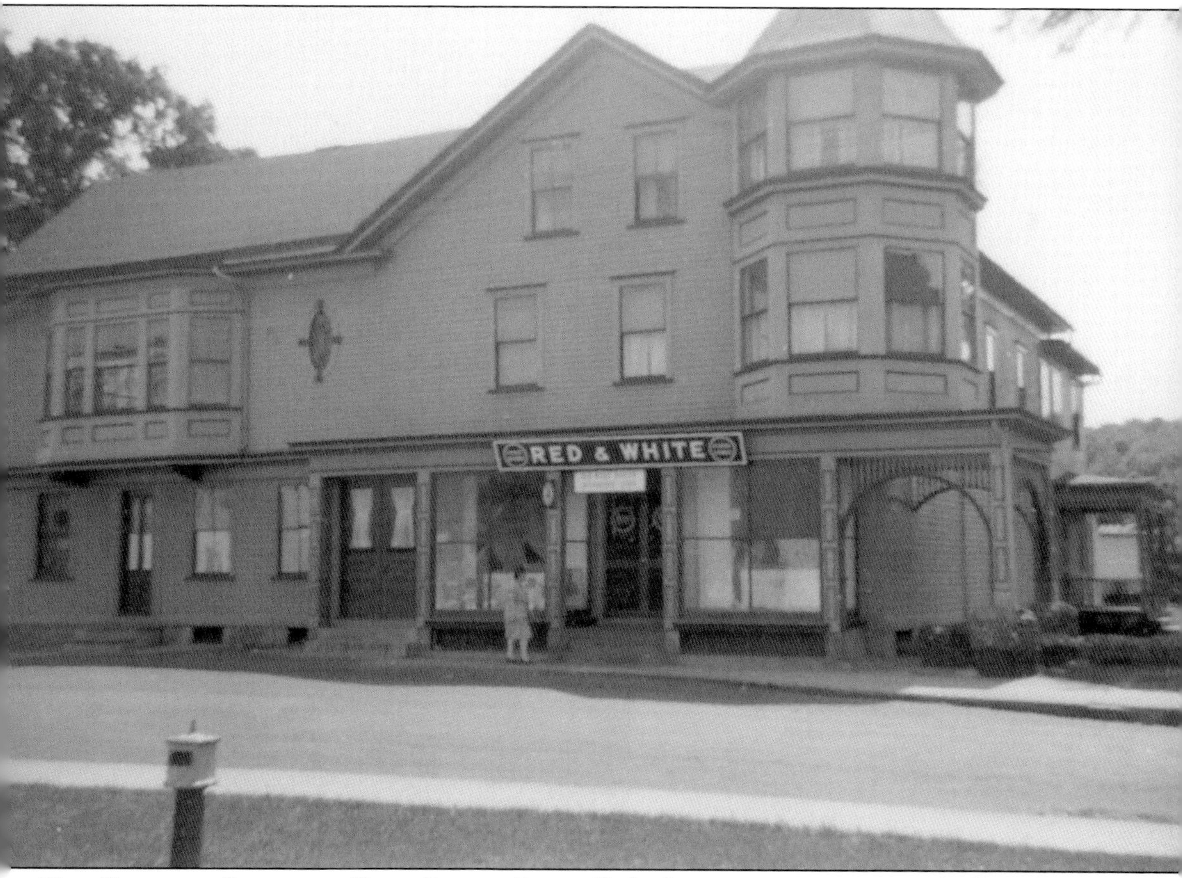

The Goodyear Store and Post Office. Originally built as a company store and office, this building later became a private residence. Annie Clarie owned the A.M. Clarie Store, where the post office was also located. Alma Forcier was the first postmaster in 1919, followed by Edgar Proulx. In 1946, the building was purchased by Francois Sarault. It was torn down in the mid-1960s to make room for the expansion of the Rogers Corporation.

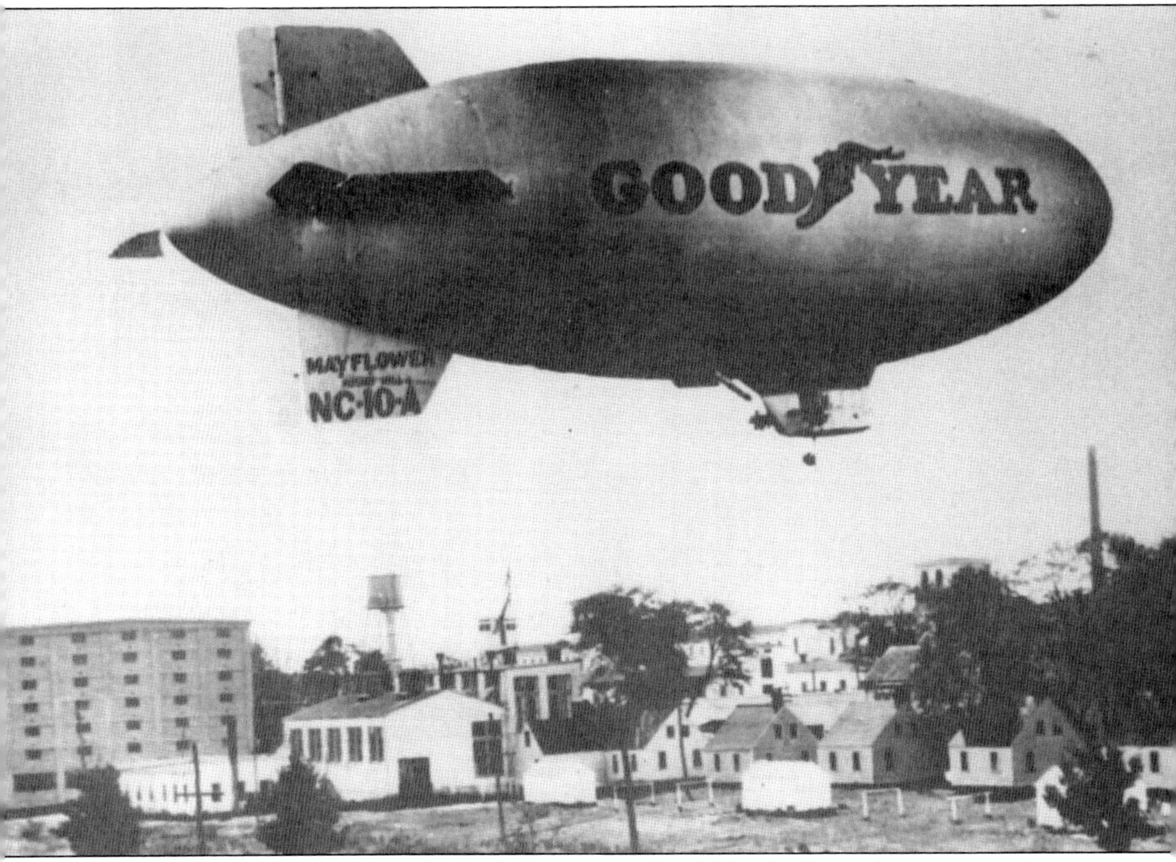

THE GOODYEAR BLIMP *MAYFLOWER*, OCTOBER 10, 1929. As the welcome visitor hove into sight over Goodyear, the mill whistle bellowed forth ten long blasts in official recognition. Shortly thereafter, the village was swarming with people anxious to see the first lighter-than-air craft ever to land in Killingly.

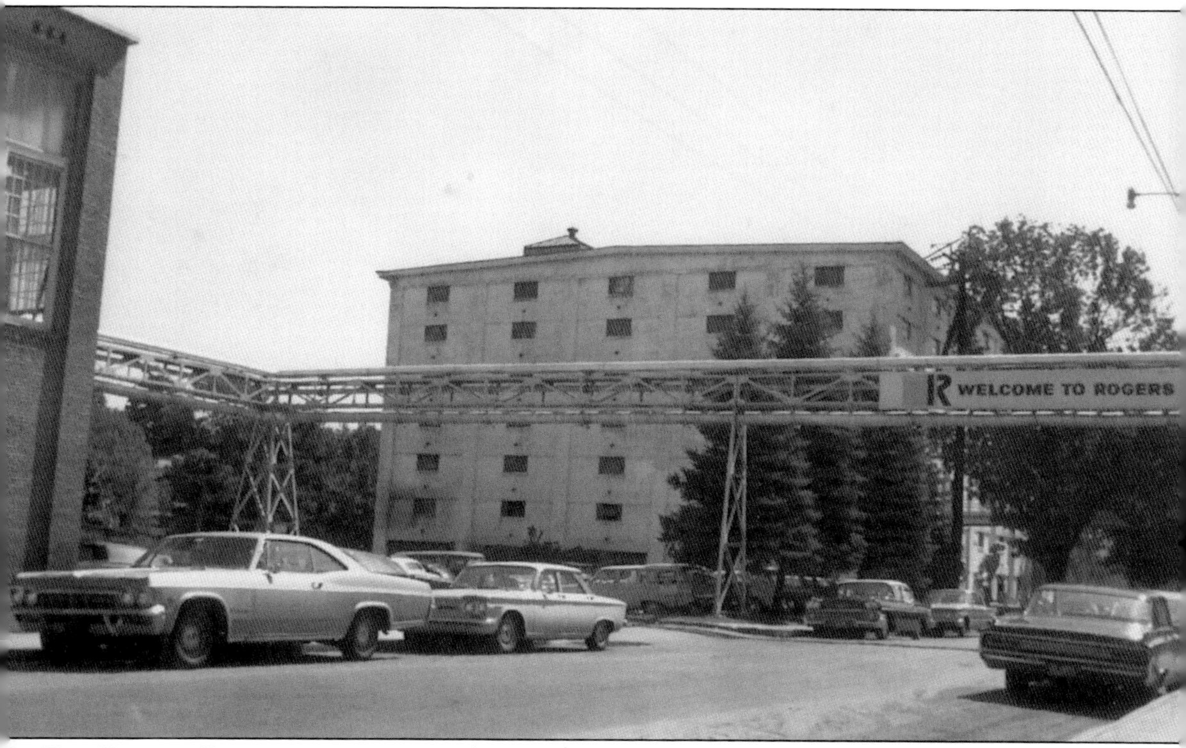

THE ROGERS CORPORATION, 1935. The Goodyear Company closed its operation in 1932, during the Great Depression. Powdrell & Alexander speculatively bought the village and sold it in 1935 to the Rogers Corporation, a paper and chemical producer. The houses were sold individually. The Rogers Corporation continued to add on to the plant and to prosper. It produced electrical and electronic insulation, gaskets, shoe board, and fiberboard. In 1954, the village changed its name from Goodyear to Rogers.

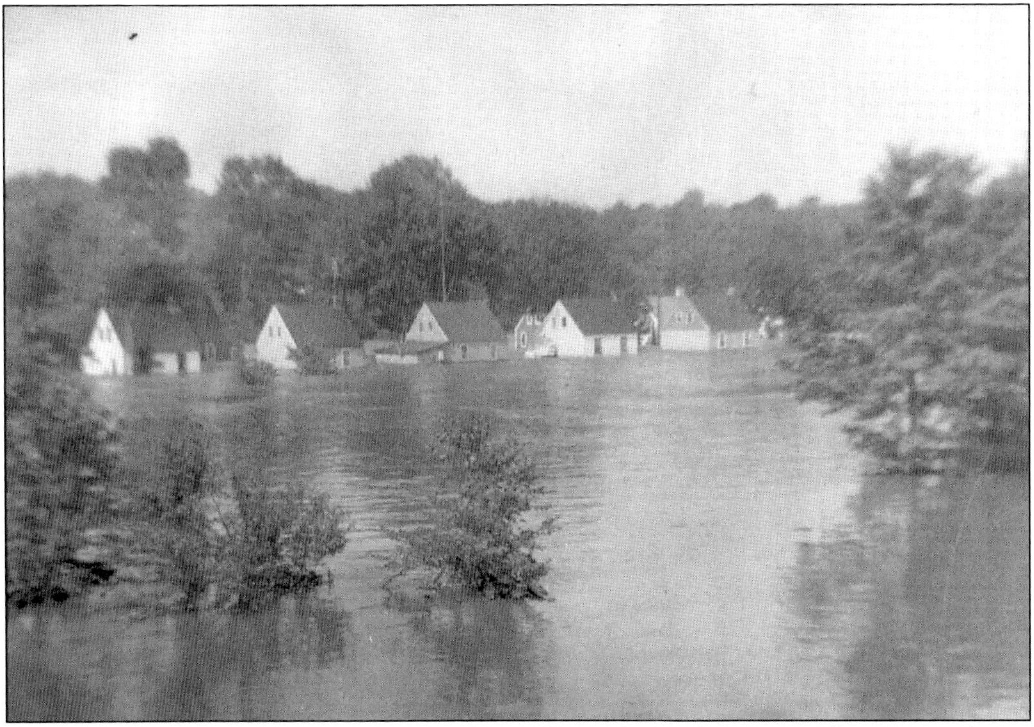

A Flood of the Lower Village, 1936. Police had to order residents out of these homes during the March 1936 flood. Early in the morning, the water had reached the doorsills.Late in the evening of that same day, the first floors were under water. Residents were hurriedly evacuated.

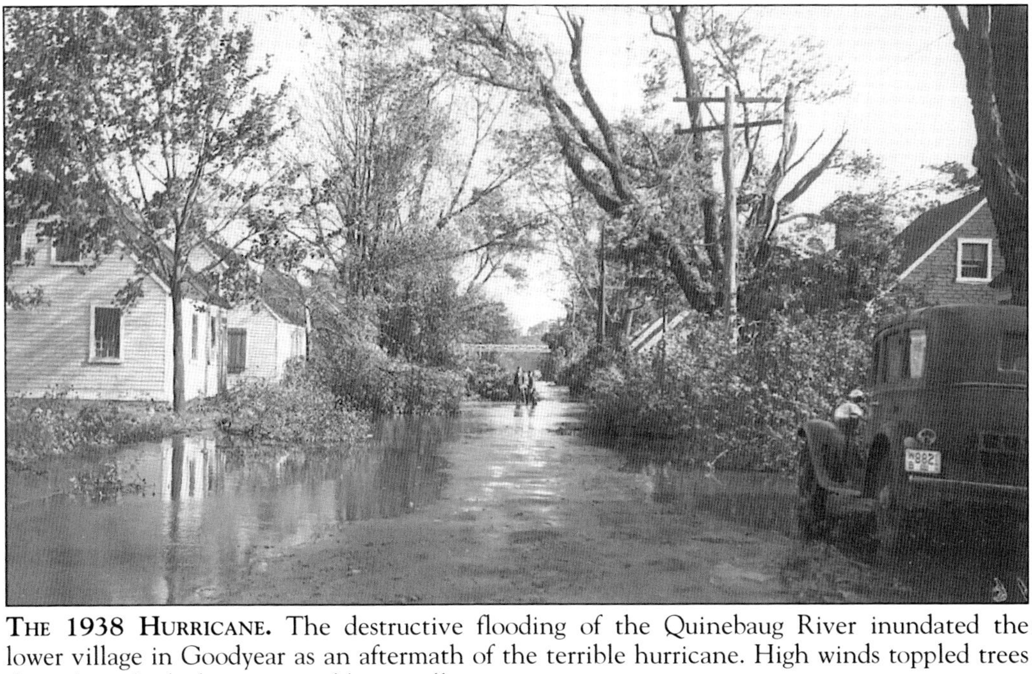

The 1938 Hurricane. The destructive flooding of the Quinebaug River inundated the lower village in Goodyear as an aftermath of the terrible hurricane. High winds toppled trees throughout both the upper and lower village.

Seven

South Killingly:

Tunk City, Mashentuck, and Horse Hill

A Summer View of South Killingly. The South Killingly area was probably one of the last

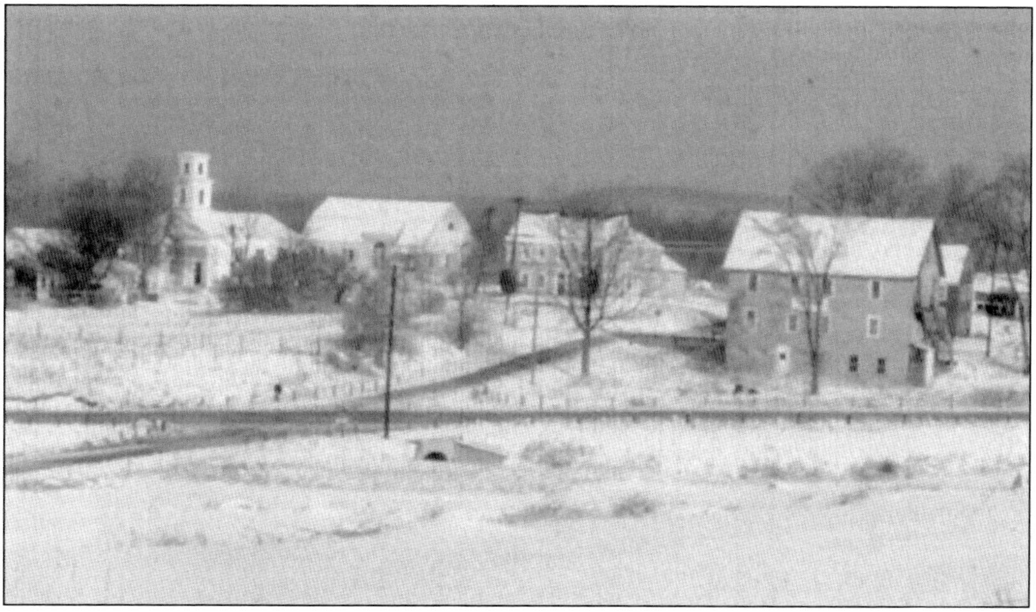

A Winter View of Tunk City. South Killingly was often called "the city," even though it had only a church, tavern, school, general store, and several homes in the 1800s. Capt. Alexander Gaston ran a mercantile operation supplied by wagon loads of goods from Providence. He donated a 700-pound bell for the church. The bell was discovered to have a crack, which made its ring sound like "tunk, tunk, tunk." That led to the nickname "Tunk City."

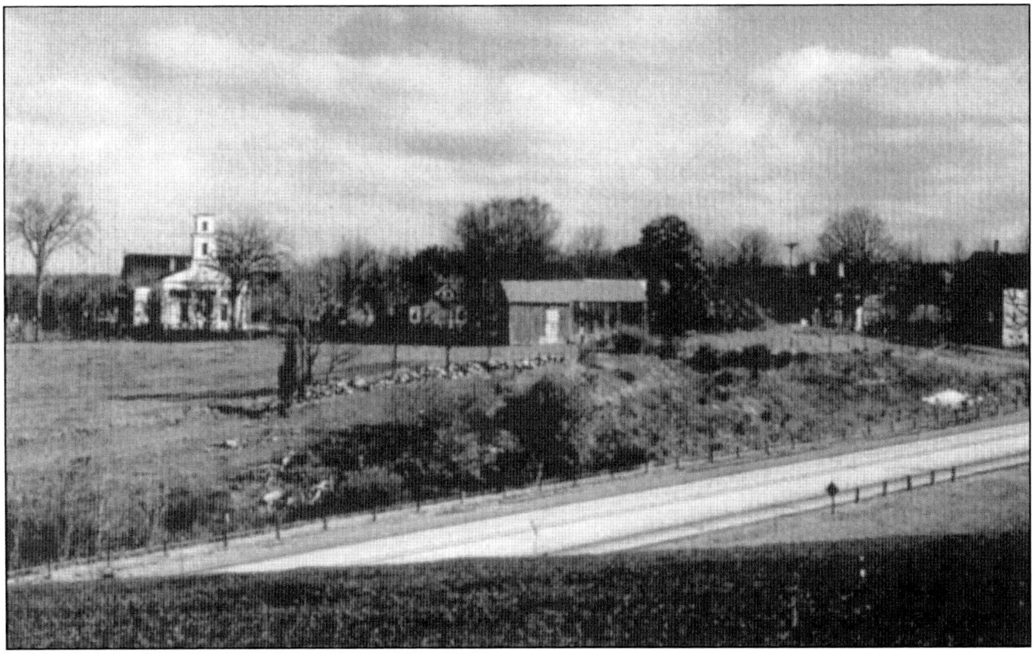

parts of town to be settled by more than a few individuals. The first settler was Jacob Spaulding of Plainfield in 1721. The largest settlement is the area clustered around the 1837 Congregational Church. Twentieth-century farmers in the area operated dairy farms and orchards. After World War II, many farms were converted to poultry operations.

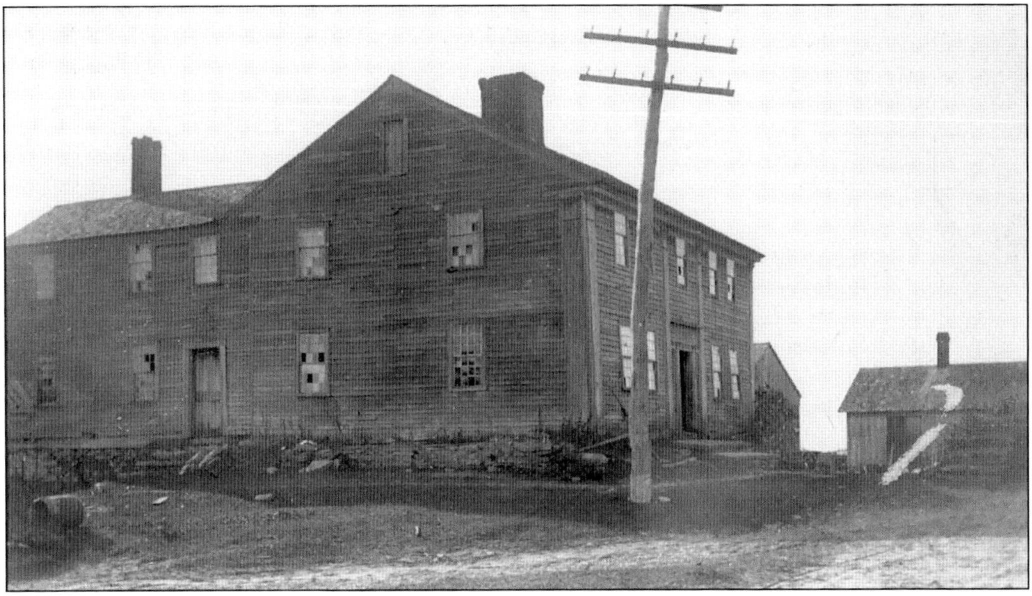

THE LOWELL GRAVES TAVERN. South Killingly had one tavern that was located on the stage route to Providence. This tavern was on the south side of Hall's Hill Road, across the corner from Steve Douglas's Store. Operated at one time by Lowell Graves, the tavern was the original business exchange where townspeople learned about local trade and local scandals. The old tavern has been gone for many years.

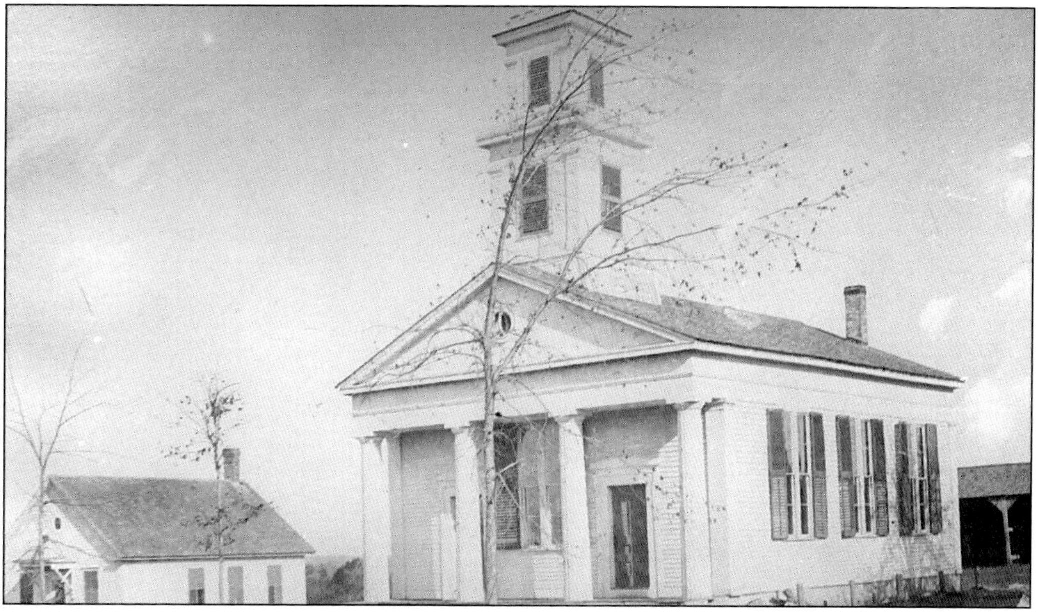

THE FIRST CONGREGATIONAL CHURCH OF SOUTH KILLINGLY, 1837. The Separatist congregation was organized in December 1746. Because of the distance to the First Society meetinghouse, early South Killingly residents found it difficult to attend public worship, especially during winter months. The handsome Greek Revival Congregational church was built in 1837, a little east of the first structure. There have been no major alterations, except for the addition of a basement and office in 1956.

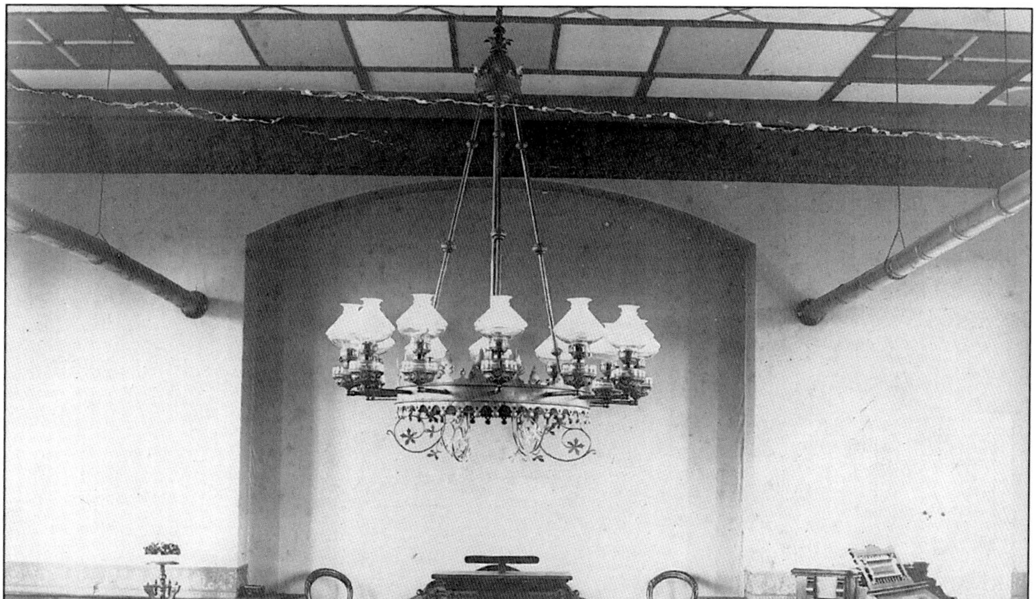

THE INTERIOR OF THE SOUTH KILLINGLY CHURCH. This view of the inside of the church shows the details of the tin ceiling, which was popular in public buildings. The various squares were decorated in splendid colors, some of which were listed on the invoice as Chinese red, green, blue, and yellow.

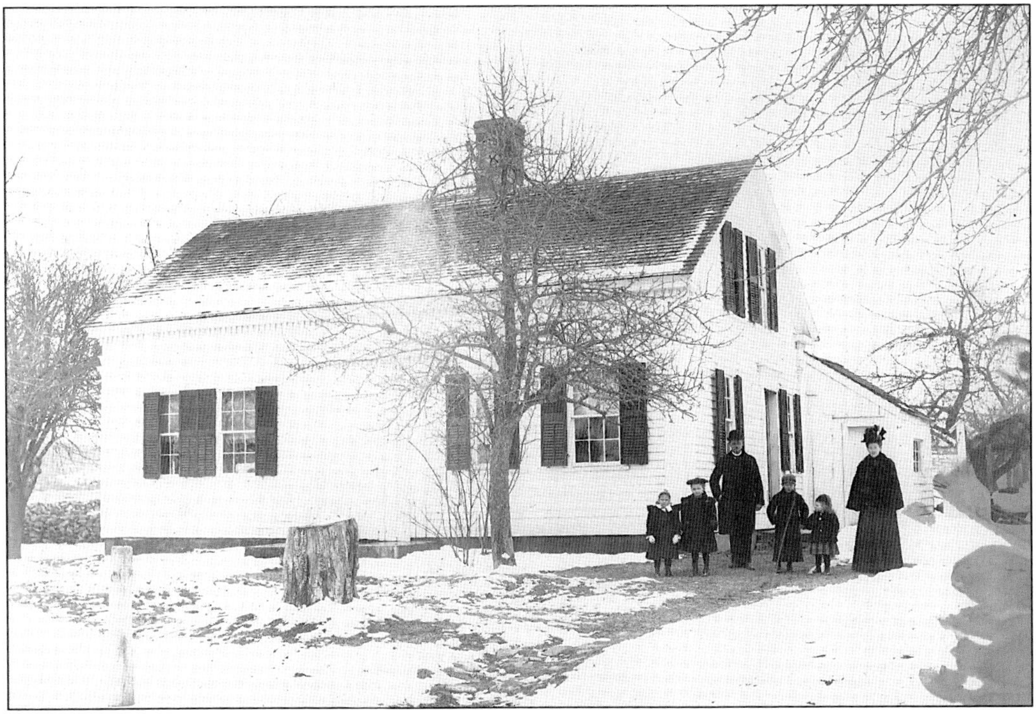

THE CONGREGATIONAL PARSONAGE, 1847. The J.D. Rood House is located immediately north of the historic South Killingly Cemetery, on the southeast corner of Terwilliger and Cook Hill Roads. J.D. Rood built the house on a lot he purchased from Siloam Short. The house was sold to the South Killingly Congregational Church in 1869 for a parsonage. It is now a private residence.

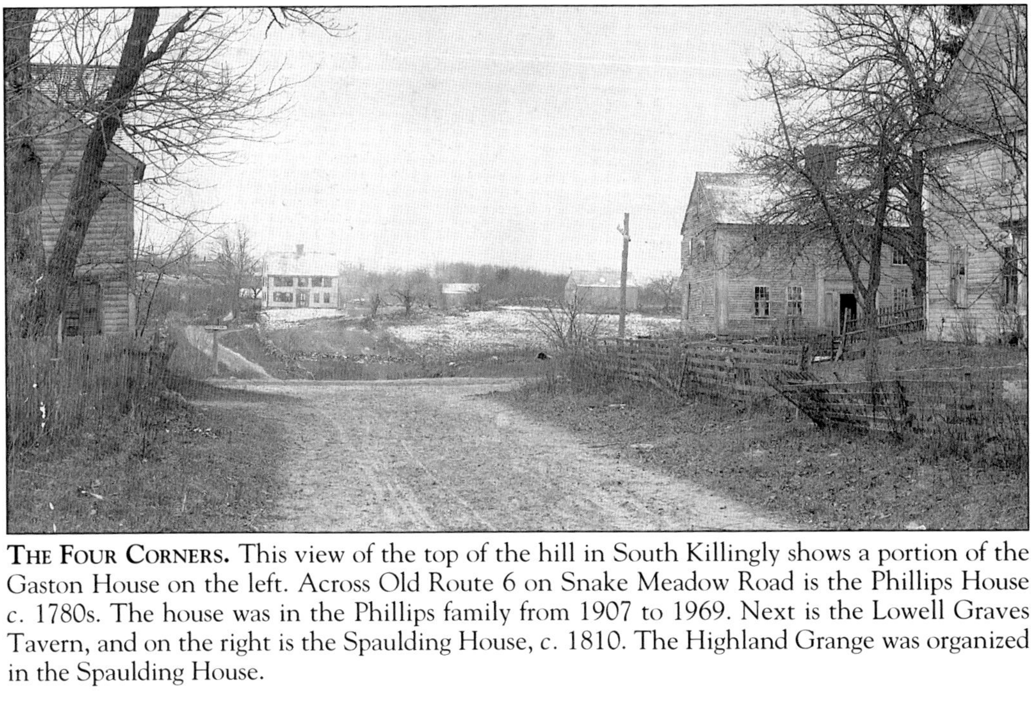

THE FOUR CORNERS. This view of the top of the hill in South Killingly shows a portion of the Gaston House on the left. Across Old Route 6 on Snake Meadow Road is the Phillips House *c.* 1780s. The house was in the Phillips family from 1907 to 1969. Next is the Lowell Graves Tavern, and on the right is the Spaulding House, *c.* 1810. The Highland Grange was organized in the Spaulding House.

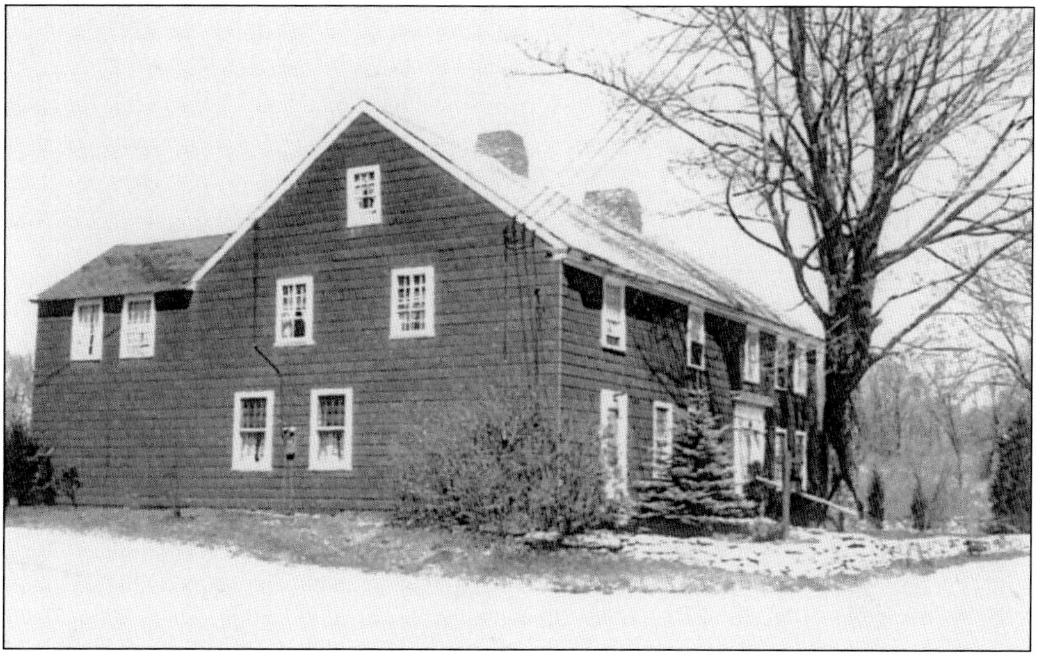

THE GASTON-HOVEY HOUSE, C. 1790. On the northeast corner of Halls Hill and Cook Hill Roads sits the oldest house in the South Killingly village. Alexander Gaston, a prominent merchant, acquired it in 1802. Gaston sold the dwelling to Dr. Daniel Hovey, a respected physician in the community, in 1838. William Gaston willed it to the South Killingly Congregational Church in 1912 for use as a parsonage.

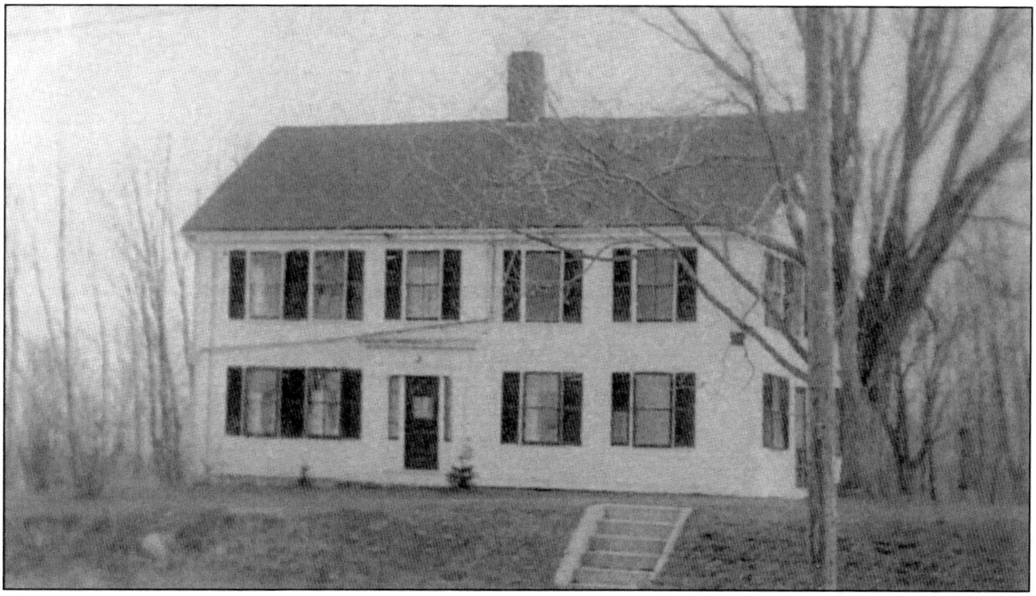

THE DAY HOUSE, C. 1795. The Day House is located at the eastern intersection of Halls Hill Road and Route 6. For most of the 19th century, the house was associated with the Day family, who operated a tavern. During the 1920s–30s period, rooms of the house were rented to workers building the "new" Route 6. An early owner was Stephen Douglas, who ran the store on the four corners. In 1935, Raymond Barlow owned it.

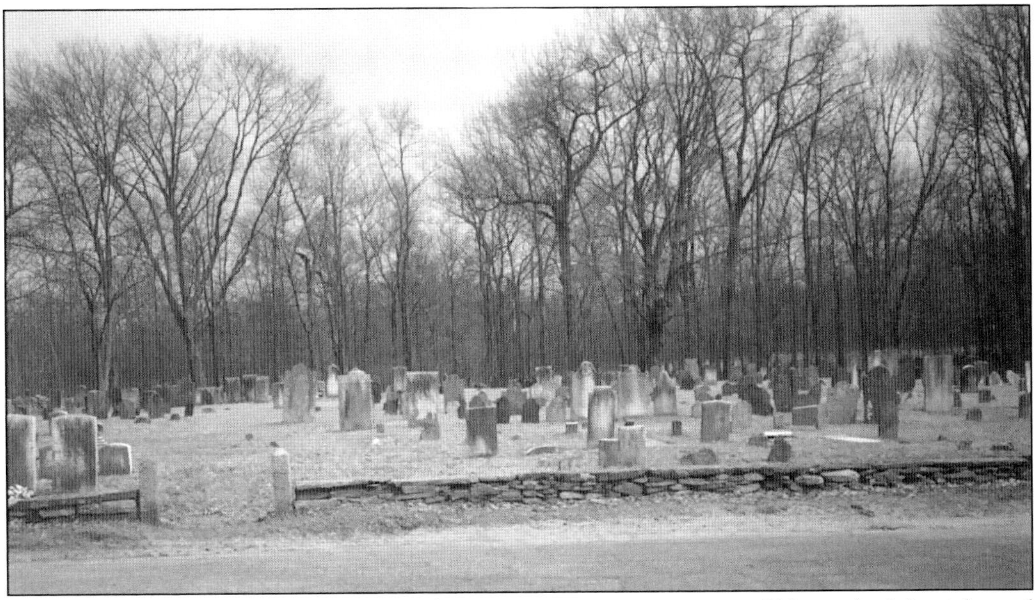

Old South Killingly Cemetery. This cemetery contains over 300 marked burials and dates back to at least the mid-1700s. The last burial was in 1920, that of Jacob Pidge, the last stagecoach driver in the region. A memorial stone for Mary Dixon Kies was set beside that of her husband, John Kies. In May 1809, she was awarded the first known patent issued to a woman in the United States.

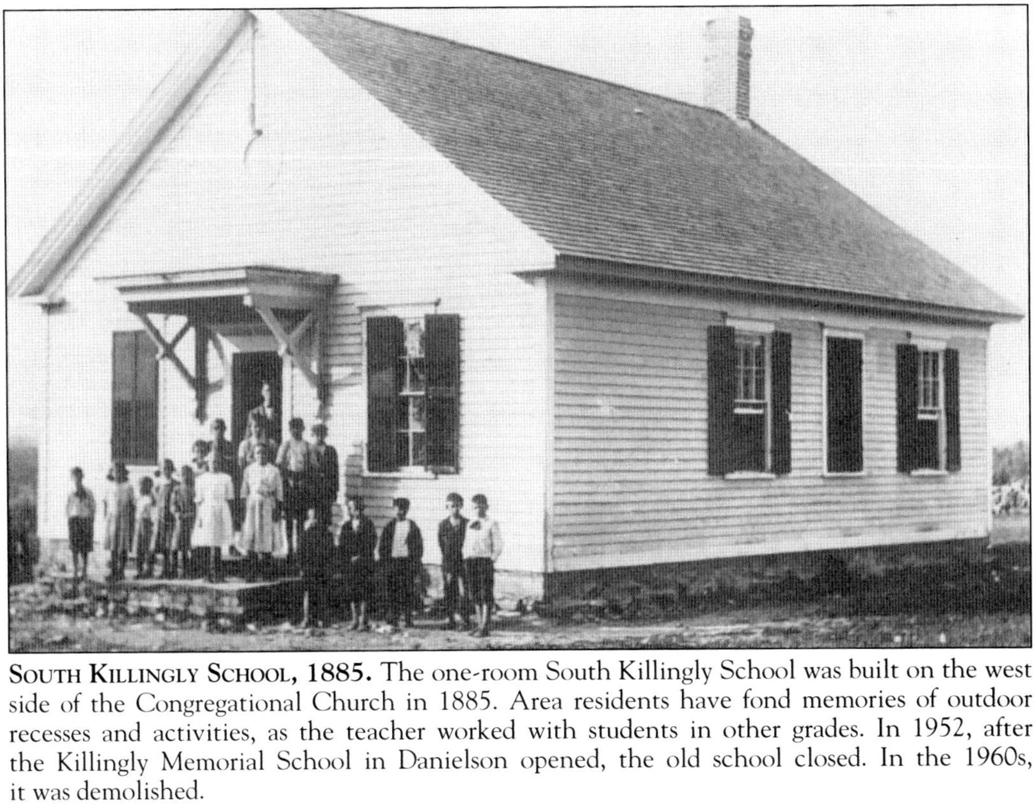

South Killingly School, 1885. The one-room South Killingly School was built on the west side of the Congregational Church in 1885. Area residents have fond memories of outdoor recesses and activities, as the teacher worked with students in other grades. In 1952, after the Killingly Memorial School in Danielson opened, the old school closed. In the 1960s, it was demolished.

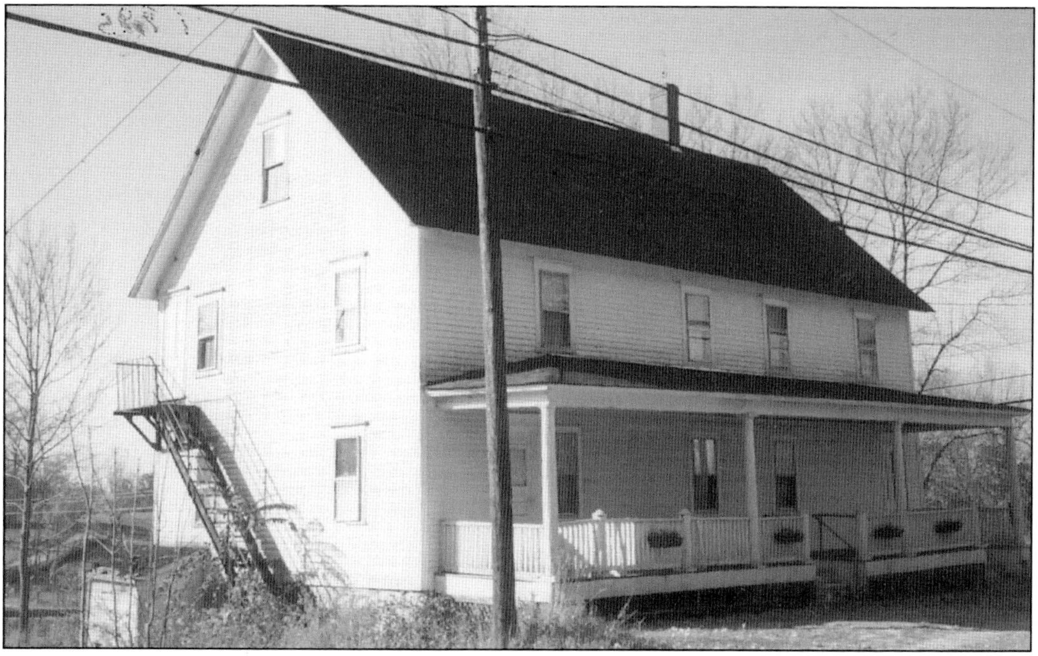

HIGHLAND GRANGE #113, ORGANIZED 1890. Early grange meetings were held in the homes of the members. Here the grange met at Albert Grover's home on Hall's Hill Road in South Killingly. Members included 17 men and women. William H. Fiske was the founder of Highland Grange and served as chairman of the committee to build a new grange hall. Shares were sold to cover the cost of the building, which came to $900. A porch was added in 1910.

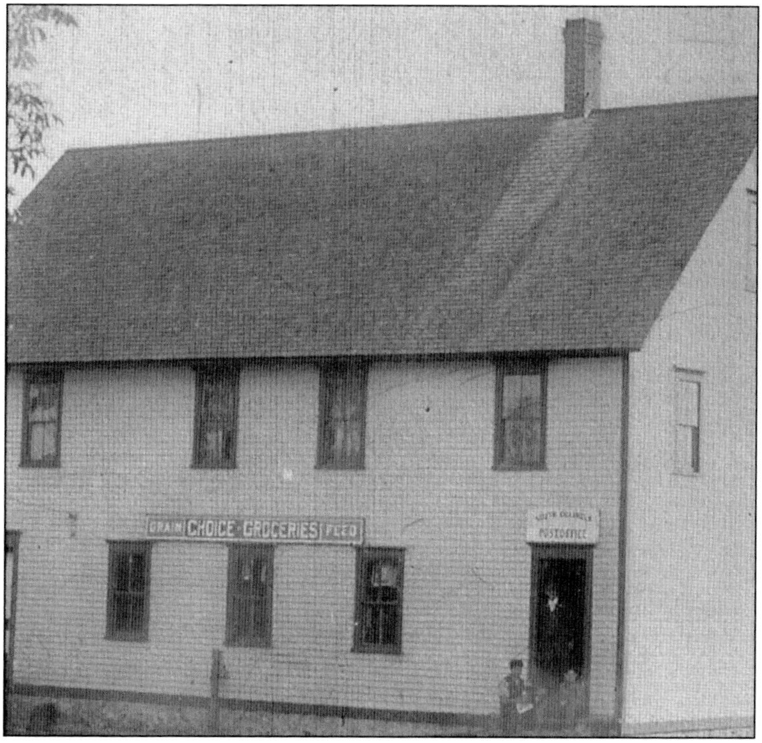

STEVE DOUGLAS'S STORE AND POST OFFICE. Highland Grange #113 erected this building in 1893 at a cost of $900. The store and post office were located on the first level; and the grange meetings were held on the second floor. Cyrus Day was the first postmaster in 1836. For a time, firefighting equipment was housed in the basement. There was also a gas pump out front in the early 1900s. The original painted curtain still hangs in front of the second-floor stage.

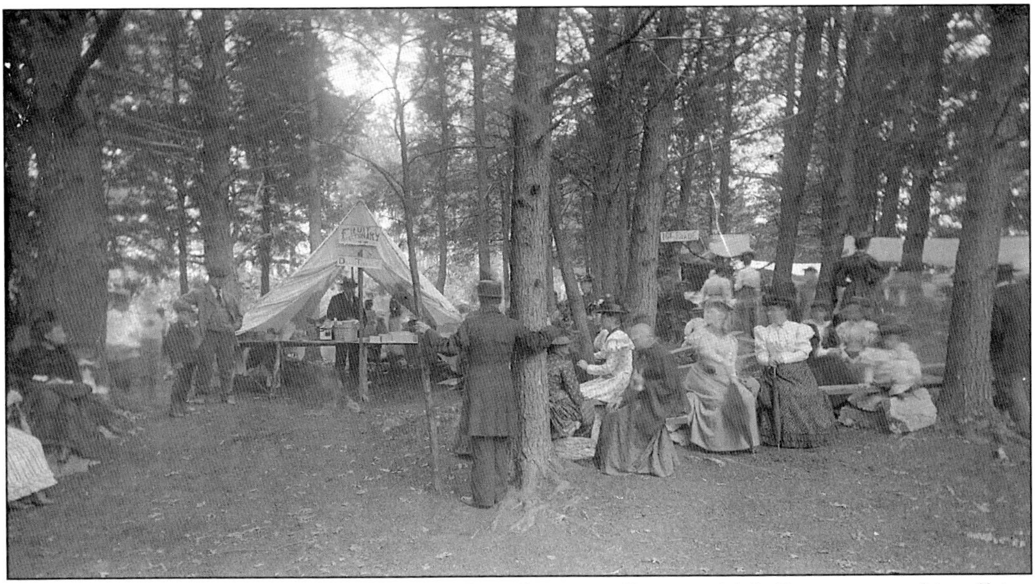

A South Killingly Church Picnic at Old Furnace Park, 1894. Picnics were big affairs. Seating was provided for 307 people. Men were detailed to hitch the horses for the ladies. Transportation was provided from the train depot to the picnic grounds. The menu included baked clams, quahog chowder, crackers, bread and butter, tea, coffee, lemonade, cake, pie, watermelon, and ice cream. Chowder and crackers cost 15¢, cake or pie slices 5¢, watermelon 3¢, and ice cream 10¢.

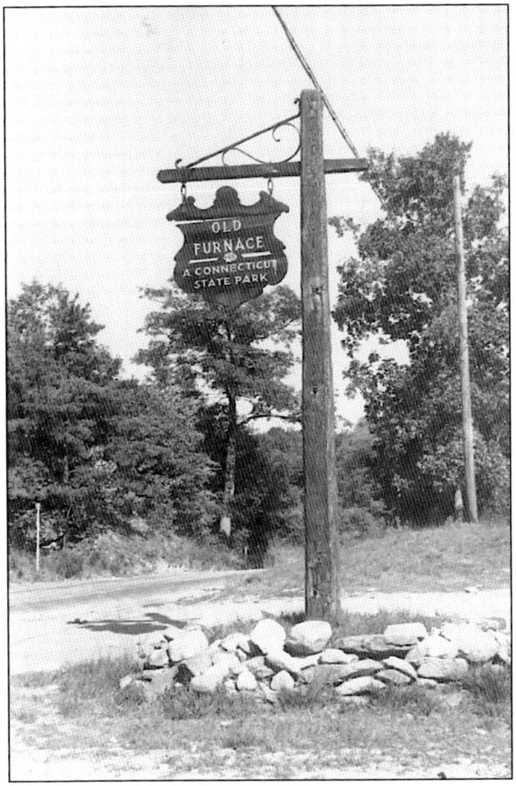

Old Furnace State Park, 1944. The name of this area was derived from the iron foundry established by the Brainard Brothers in 1835 on Fall Brook. The foundry made stoves. Later, Old Furnace became a popular picnic grove. In 1944, during his term in the Connecticut State Legislature, the Rev. Charles X. Hutchinson Jr. of the Danielson Methodist Church sponsored a successful bill to have Connecticut take over Old Furnace as a state park.